Why Be Jewish?

Intermarriage, Assimilation, and Alienation

Rabbi Meir Kahane

Why Be Jewish?

A battle plan for Jews who do not want to disappear.

"This column is dedicated to encouraging the reader to acquire *Why Be Jewish?* and to digest its contents. Read the book. You'll be shocked, and better yet, enlightened."
—*Jewish News*

"Important reading for all people who are asking themselves 'Why Be Jewish?' and for parents and teachers concerned about how to develop youth who are actively Jewish."
—*American Jewish World*

"Rabbi Kahane throws down the gauntlet to all Jews to accept with renewed vigor the truths of Jewish faith and tradition."
—*ALA Booklist*

"I am convinced that Rabbi Kahane's argument is valid and the Jewish community will be well-served heeding it most carefully."
—*Judaica Book News*

Other books by Rabbi Meir Kahane

Never Again

The story of the Jewish Defense League

Time To Go Home

Forty Years

Our Challenge

Listen World listen Jew

They Must Go!

Uncomfortable Questions for Comfortable Jews

Israel: Revolution or Referendum

On Jews and Judaism

The Jewish Idea vol. 1 & 2

Contents

"Neither shalt thou make marriages with them: thy daughter thou shalt not give unto his son, nor his daughter shalt thou take unto thy son."

—*Deuteronomy 7*

"Now therefore give not your daughters unto their sons, neither take their daughters unto your sons. . . . Shall we again break Thy commandments, and make marriages with the peoples that do these abominations? Wouldest not Thou be angry with us till Thou hadst consumed us, so that there should be no remnant, nor any to escape?"

—*Ezra 9*

A Challenge

Ever so seldom in history, moments emerge that are pregnant with greatness. The pity is that to only a few are they starkly obvious. Most men, so long engrossed in the petty aspects of their own lives and personal trivia, become as small as the things that surround them and thus blinded to greatness—incapable of recognizing it. Nevertheless the moment exists and, while promising spectacular benefit if seized at the proper time, it offers only spectacular disaster when allowed to pass by. The duality of the Moment of Greatness is clear and indisputable. Either we grasp it for monumental good or it seizes us for monumental disaster.

When does such a moment arise? Only in times of transcending crisis. At an age when people have become lost, disillusioned, and begin groping desperately for answers. After they have tried all manner of illusion only to learn its name, and after they have eaten and drunk from all kinds of strange dishes and wells only to discover that they are hungrier and thirstier than ever. At a time when they are driven and obsessed by a frustration and boredom of the soul that gives them no respite. And when the idols and icons of their time lie broken and shattered, having failed to give them the answers and solutions so eagerly promised. It is at times like these that the Moment of Greatness arrives and the future and fate of humanity teeter for a moment on the precipice of history, awaiting the answer to the question: Will man seize the opportunity and grasp truth?

For let it be clear. It is at such moments, when all the falsehoods are momentarily laid bare and all the illusions lie shattered before his eyes, that man has the chance to return to sanity. If he does, the world is uplifted, redeeming both soul and mind. If he does not, it is doomed to plunge into a whirlpool of madness and anarchy, the product of a frenetic and mindless attempt to escape mankind's horror of being lost.

We live today in such a moment. We teeter, now, on the brink. It is true for all mankind and truer yet for the Jew. We have emerged from a frantic and exhausting period of Jewish history that saw us run pell-mell down the path of escape from ourselves and our heritage. When the gates of the Ghetto were flung open and the walls that shut the Jew out of the Gentile world came crashing down; when Emancipation beckoned as some Greek siren offering the pleasure of this world for payment in the next; when the Jew was suddenly given the opportunity to be a Gentile and surpass him at it—how eagerly we threw overboard all our Jewish spiritual baggage.

How we believed all the false prophets and how we drank eagerly from all the poisoned water. How we ran toward all the glittering frauds and away from the strong and eternal Jewish verities. How we believed in Reform and Assimilation and Enlightenment and Cultural Pluralism and Liberalism and Democracy and Socialism and Marxism and Participatory Democracy and Chairman Mao and Comrade Trotsky and Rationalism and the inherent decency of man . . . . All of it died in the flames of Auschwitz and the mockery of Stalinist trials and the madness of an irrational mob.

In a way, it is good. The self-deceptions have been laid bare, the fraud exposed, the answers shown to be cant. And millions of Jews stand today with no more of an answer than they had a hundred years ago, yet with much more than those of the past century had. For we, at least, know at last what is *not the way*. We need not be betrayed by false priests and falser doctrines. At least we should know that all the escapes from Jewishness are dead ends and worse. If so, we have taken our first step out of the darkness and into the light of sanity. We stand at the moment of truth and have the opportunity to create great things in ourselves and from ourselves. If we only listen; if we only open our hearts; if we only have the courage to break with the little people who lead us.

One
THE TRAGEDY:
WHAT MAKES BERNIE RUN?

1
Bernie and Bridget

Every normal human being feels attachment to his own nation. This is a natural and universal social instinct. The Jew, however, is in many respects remote from this norm. His attachment to his nation is full of contradictions and fractured.—*V. Medem, leader of the Jewish Socialist Bund.*

None will chant a mass, no *kaddish* will be read; nothing sung, nothing said, at my dying bed . . .—*Heinrich Heine, German-Jewish poet, baptized as a Christian.*

Once there was a television program which centered on the theme of intermarriage. The heroes of the piece were named Bernie and Bridget. The American Jewish Establishment put great pressure on the network that televised the series and the program was ultimately dropped. Bernie and Bridget were no longer. They had been cancelled . . . .
How relatively simple it was to cancel Bernie and Bridget on television and how much more difficult to struggle against the intermarriage and assimilation that exist in real American Jewish life. How simple to picket a television series to death and how hard to stamp out the disease that daily afflicts the real-life existence of American Jewry. If we no longer find Bernie and Bridget strolling hand-in-hand across our television screens, we need only look at our campuses, at our streets, at our neighborhoods. Bernie is alive and well.
What makes Bernie run? What makes him run after Bridget? What makes Bernie run away from Judaism and cut the chain of generations? What makes Bernie run away from the Judaism that

his great-grandfather clutched, at the risk of loss of happiness, of material wealth, and, so often, of life? What makes Bernie run?

When President Jimmy Carter was preparing to take office he put together a Cabinet that included a woman, two blacks, and—in a manner of speaking—several Jews. Actually, Mr. Carter nominated to the Cabinet and other high posts one Jew who had converted to Protestantism, one whose mother was Jewish and father Christian (with the son dutifully obeying the call, "Honor thy father,") and two Jews who were married to Christians. It was a mind-boggling lesson in Jewish disappearance—in what makes Bernie run.

The most intriguing of these nominees is W. (for Werner) Michael Blumenthal, chosen to be Secretary of the Treasury. Blumenthal's case resembles that of the classic, stereotypical German Jew, many of whom called themselves "Germans of Mosaic persuasion." Born in Germany, his parents were already among the tens of thousands of Jews who were busily dropping their Judaism as needless and, perhaps, unwanted baggage. A Blumenthal aide described them as "completely secularized and nonreligious," a condition that clearly made no impression on the Nazis whom they fled, leaving behind a prosperous clothing store and, one would imagine, their illusions.

If so, apparently illusions have a way of being reincarnated in the next generation, for Blumenthal, doing well, married a Presbyterian named Eileen Polley and raised a corporation called Bendix. As its successful chairman and president, Blumenthal, according to the *Detroit Jewish News*, had a "heavy record of compliance with the Arab boycott" but at the same time, according to Dr. William Haber, president of the World ORT Union, "he is not *unfriendly* to Israel."

The convert is James Schlesinger, selected as Energy Chief. Born a Jew in New York, he followed his Bar Mitzvah some years later with a trip to Europe, where he became a Lutheran.

Named by Mr. Carter to head the CIA (a nomination that later ran into trouble for nonsectarian reasons) was a semi-Semite, Theodore Sorenson. His mother, Annis Chaikin, an immigrant from Russia, was active in pacifist and feminist movements in the years during and after World War I and married a Christian while a student at the University of Nebraska. Sorenson professes Christianity.

The last of the assimilating Jews is *wunderkind* Harold Brown, named to run the Defense Department. Married to an Episcopalian, Brown has nothing to do with Judaism except having had to suffer the indignity of applying to the exclusive and restricted California

Club and waiting for more than three years now while his name is "still in the works."

In essence, the conversion and intermarriage drama that was highlighted on the Washington government level was a rather awesome manifestation of a phenomenon that is raging through the American Jewish community. The escape from Judaism and Jewishness is seen at all levels and while it is many times motivated by opportunism, insecurity, or self-hate, increasingly its roots are simply *indifference*.

On the name-dropping level, intermarriage is an accepted thing; among the famous and near-famous, it is so accepted as to be as natural as any other kind of union. Thus, the August 20, 1973, issue of *New York* magazine fascinated its predominantly Jewish readership with a number of intermarriages to help the bored housewife pass the time of day. And so we learned of:

> Paul Wexler, marrying former nun Jacqueline Grennan (later president of Hunter College);
>
> Eli Wallach, married to actress Anne Jackson;
>
> Richard Schaffer, married to Katherine Lindsay, daughter of the former Mayor of New York;
>
> June Rossbach, marrying Congressman Jonathan Bingham (he continues to be a staunch supporter of Israel);
>
> CBS boss William Paley, married to the former Barbara Cushing;
>
> Jonas Salk, who gave so many Jews *naches* by discovering the vaccine that bears his name, giving others palpitations when he married Françoise Gilot;
>
> Melvyn Douglas, married to former Congresswoman Helen Gahagan Douglas;
>
> Irving Berlin, who learned firsthand about white Christmases and Easter parades from Ellin Mackay;
>
> Arthur Schlesinger, Jr., who escaped the Vietnam debate and married Alexandra Emmet;
>
> Giancarlo Uzielli, married to the former Anne Ford (it is Uzielli who is the Jew, converted to Christianity);
>
> Irma Deutsch, who showed that Jews and Puerto Ricans *can* coexist by marrying Congressman Herman Badillo.

And of course, there is Muriel Murphy, who, in the best tradition of enlightenment, runs the finest salon in the East. In a fascinating article in the *New York Times* (July 23, 1975), we learn about the

kind of exciting and compelling evening one can spend there if so
fortunate as to be invited. Lady Annunziata Asquith, the great-
granddaughter of the British Prime Minister, apparently mentioned
to her friend Mrs. Elizabeth Balfour (daughter of Prince Paul of
Yugoslavia and Princess Olga of Greece) that she was going to New
York. This elicited a shriek of delight from Mrs. Balfour and the
urgent advice that she, Lady Annunziata, must visit Mrs. Murphy's
salon. Three nights later, the Lady and seven suitcases arrived to be
greeted by one Harry Craig, described by the *Times* as an Irish-born,
Italian-resident, frequent houseguest of Mrs. Murphy, who writes
songs. The *Times* then goes on to say:

> She [Lady Annunziata] says that Mr. Craig talks about Mo-
> hammed, that Mrs. Murphy and Arturo Ripstein, a Mexican
> [?] movie director, argued violently about whether or not
> animals could cry, and that Jean Gimpel (a Frenchman with a
> London art gallery) raged on about art. Sometime during the
> evening, someone said that Faye Dunaway was on the phone.

The exciting Mrs. Murphy, born Muriel Oxenberg, is the
daughter of Russian Jews who became wealthy "by selling smoked
fish."

What makes Bernie run? Who put Muriel in Mr. Murphy's
chowder?

As in so many things, the *New York Times* is a barometer, micro-
scope, and telescope for the events of our time. And so, a cursory
glance at the wedding and engagement announcements reveals:

> Priscilla Lee and Louis Adam Goldman . . . were married
> yesterday at Antun's restaurant in Queens Village by Rabbi
> Roy Rosenberg. The bride is the daughter of Mrs. Robert C.
> Lee of New York and Hong Kong. . . . She is a granddaughter
> of the late Frank W. Lee, former Acting Foreign Minister of
> China. . . .
> Mr. Goldman's parents are Mr. and Mrs. Morris H. Gold-
> man. . . . His father is in real estate.

What makes Louis run to Hong Kong . . . ?
And again:

> Gail Merrifield was married here yesterday afternoon to
> Joseph Papp, producer of the New York Shakespeare Festival.

. . . Justice Samuel J. Silverman of the State Supreme Court performed the ceremony. . . . Mr. Papp, son of the late Mr. and Mrs. Samuel Papirofsky of Brooklyn. . . . His father was a trunkmaker. The bride . . . is the daughter of Richard Merrifield of Keene, N.H.

What makes Joseph so keen on New Hampshire . . . ?

And the list goes on and on: In the United Congregational Church at Little Compton, R.I., Episcopalian Nancy Susan Noye marries Mark Lee Weissler of Fresh Meadows, Queens, in a ceremony performed by the Rev. Harrington M. Gordon, Jr., with Rabbi Philip Schechter assisting. Walter Cronkite's daughter marries Gifford Cochran Whitney in an Episcopalian ceremony and Judaism is united with the grandson of Cornelius Vanderbilt Whitney. The *New York Times* managing editor, A. M. Rosenthal, gives away his son Daniel Michael to Amy Margaret Rhodes, as her sister Katherine Clancy attends; and Hank Greenberg either hits a home run or strikes out (depending on one's outlook) as his daughter Alva Gimbel marries Frederick Bill Gahagan, in an intermarriage performed by one of the rabbinical deans in that field, Rabbi Sam Silver of Stamford.

What makes all the Bernies and Bernices run—after Nancy, Gifford, and Bill? Whatever the cause, it is abundantly clear that intermarriage and assimilation are exploding in America, and not only do the young people who intermarry no longer manifest their once prevalent guilt feelings, but parents are more inclined to accept the fact. More and more rabbis will marry the couple, and there is a subtle tendency on the part of some of the major Jewish Establishment groups to play down the gravity of the problem on the grounds that many of the Gentile partners are good "Jews" in the sense that they become active in the Jewish community. The willingness of the Establishment to give intermarriage a better "image" may, of course, come from the fact that so many of them, and especially their children, are in fact intermarried. In any event, it is a rather poor joke that increasingly, Jewish parents (from liberal suburbia, naturally) "comfort" themselves with the thought that "at least he (she) is white . . . ."

Speaking to some 1,000 persons at the 78th annual meeting of the National Conference of Jewish Communal Services (NCJCS), Milton Himmelfarb, of the American Jewish Committee, characterized American Jewry as "an endangered species" and said that it faces "extinction." How many Jews intermarry? According to the *Jewish*

Post and Opinion, a weekly newspaper, one out of every three marriages involving a Jew also involves a Gentile. Golda Meir, in a speech before the Zionist Organization of America in 1972, quoted World Jewish Congress figures of 40 percent. The difference in figures most probably results from the fact that the lower estimates count only those marriages in which there was no conversion ritual —even symbolically—on the part of the Gentile partner, while the higher figure includes marriages in which the Gentile went through a "conversion" process. For the most part, the conversion is a rather farcical arrangement made without the slightest desire to become Jewish, but rather to pacify the Jewish parents, and usually under the auspices of a non-Orthodox rabbi who will make the process relatively swift and "painless." In effect, it is a fraud in which rabbi, couple, and parents all acquiesce, and the primary victim is Judaism.

Frantic efforts on the part of parents and their Jewish Establishment groups have clearly failed to stem the tide. All the arguments have been tried. *Intermarriages cannot work and the chances for divorce are very high.* The youngsters, holding hands, listen to the statistics much in the way that they listen to the figures that "prove" that cigarette smoking causes cancer. Bernie continues to smoke and to marry Bridget. *How can you do this to us?* Bernie somehow does it. *This will kill your mother (father)!* Bernie gambles (correctly) that it will not. *You owe it to your people!*

Ah, Bernie's "people." Bernie owes the Jewish people a sacrifice. He owes it to Judaism and to Jewry to give up the good-looking *shiksa.* There is only one flaw in this argument: Bernie does not really feel that he owes anything to the Jewish people because he sees no overwhelming reason to be Jewish, let alone to give up his Irish (or Episcopalian) rose.

Some time ago, a young Jewish girl wrote a letter to one of the English language Jewish weeklies. In it, she stated:

> I am a sophomore in college. I received a Talmud Torah [Hebrew school] education, after five years of which I was Bat-Mitzvahed. When my formal Jewish education ended, I remained active in my synagogue through the youth group and intertemple activities (basketball league and dances).
>
> My parents are warm, loving people who have always been active in Jewish life. My father is past president of his synagogue, active in B'nai B'rith, UJA, Israel Bonds, and so on. My mother has given of her time to her sisterhood, Hadassah,

and various other women's organizations. In short, my home was always a hub of Jewish activity and involvement. Through their life-style, my parents have demonstrated their commitment to Judaism.

And yet, after much soul-searching, I had to admit that, for me at least, this way of life holds no meaning. I seek something more to offer, on every level. Because of this, I must conclude that religion is meaningless. Please be assured that I am not making a value judgment without having searched my heart and mind. For the past two years I have been in constant quest . . . a quest that has led me to study many religions and philosophies. All my study has led me to just one conclusion.

In order for man to derive meaning from his existence, he must take those values which are universal, those values which are the common denominators that enhance the brotherhood of man, and live by them. Man, for his very survival, must allow those universal values to guide him to a better understanding and love his fellowman. It is only in this way that we may survive and our lives will have meaning. Therefore I believe that we must renounce all religions, for they serve to divide and destroy rather than to unite man. Man must have only one credo to live by, and that credo must be universal brotherhood.

Little wonder that in the face of such feelings and upon meeting a handsome (pretty) Gentile, and "falling in love," that this love conquers all—including archaic Judaism with its "reactionary proscriptions against intermarriage." And so nice Jewish girls even marry nice Arab boys. In a discussion of three such marriages, the *New York News* (April 28, 1974) wrote of Marcia, "a Jewish intellectual from a wealthy Long Island borscht-loving family," married to Jusuf, a Syrian Arab. When the Yom Kippur War broke out, says Marcia, daughter of Sarah, Rebecca, Rachel, and Leah, "my parents were overly emotional. They kept insisting 'Israel must survive.' I kept saying, 'Who's talking about Israel not surviving? The Arabs never attacked Israel—they could have, but they didn't drop bombs on Tel Aviv. They attacked their own lands.' " Marcia, the intellectual, for whom love conquered all, including common sense and concern for her people. What makes Marcia run after Jusuf?

Clearly the same thing that made a young Jewish woman tourist marry terrorist Faik Hassan Bolot, in a Moslem ceremony at Ramle prison. Bolot was captured in a raid on a PLO camp and sentenced to seven years imprisonment for terrorist acts. The young Jewess met him, fell "in love" with him, converted to Islam, and married him. What makes Bernice run after PLO terrorists?

Not every American Jewish youngster would subscribe to every statement in the Jewish girl's letter, but surely the vast majority would agree that there is no really sound reason not to marry a Gentile whom you *love*. Indeed, in a speech at Baltimore's Temple Oheb Shalom, Reform Rabbi Samuel Sandmel told his audience to revise their thinking on many Jewish problems, including intermarriage. Said Sandmel: "Ninety-nine percent of Jewish youngsters see nothing wrong with intermarriage, and while it is a serious problem for Jews, I have no solution for it."

And so it grows and rages on. According to a National Jewish Population Study conducted by the Council of Jewish Federations and Welfare Funds (CJFWF), 31 percent of the Jews who married between the years 1966 and 1971 married Gentiles. Erich Rosenthal in his "Studies of Jewish Intermarriage in the United States" examined marriage records in the two states that included the religious identification of the registrants, Iowa and Indiana. In Iowa, he found that 42.2 percent of all marriages involving Jews were intermarriages, while in Indiana, the figure was 48.8 percent. Harold Taylor Christensen and K. E. Barber, in the August 1967 *Journal of Marriage and the Family*, found a 47.3 percent rate of Indiana Jewish intermarriages.

Furthermore, it is clear that intermarriage among young second- and third-generation American Jews is escalating, proving correct Rabbi Sandmel's curiously calm dictum that ninety-nine percent of Jewish youngsters see nothing wrong with intermarriage. Thus in 1956, Rosenthal showed that Jewish intermarriages among foreign-born Jewish husbands was 1.4 percent, among first-generation husbands it had gone up to 10.2 percent, and among second-generation husbands it had shot up to 17.9 percent. And let it be borne in mind that all of the Rosenthal and Christensen-Barber figures are between 15 and 20 years old and that they are certainly higher today. In a survey conducted in Boston in 1965, it was shown that in all marriages in which the Jewish husband was below age 30, the rate of intermarriage was 20 percent, rather than the lower 7 percent for husbands between 31 and 50. In 1970, Marshall Sklare, the leading sociologist on the American Jewish scene, said this concerning the Boston figures: "If by 1965 one in five young Jewish couples in Boston constituted a case of intermarriage, we can safely assume that the figure is now approaching one in four."

It is important to note that many of the surveys deal with Jewish husbands only. This is because for years there was an extremely low rate of Jewish women marrying Gentile men. In the words of Rabbi David Eichhorn, (*The Reconstructionist*, December 1968):

> This was true until about ten years ago but it is no longer true. Time was when a Jewish daughter was subjected to much stronger family and communal pressure in an intermarriage situation than was a Jewish son and many a fearful Jewish girl chose to be an old maid rather than marry a dearly beloved non-Jewish boy. This particular aspect of Jewish female is getting rarer.

Indeed.

It is clear that the future bodes only more intermarriage. Freedom and equality have brought the Jew the right to do everything that Bridget's father does, and to marry his daughter, too. Jews have broken out of the Ghetto with a vengeance and mix with the Gentiles in every sphere. Witness the tremendous percentage of Jewish youth who attend college and university—the most powerful force for intermarriage possible. There the young Jew is at the mercy of a scholastic atmosphere which is unfavorable to religion and all "parochial" trends and which radicalizes him into questioning the importance of a heritage he knows about only on a Bar Mitzvah child's level. He meets Gentiles who are his peers and finds them remarkably similar (there are, he discovers, quite a number of bright Gentiles), and he shares a major part of his life with them for at least four years.

In a study prepared for the American Jewish Congress by Caplovitz and Levy (*Interreligious Dating Among College Students*, 1965), it was seen that:

> The transition from high school to college represents for most young people a lessening of the influence of their family and an increase in the influence of their peers and professors who hold out to them a world of secular knowledge. Religion and other traditional beliefs reinforced by the family of origin are apt to become weakened in the college setting.

The effect on the educated Jew is also evident. Concluding their survey, the authors say:

The proportion of Jewish academics and professionals will undoubtedly increase in the future and it is precisely in these sectors that the religious tradition appears to be weakening, being replaced by an ideology of secular liberalism that views intermarriage permissively.

And the May 5, 1964, issue of *Look* magazine featured an article titled "The Vanishing American Jew" . . . .
More than true. In 1975, in an era of exploding world population, the world Jewish community *lost* more than 80,000 of its total population. It is not only because of intermarriage and general assimilation. It is because of the Jewish liberal Bernie and Bernice, who are the world's leading advocates of birth control and voluntary sterilization. There is overpopulation in India, and Egypt has too many babies. The progressive Bernice is horrified. What does she do? She, the Jew, stops having babies. Zero population growth is the banner raised high as the Jewish woman opens her mouth for India by shutting her womb to Jews.
In the words of William Berman of the Jewish Population Regeneration Union (PRU):

> To maintain its numbers, any group must average 2.5 children per family. The Jewish birth rate, however, is estimated at 1.5 per family. Coupled with an intermarriage of 40 percent in the United States, a dismal picture emerges. American Jewry will be reduced to a paltry remnant within four generations . . . with the present rate of decline calculated at more than 100,000 per year.

And if by chance there should be conception by "an accident," who among the major faiths in America is the leading proponent of abortion? Bernice, of course. What makes Jewish lemmings like Bernie and Bernice commit suicide? What drives them to destroy the Jewish people through birth control, abortions, intermarriage, and assimilation? What makes Bernie and Bernice run wild? This is the question that drives the American Jewish Establishment to frantically set up committees, study groups, surveys, and commissions. This is the question that drives them to study the problem again and again and then again. This is the question to which they allocate so much time and so much communal money. This is the question that is at the top of their puzzled order of priorities, over which they scratch their collective well-groomed heads: *What makes Bernie run?*

All the efforts to solve the problem are doomed to failure from the start because they so totally miss the point. The former Prime Minister of Israel, the grand old *bubbe*, Golda Meir, on whose words of wisdom hang so many Hadassah women (once Jews worshiped a golden calf; today it is a Golda one), told visitors from an American Jewish organization: "The answer to assimilation is to teach your children Hebrew." As if the Israeli Arabs, the Pope, the Pilgrim fathers, and Balaam's donkey had not all spoken Hebrew without remaining anything but Arabs, Popes, Pilgrims, and donkeys . . . .

Or we build huge temples, Jewish Community Centers, and Y's with gymnasiums and recreation areas where Jewish youngsters can play together, dance together, and, hopefully, marry together. And then they grow up and find other playmates in other places and we learn, at great expense, that not by AZA basketball and dances do Jewish youth live.

Or we find a new phenomenon. "If we are going to lose our people to *them*, let us try to get their people to *us*." And so we find the foolish Jew talking of Jewish proselytizing, of going out to actively convert Christians to the suddenly "true faith." And shall we soon hear of our answer to the "Jews for Jesus" in the form of "Christians for Moses?" And will there emerge from South Israel an Oriental Jewish version of Rev. Moon (according to the Jewish lunar calendar)?

Milton Himmelfarb tells the NCJCS that there will be an increase in Jewish proselytizing and not to feel "uncomfortable" with this because it is "in the Jewish interest." Indeed? After generations of condemning Christians for trying to snatch Jewish souls and priding ourselves on the Jewish tradition that bars seeking converts and even bids us to discourage those who come voluntarily lest we turn into a competitive, spiritual supermarket, suddenly we find that it is in our "interest" to do the opposite. Say that it is in the interest of the Reform and Conservative Jewish movements whose organizations and members are being decimated by intermarriage, but do not tell us that the disgusting missionary practice that will net us the kinds of misfits and psychotics that Christians are able to dreg (if I may coin this as a verb) from us, will be good for the Jewish people.

Conservative rabbi Gilbert Kollin of Flint, Michigan, proposes a "worldwide program of conversion," telling us that there are countless Gentiles who would be "delighted to become Jewish if only someone asked them." Says Rabbi Kollin: "Every convert represents a potential member for our shrinking synagogue rolls, a potential parent of children to send to our dwindling schools, a potential *oleh* [immigrant] for Israel." Moreover, "a convert as Jew-on-the-way-in cancels out the negative effect of the all-too-familiar Jew-on-the-way-out."

The bankruptcy of Jewish leadership was never more clearly seen. Admitting that he and rabbis like him have failed, Kollin has no answer except to convert Gentiles. As a rabbi he cannot save Jews, so he becomes an accountant and makes up the loss by saving Gentiles. He has no answer to the Jewish Bernies who flee his synagogue, his religious school, or his Israel (the thought that perhaps emigration to Israel might start with himself has probably never crossed his mind), for he *creates* Bernie.

Kollin continues, undaunted, saying that "the phenomenon of so many Gentiles eagerly 'wanting in' might stimulate large numbers of indifferent Jews to take another look at their Jewishness."

One can see the conversion supermarket opening in every Gentile neighborhood. Perhaps we can offer a free television set to one who converts and brings three friends. Synagogues can be requested to mail in their gross loss of Jewish members so that the new Gentile-Jews can be allocated to them properly. As Bernies leave, we can welcome new potential Bernies, and will they in turn be taking their leave of us sometime in the future? What a wonderful religion it is that opens its doors to Gentiles because it cannot hold on to its natural-born sons and daughters! What a magnificent faith that needs to give a morale boost to its own non-Jewish Jews by saying: "See, look at all the Gentiles joining. It *must* be good because it's the 'in' thing!"

But worst of all, we find the Jewish parents pathetically struggling against intermarriage and then rationalizing away surrender in a thousand sad ways. The proscription against intermarriage was once so clear and awesome that parents would go into mourning for a child who married a Gentile, equating this with spiritual death. But it takes a parent who truly believes to feel so strongly. When, on the one hand, the parent's faith is as weak as the child's (the difference is that Bernie is more honest) and, on the other, the parent is caught up in the great American ethic, "Love thyself," the prohibition against intermarriage begins to sag.

"Love thyself" means "Look upon life as an opportunity for

personal happiness." The young Jew sees his personal happiness with the pretty Bridget, and his parent, who lives to give Bernie everything in life (especially those things he/she did not have), is caught up in the dilemma: On the one hand, there is the Jewish prohibition that was proclaimed to save the Jewish people from spiritual genocide. On the other hand, there is Bernie's personal happiness as well as that of his parents (will they never see their Bernie again? Will they never share the joy of a grandchild?). Is all this really worth standing by a Jewish precept, especially since there are a million and one other precepts they do not observe?

And so they rationalize. They tell themselves that times are "different" today. And that she is really a wonderful girl, so intelligent and sweet. And that everyone is doing it, and "at least she is white." And that it is better to be friendly than to drive Bernie away entirely. And the Reform and Conservative rabbis aid in the charade by "conversions" that are patently fraudulent, one more false layer on a "Judaism" from which Bernie ran away in the first place, in such great measure because of its lack of honesty.

In his article "Intermarriage in the United States," (*American Jewish Yearbook*, 1970), Arnold Schwarts wrote:

> As the proscription [against intermarriage] is breached with increasing frequency, conversions, too, increase but grow ever more formal, until they come to be regarded as only a formality. Eventually, conversion is seen by the marrying couple, their peers, their parents, and, in some instances, by their rabbi, as dispensable and unnecessary.

All the Jewish wiles are used in an effort to delude themselves. But deep in the Jewish parents' hearts is the knowledge that Bernie has married a Gentile, that Bridget has no part in the People of Israel, that their son has somehow betrayed his people and snapped a chain of four thousand years, and—most of all—that *they*, the parents, have tragically and awesomely failed as parents and as Jews.

What does make Bernie run? The truth is that huge numbers of Jews simply find nothing of importance in the concept of being Jewish. It is, at best, irrelevant to them and, in a number of cases, distasteful to their view of life. In essence, the young American Jew, born in the United States and more than a step away from the Orthodoxy of his grandparents (or by now, perhaps, his great-grandparents), is prepared to ask himself the questions that his parents may be afraid to ask and to draw his conclusions from the lack of an answer. Surely, Bernie runs after Bridget to the extent that he runs *away* from Judaism.

In 1961, *Commentary* magazine, the prestigious and intellectual organ of the American Jewish Committee, published a symposium. Some of the bright and (then) upcoming intellectuals and writers on the American Jewish scene were asked their views on being Jewish, anti-Semitism, the possibility of their children converting or marrying out of their faith, and the State of Israel. Those who were asked are, for the most part, well-known names today. Their answers were shocking to the Jew who sought nothing more than to have his diluted Judaism without being bothered by inherent contradictions. They were incisive, brutal, and, in many ways, stripped the American form of Judaism naked.

Raziel Abelson, professor of philosophy at New York University, proceeded to the heart of the question by answering with a question (and thus, ironically, immediately demonstrating his Jewishness). "You ask me about being a Jew," said Abelson, "I will ask you a question: What is a Jew? Is being a Jew an essence . . . or is it an accidental trait like being a New Yorker?" What Abelson was getting at was that after a Jew stopped believing in and practicing Judaism, what was there that made it so important to be a Jew? The implications of the question are clear. And what but the grossest form of racism stops him from marrying a Gentile?

Jason Epstein responded: "That I am also a Jew seems relatively unimportant. . . . My son . . . may become a Jew or anything else he chooses. I doubt that I'll care, though I don't understand the religious impulse and would be puzzled to find it in him. . . . I have the impression that the traditional human groupings are on the way out. As we hear of new cultures and watch new societies grow, the old ones seem less inevitable." It should be pointed out that Mr. Epstein's reply was sent from Lagos, Nigeria. He added, "Jews are also human before anything else." It is a statement that more and more Bernies echo daily.

And Philip Green tells us that "a Jew can best fulfill his moral obligations *not* by becoming especially involved in the Jewish community . . . but by joining the community of radical political action." Furthermore, "where elements of Judaism conflict with the necessities of radical action and thought, I would drop them instantly." Why? Here is the crux of Bernie's feelings:

"For the commitment to broaden the contours of human freedom and justice must take precedence over everything else; *to me, the*

Jewish tradition has no meaning except when it is incident to that greater tradition" (italics mine).

Lionel Rogosin wants his children to be "familiar with the values inherent in all traditions and aware of the fallacies in all traditions," and he adds, "Given my beliefs, this possibility—that my children may convert to another religion—does not concern me."

Edgar Rosenberg objects to apostasy and then adds, "I've nothing whatever against intermarriage." Samuel Shapiro would be "rather surprised if any of my children become Mormons or Methodists; but I should point out that if they were to become synagogue-going Jews, this would also amount to conversion to another religion."

The uniform thread that goes through all the replies and comments is: There is nothing special about being a Jew; there is something reactionary about cleaving to parochialism and nationalism; in our days the struggle must be for a universal ethic and a universal One World.

Given such a negation of Judaism and Jewishness, is it any wonder that Bernie marries Bridget? Is it surprising that Bernie finds his parents', rabbi's and Establishment's criticism inexplicable? Bernie has transcended Judaism; it is too narrow and constricting. He has become a *human being.*

And this human being will marry another human being and Bridget is, indeed, that. His intermarriage is intimately tied to his rejection of Judaism as the most important part of his life, as a thing to which he owes loyalty and attachment. Bernie runs to Bridget and intermarriage because he runs away from Judaism.

2
Jews for Nothing, Everything, and ?

But what is happening in the United States today is more—far more —than just intermarriage and conversion. It is assimilation on the grand scale.

It is the Jews who are for everything—*but* Judaism. Who struggle for political causes that are non-Jewish and, many times, anti-Jewish. It is the Jews who desperately need spiritual answers and who turn to Christianity or to Eastern Mysticism or to Satanism. It is those who turn to drugs and to alcohol and to every conceivable solution because they neither know nor care to know about their heritage. And it is the young Jew who may—quite by accident—marry another Jew, simply because he or she happened to "be there." It is the Jew whose Jewishness is not a thing to be despised but simply something that is utterly and totally irrelevant—counting for no more than the color of the Jew's hair. He marries a Jew but could just as easily have fallen in love with a Gentile.

Glancing through the newspapers at random, one can sometimes suddenly grasp an overall picture. One need only have the eyes to see and the capacity to feel. And so, over the space of a short time, there appeared in the news media the following:

> Susan Stern. . . died Saturday at University Hospital in Seattle after suffering an apparent heart seizure. She was 33 years old. Mrs. Stern was born Susan Tanenbaum in Brooklyn in 1943. Her life was of the type that often bewildered middle-class parents of the 1960's. . . . She later became associated with the Weathermen, one of the most radical of the left-wing activist groups. Her life was often one of contradictions. She was a feminist who would dance topless . . . a political activist . . . who

by her own description never was really convinced by her own political line, a clear-headed observer who consumed hallucinogenic drugs . . . .

And:

Gary Davis, who declared himself the first "citizen of the world" in 1948, arrived here (Ben Gurion Airport) yesterday (in 1976) with a friend to find that Israel would not honor their passports, issued by the "World Service Authority. . . ." In 1948, he [Davis] burned his American passport in Paris, declaring himself a citizen of the world . . . ."

And:

B'nai Yeshua (children of Jesus), described by its founder as a "born-again Jewish-Christian movement," has purchased the former Stony Brook [Long Island] School for Girls as its new national headquarters. The group expects to run three programs a year with each attended by up to 60 "Jewish students that want training for the ministry," according to Michael Evans, the founder of the organization. . . . "We are just Jewish people that believe in Jesus," he said. Evans added, "I personally did not have strong faith in my Jewishness until I believed in Jesus . . . ."

A litany of Jewish spiritual genocide, of young and once young Jews, lost, searching, indifferent to and alienated from their Jewishness. Radicals, topless dancers, drug users, world citizens who see no need for Jewish exclusiveness, followers of a Jesus in whose name their ancestors were burned, and disappearers. The picture is a suddenly stark one—transcending intermarriage. It is the loss of a youth, the collapse of Jewish identity, the tragedy of Jewish spiritual suicide and genocide. Bernie runs not only into the warm arms of Bridget but into the passionate embrace of causes and peoples who have to be saved by him. All peoples, except his own. Bernie, the Jew turned "human being" . . .

Their names were Schwerner and Goodman and while the Jews of the Soviet Union were being throttled and denied the elementary right to live as Jews or leave for Israel, they and thousands like them were fighting for the cause of the Blacks. Jewish youth from Great Neck and Forest Hills and Scarsdale went South to undo the wrongs of the Wasps, and they sat down and sat in (jail), and Schwerner and Goodman were killed. And what did it matter to the suburban Jewish youth that Soviet Jews and Syrian Jews and observant Jews of Israel were struggling for *their* rights and that poor and elderly Jews in Brooklyn and the Bronx and Mattapan and Dorchester could not enjoy such elementary civil rights as walking the streets without fear of mugging or rape? The main thing was that "humanity" would be liberated and that meant Blacks and Puerto Ricans and Chicanos and lettuce and grapes. And that meant Cuba and Vietnam and Africa; and what "human being" had time for Jews?

And so Jerry Rubin and Abby Hoffman and Rennie Davis and all the Yippies and Hippies and fighters for freedom fought police in Chicago and New York and marched for Castro and "Ho, Ho, Ho," and went out to cut sugar in Cuba, and ran from military service in Vietnam and showed the world how much Jews loved them. And, indeed, greater love had no people. For though Le Roi Jones could write poems about knuckles in Jewish bodies and Stokely Carmichael and H. Rap Brown could attack Israel as enemies of the Black people—Jews refused to be thrust aside. They continued to march and the young white Jewish godesses from Yellowstone Boulevard continued to show their humanity by sleeping with them. But no one saw them marching for Jewish causes, for Bernie and Bernice had transcended that.

And when anti-Semitism erupted against Jewish teachers in New York City in 1968, and Jewish teachers who had earned their jobs by merit and Civil Service exams, and who had gravitated into teaching in the first place because of anti-Semitic denial of professional and private business opportunities, were faced with dismissal in favor of militant Blacks and physically threatened, there was, of course, a Council of Jews for Racial Justice. They were prepared to condemn the *teachers* and say that "an anti-Semitic scare is used to disguise the raw denial of democratic rights to minority groups in this city."

Bernies of all kinds were dropping a Judaism that was increasingly irrelevant and fighting for "human beings" even as they *became* human beings. Of course, Gary Davis, citizen of the world, *had* to be Jewish, a Jew who had outgrown his Judaism. Of course, for him there are no boundaries or nations, only a world in which all are citizens. While Blacks and Browns and Yellows are struggling for their own states and identities, while Scotch and Welsh and Bretons and Corsicans and Quebecois are formulating their proud new demands for independence, Gary Davis is giving up his. It is the story of millions of Bernies who suffer from spiritual and national malnutrition. They are starving to death even as they sit in their luxurious, well-upholstered suburban homes.

In the fall 1974 issue of *Response*, a young Jew named Bob Lamm wrote of what life in Westchester County was for him:

> Jewish institutions abounded, their main purpose being to promote our cultural, intellectual, and sexual inbreeding. To keep us away from *them*. I became disenchanted with my temple youth group, which stressed religious and cultural activities and "parochial" Jewish concerns [like Israel]. . . . My disgust with the parochialism and the racism of these upper-middle-class Jews led me to feel ashamed about being a Jew.
>
> My friends and I became increasingly hostile to the comfort and smugness of our Jewish community. We rejected the temple youth groups and created a dynamic and humanistic Jewish youth organization at the local YM-YWHA. Our concerns were equal rights and civil liberties, our heroes were from the early SNCC and our culture came from the protest songs of Dylan, Phil Ochs, and Tom Lehrer . . . .

It was a mass escape for the Bernies of America, and the Vietnam War sharpened the humanism and universalism of the escaped prisoner of Judaism. What did Israel's narrow escape from destruction in 1967 matter when Vietnamese were being butchered? "Hey, hey, LBJ, how many kids did you kill today?" Bernie marched and shouted obscenities and fought for his Vietnamese brothers (North, of course) and it made no difference that Hanoi Radio and Peking's news media attacked Israel as the "running dog" of the imperialists and pledged their undying "support of the Arabs." For Bernies had learned not only to march for *non*-Jewish causes, but even for *anti*-Jewish causes, and in the ranks of the many "human beings" there were also the Bernies who made up so much of the ranks of the Marxists.

In the middle of May 1967, Egyptian dictator Gamal Abdel Nasser suddenly sent two divisions of troops into the Sinai, ordered the United Nations Expeditionary Force out, and blockaded the Israeli port of Eilat. From all about the Jewish state came exuberant and hysterical Arab calls for "throwing the Jews into the sea," and in every Arab capital mobs shouted about "washing the streets of Tel Aviv with Jewish blood."

As the Arabs mobilized for war, Jews all over the world shuddered at the impossible thought: "Again . . . ?" What happened is history: the Israelis did not wait for genocide but smashed the Arab armies in six days, saving two and a half million Jews from the fate of their six million brethren. As the incredible news of the miraculous victories flashed across the world, Jews in every country (perhaps most especially those of the Soviet Union) erupted in a spontaneous explosion of joy and thanksgiving. Never in many years had all of world Jewry been so united—but not quite all.

In June 1967, a bare ten days after Israel was saved from extinction, a young woman named Rita Freed, in her capacity as chairwoman, addressed a large group of people in Manhattan's Academy Hall, off Union Square. Rita Freed was Jewish, as were the vast majority of those in attendance. On the wall were posters proclaiming "defeat and destruction of Israel" and "hands off Arab territory." In the front of the room stood a table heaped high with literature published by the Palestine Liberation Organization, the Syrian Government, and the Arab Information Center (a sample paragraph: "Violence, the killing of peaceful Arabs in their own homeland, operations of Zionist subversion, are all facts with which world opinion should be acquainted . . .").

The meeting was called by a Trotskyite group known as Workers World, many of whose leaders and activists were Jewish. Mrs. Freed became the chairwoman of a front group called the Committee to Support Middle East Liberation (CSML), almost all of whose members were Marxist-Trotskyite Jews. CSML flooded campuses with pro-Arab literature, demonstrated at the Israeli Consulate in New York, and published its own pamphlets, including: "The War in the Mideast—What Are the Forces Behind It?" by Freed, and "An Israeli Worker's Answer—An Alternative to Zionism," by Mike Rubin. Demonstrators against Israel included such Jews as David Axel, Joel Myers, Naomi Goldstein, Siggy Klein (also a member of the Veterans for Peace in Vietnam), Ed Vogel, Maryann Weissman, and the leading ideologician for Workers World, Sam Ballan, who writes under the name Sam Marcy.

There was not the slightest doubt what these Jews wanted—the end of a Jewish State and its replacement with a "Palestinian" one. That which every oppressed people in the world was entitled to and for which the Jewish revolutionaries spent so much time and effort, they refused to acknowledge to their own kind. Thus, in a leaflet prepared by Freed:

> The Committee to Support Middle East Liberation is holding a demonstration today in solidarity with the people of Palestine who were kicked out of their homeland and made into a nation of refugees when Israel was established.
>
> To demand more U.S. military and economic support of Tel Aviv [sic] is to demand more bullets and bombs to "help" American GIs in Southeast Asia. We must demand the withdrawal of the Jewish working people from the death trap which is Israel. For those Israelis who would refuse to live in a secular and democratic state, we call upon the U.S. Government to open the doors of America . . ."

Total support of the PLO call for the elimination of a Jewish state is Trotskyite policy, and the Jewish leaders of the various Trotskyite groups advocate it without qualms. Thus, men like George Novack, Harry Ring, and Dave Frankel enthusiastically support the official stand of the Trotskyite Socialist Workers Party on the Middle East:

> The struggle of the Palestinian people against their oppression and for self-determination has taken the form of a struggle *to destroy the state of Israel.* We give unconditional support to this struggle of the Palestinians for self-determination.

The support by Jews of the Arab efforts against Israel are tragic evidence of the spread of a malignant Bernie-ism in American Jewish life. Jews like Leo Huberman in the *Monthly Review,* Hal Draper in *New Politics,* and Irving Beinin, editor of the *Guardian,* all led the struggle against Zionism after the 1967 war. It is not surprising that the Jewish Marxists applauded the arrival of Yasir Arafat in New York in 1974. *Workers World* headlined its editorial (November 15, 1974) "Welcome Palestinians!" and wrote: "We welcome the Palestinian delegation to New York and applaud their courage in pressing their views here in the very bastion of imperialism." It is not surprising that Sam Marcy, Judith Stoll, and P. Meisner were avid attackers of Zionism and that the United Nations resolution branding Zionism as "racism" was called "a resounding defeat for the United States and all its imperialist allies."

For it is not on the issue of Israel alone that the Jewish radicals have totally supported anti-Jewish, Jew-hating groups, causes, and individuals. In the late sixties there burst into the open a long-smoldering Black anti-Semitism that shocked, most of all, the many Jews from Great Neck, Greater Neck, and Greatest Neck (this is how Jews conjugate their suburbs), who had spent so much of their lives raising up the "natives."

The focal point of the outbreak was the New York City school system, where a large percentage of the teachers were Jewish, in great measure because they were victims of discrimination in the years until the end of World War II and had been barred from other professions and by many private firms. In the Bedford-Stuyvesant and Ocean Hill-Brownsville areas of Brooklyn, Black militants began demanding "community control" of their schools, which meant, for all practical purposes, the firing of the teachers who had won their hard-earned jobs through merit in the Civil Service examinations.

The most outrageous kind of open anti-Semitism began to appear in the Black community with a group placing hate material in the boxes of Jewish teachers, threatening them and warning them to "get out." The official Black teachers group, the African-American Teachers Association, became the leading force for anti-Semitism; the lead article in the November-December issue of its organ, *Forum*, was blatantly Jew-hating. Written by a P.S. 68 teacher named John F. Hatchett, it was titled "The phenomenon of the anti-Black Jew and the Black Anglo-Saxon" and began:

> We are witnessing today in New York City a phenomenon that spells death for the minds and souls of our Black children. It is the systematic coming of age of the Jews who dominate and control the educational bureaucracy of the New York public school system.

Hatchett went on to charge that Black children were being "educationally castrated."

A leading official of the Black teachers group, Leslie Campbell, who taught at Junior High School 271 in Brooklyn, read a poem over radio station WBAI which began with the words: "Hey, Jew-boy, with the *yarmulke* on your head; you pale-faced Jew-boy, I wish you were dead." In the face of this provocation and of open threats of violence against Jewish teachers and the transfer of 17 Jewish teachers from their Brooklyn jobs by a Black community control chief, the Jewish radicals wrote in the June 26, 1969, issue of *Workers World*:

> The issue of "anti-Semitism" is also being dragged in by the hair. . . . No Jewish progressive gives even a modicum of confidence to any such charges against the African-American Teachers Association.

The Jewish Trotskyites were not only not appalled by the Jew-hatred of the teachers above, but a July 1968 conference of the Coalition for an Anti-Imperialist Movement at the Hotel Diplomat in Manhattan saw the platform again graced by Rita Freed, who "exposed the role of Israel as a watchdog for U.S. oil interests," as well as by Maryann Weissman, of the Trotskyite Youth Against War and Fascism, and Ralph Poynter, associated earlier with the threatening leaflets and now head of something called the Teachers Freedom Party. In an article describing the conference, Naomi Goldstein called Poynter a "militant fighter for self-determination for the Black people."

As for the author of the anti-Semitic article in *Forum*, John Hatchett, he was chosen in 1968 to head the Martin Luther King, Jr., Afro-American Center at New York University. When a furor arose over his hiring, Hatchett was reluctantly fired, which brought out a large number of white protestors—the vast majority Jewish—who struck the school and shouted: Join the Strike to Reinstate Hatchett! Not even the fact that the striking Black students would not allow the white Jews to seize the same buildings as they, had any apparent effect on the Jewish radicals.

Opposition to Israel and negation of any ties with the Jewish people are characteristic of the Jewish radicals. In the words of Ned Polsky (in the 1961 symposium in *Commentary*—see Chapter 1):

> Unless one defines a Jew in strictly racist terms—i.e., as anyone born of Jewish parents—I am not a Jew and since childhood have not thought of myself as such. . . . I see no virtues unique to the Jewish tradition and some evils. . . . All religions rest on false assumptions. I hope any children I have will become atheists. . . . I am anti-Zionist. Jewish chauvinism is no less despicable than other kinds of chauvinism—and more despicable than many, since it is based on racist ideology. . . . In the dispute between Israel and the 900,000 Arab refugees it has driven from their lands, I support the Arabs.

It is the words of Leon Trotsky to a Jewish delegation: "I am not a Jew but an internationalist!" It is the words of Hyman Lumer of the Communist Party, U.S.A., writing in the January-February 1976 issue of the party organ, *Jewish Affairs*. Describing his reaction to the words of a disillusioned Jewish Communist who had said: "First of all and before all I am a Jew," Lumer wrote:

> I was so shocked and hurt that I think I did not listen any more. A Communist speaking to Communists and saying: "First of all I am a Jew!" Such is the impact of the poison of nationalism even on veteran class fighters! A Communist is first of all and second of all and last of all a Communist.

And so they continued down the road of self-destruction and self-hate, overlooking and ignoring and rationalizing all the Jew-hatred and contempt, and joining in with the enemies of their own people and in the destruction of Judaism and Jewishness.

This phenomenon of self-hatred is a complex one as are all the other examples of Jewish *selbsthass*. At times it is the pathetic kind of a Dr. Karl Landsteiner, Jewish-born Nobel Prize winner, who fled Hitler's Germany in the 1930s and arrived in the United States to file an injunction against *Who's Who in American Jewry* from including his biography. As an explanation, he wrote:

> It will be detrimental for me to emphasize publicly the religion of my ancestors, first as a matter of convenience, and secondly, I want nothing in the slightest degree to cause any mental anguish, pain, or suffering to any members of my family. My son is now 19 years old and he has no suspicion that any of his ancestors were Jewish.

The realization that if not his son, then at least Hitler had discovered the "secret," had no effect on Landsteiner. If anything, it made him and Jews like him more determined than ever to hide that "secret."

One of the most penetrating analyses of *selbsthass* is the famous essay, "Self-hatred Among Jews," written by Kurt Lewin in 1941. In it, he says:

> The self-hatred of a Jew may be directed against the Jew as a group, against his own family, or against himself. It may be directed against Jewish institutions, Jewish mannerisms, Jewish

language, or Jewish ideals. There is an almost endless variety
of forms which Jewish self-hatred may take. Most of them, and
the most dangerous forms, are a kind of indirect undercover
self-hatred.

The self-hating Jew may—and often does—come to believe what
the anti-Semite says about him. How can so many people in so many
different eras be wrong? he quietly asks himself. He believes the
defamations and he acts upon them in a variety of ways. He may
decide that he must escape such a people, and thus cuts off all contact with them. If this is not enough, he may try to prove that he is
not one of them by attacking them and trying to destroy them. Or
he may decide that the only way that he—lost, alienated, rootless,
without belief in nation or religion, lacking in clear identity, with
no motherland or fatherland, a minority subject to hatred and
persecution—can survive, is to destroy all nations and religions and
roots and identities. He can try to become a human being in a world
in which there are *only* human beings. He can adopt a kind of
Samson complex—destroying the temple of nationalism and identity
over his own head. "If I have no identity, let there be no identity
for anyone," he cries. "Let the souls of the Philistines perish with
me, who has none."
And so Bernie runs to Marx, himself a Bernie, and tries to destroy
his Judaism and himself.
A few years ago a young Jew named M. Jay Rosenberg, who himself had gone the leftist Bernie route, wrote an article titled "To
Uncle Tom and Other Such Jews." It appeared in the *Village Voice*
February 13, 1969, and read in part:

> It is becoming increasingly fashionable in certain left-wing
> Jewish circles to put down everything Jewish. These Jewish
> leftists, hung up because they were not born Protestant, find
> that they can glibly resort to anti-Jewish stereotypes without
> being referred to a good psychiatrist. It is now quite acceptable
> for the Jew to attempt to ingratiate himself with the *goyim* by
> condemning what he has always been ashamed of. . . . He
> desperately wants assimilation; Jewishness embarrasses him. He
> finds the idea of Jewish nationalism, Israel notwithstanding,
> laughable. The leftist Jewish student is today's Uncle Tom.

Strong words and sometimes accurate, but sometimes not, and,
above all, missing the point. There is self-hatred among many of the

Bernies, but there is mainly something else: in many cases, a genuine question as to why nationalism is important and why Jewish nationalism has any value. The acceptance of Black nationalism is, for the leftist Jew, a hope that Marxism will follow as the capitalist system is torn apart by racial and national problems. But the young Marxist Jew feels that *he* has gone "beyond" nationalism. There is an immense amount of condescending to the "backward" Black here as the Jewish Marxist, who has already grasped the need to drop nationalism, "understands" the need of the Black to achieve it before he can drop it.

Rosenberg is rightly angry at Jewish Marxists, but he, too, does not understand them fully. For self-hate, too, has roots that must be understood, and merely because Rosenberg feels *his* "Jewishness" (though he might be hard pressed to define it), there are countless Bernies who do not. There is almost nothing that will teach them the futility of the race they run. The same Jews who opted in Germany for assimilation and Prussianism, were repaid for their love of fatherland with Hitler's Auschwitz. The same Bernies who played so great a role in the Bolshevik revolution, who denied their Jewishness in favor of internationalism, received their "reward" too. It is said that in 1921, the Chief Rabbi of Moscow, Rabbi Jacob Maze, pleaded with Leon Trotsky for the Russian Jews and their institutions. Trotsky answered, as always, that he did not consider himself a Jew but rather a Bolshevik revolutionary. To which Rabbi Maze replied: "The Trotskys make the revolutions and the Bronsteins pay the bills."

Rabbi Maze referred to the fact that Jewish revolutionaries play such a great role in the destruction of their own people. There is another, more ironic sadness. The same Trotsky who fled his Bronstein heritage to make the revolution, in the end pays the bill—*for the Gentile still knows him only as Bronstein.* And the third sadness is that more than 35 years after Trotsky/Bronstein was repaid for his part in the revolution by a Stalinist icepick in his head, his philosophical Jewish heirs, the young Bernie/Trotskys of our time, have learned nothing and continue to run after their Marxist Bridget.

And there are other Bernies running in other races, away from Judaism, but after other things.

One of the early Christian fathers, St. John Chrysostom, wrote of the Jewish people: "Their rapine, their cupidity, their deception of the poor . . . they are inveterate murderers, destroyers, men possessed by the devil." St. Justin, at the very beginning of the Church, wrote:

"The tribulations were justly imposed on you for you have murdered the Just One." And Origen concluded: "We say with confidence that they will never be restored to their former condition. For they have committed a crime of the most unhallowed kind, in conspiring against the Saviour of the human race."

Martin Luther could say: "Set their synagogues on fire and whatever does not burn up should be covered over with dirt . . . their homes should likewise be destroyed . . . they should be deprived of their prayer books and Talmuds in which such idolatry, lies, cursing, and blasphemy are taught."

Christian deeds were stronger than words. In the year 1262, in London alone, 1,500 Jews were killed by mobs led by cross-bearing clergy. In the year 1099, the Crusaders captured Jerusalem, assembled all the Jews in the synagogue, and burned them alive, marching around to sing "Christ We Adore Thee." On their way to the Holy Land, Crusaders massacred hundreds of Jews in the cities of Worms and Mainz. There is a nearly 2,000-year history of Crusades, Inquisitions, Pogroms, Burnings, Drownings, and Massacres by a church that shouted at the Jew, "Christ-killer!"

Things are changing. If the old Jewish grandfather—zayde—was murdered for having killed Christ, some of his grandchildren are busily resurrecting Christ. The zayde preferred to lose his body and keep his soul; his grandchildren are opting for the opposite.

On the streets of Manhattan and San Francisco, on the campuses of UCLA and Michigan, a young man hands out a little pamphlet that reads: "Jesus made me kosher. . . . The Jewish Thing: He is our Messiah and our atonement. . . . Jesus is what makes some of us want to be more Jewish." The pamphlet is signed "Jews for Jesus," and the o in the word for is a Star of David. It is not a hilarious comedy, a farce or put-on. In the crazy world of Bernie, it is possible to be a good Jew—the real Jew—and believe in the man in whose name Zayde was burned by Catholics and Protestants alike. It is possible to be a real Jew, "kosher" and all, and believe in a man whose followers negated or modified kashrut at will.

And so we find one young Bernie who writes to the New York Times (March 9, 1976): "There are those of us who didn't give up the revolution. . . . We found out that Jesus was everything the Bible says he is, the one G-d of Israel manifest in human form, with real power to heal, to save, to overcome depression and worse—now." The letter is signed "Joel Stein."

Of course, the Christian missionaries have a field day with the Bernies who embrace the real Christ-killers, those who kill in the name of Christ. The American Board of Missions to the Jews, among others, subsidizes the "Christian" Bernies. Having found one such Bernie named Martin Meyer Rosen (his name progressively became Judaized so that he now calls himself "Moishe"), they published his little booklet called *How to Witness Simply and Effectively to the Jews.*

Other Christian missionaries have understood the possibilities of using the Bernie syndrome for conversions. Out of a camp in Texas, comes a bulletin of the B'nai Yeshua. Dated September 1976, it tells in glowing words of a golden opportunity to purchase a huge building on Long Island to serve as a center for missionary activity among Jews. In the bulletin of these Jewish Bernies, we find a report from Marvin Pressman:

> We continually receive salvation reports from our Jewish believers across the country who are reaching the Messiah through our materials. We recently received a letter from a young Jewish man who is in prison: "I read all the materials you send. You have made it easier to understand the things of G-d." If you know of any Jewish believers, please send me their names and addresses this month so we can send them our tracts and material to reach Jewish people for Jesus.

Song groups known as The Psalms of David and The Wailing Wall are used for concerts that attract young potential Bernies. We are asked by B'nai Yeshua: "If your are interested in having our group at your Fellowship, Congregation, or college campus, simply write to Deacon Silverman [sic]."
And:

> As you are aware, we have completed our Shechinah '76 film and it is already being sent out to the different broadcasting stations. Ed Rosen, the Director of Shechinah '77, is working very hard on the conferences. . . . Please pray for the Shechinah conferences because they are going to be held with G-d's grace in cities like Los Angeles, Philadelphia, Cincinnati, Miami . . . and many more cities across the United States.

But, of course, it is New York, with the most Bernies in the world, that is the main target, and the "Christian" Bernies write: "We are believing G-d that within eight or ten weeks we can all be moved

in and begin harvesting the fruit among the largest population of
Jewish people in the world."

By October 1976, *Newsday*, the Long Island newspaper, could
report that B'nai Yeshua—described as a "born-again Jewish-
Christian movement"—had purchased a former school for girls in
Suffolk County for no less than $480,000 (later repairs and renova-
tions upped the total cost to $800,000). The plans are to take the
12-acre property and build there a school for 60 Bernies who would
be trained to "witness" to the Jews.

B'nai Yeshua is not the only such group "among the largest
population of Jewish people in the world." The Christ Lutheran
Church in East Meadow, Long Island, is the home of the "Hebrew-
Christians." Wearing *talaysim*, (prayer shawls) and *yarmulkes*, they
will listen to their leader make a traditional Hebrew blessing and
then announce baptism schedules. The leader is a Lutheran
minister, Jack Hickman, a Bernie par excellence. The son of a
Jewish mother, he was raised in Portland, Oregon, as, in his words,
a "Marrano" (the Spanish Jew of the Inquisition period who posed
as a Christian to escape the rack but who practiced Judaism
secretly). Several hundred Bernies have joined this example of confusion in our times—a "Jewish" service that includes Communion
and prayers to Jesus.

The head of the youth arm of the Hebrew-Christians, known as
Genesis, is 27-year-old Robert Gross, who says:

> I went the whole route of going to Hebrew school, reading
> the Torah, and never having it translated. I became
> alienated. . . . Like a lot of young people I got involved with
> different social movements such as radical politics in college. I
> was looking for quality life, life with some real purpose and
> meaning. Through that process I became open to new ideas
> and I came into an understanding of Messianic Judaism.

The Hebrew-Christians established a storefront counseling center
in East Meadow, known as Rebirth (with the large Hebrew letters
that spell out the Hebrew equivalent) as well as a coffeehouse and
full-time elementary school in North Massapequa.

Excited by the influx of Bernies, Christian missionaries have
thrown millions of dollars into the drive to make Bernie run even
faster in the direction of Jesus. At least 80 missionary groups are
working in the New York area alone, and Jewish Bernies and

Bernices such as Moishe Rosen, Herb Zwickle, Sue Perlman, and David Mann happily crucify themselves daily as their frantic parents, rabbis, and Jewish organizations scratch their bewildered heads and shout: What makes Bernie cross?

The most grotesque of Bernie's love affairs with Christianity is the one which finds him reverently baying at the Moon. In this case, the Moon in question is Sun Myung Moon, head of a phenomenon known as the Unification Church. Backed by huge amounts of money (growing evidence points to the South Korean government as the source), the Unification Church speaks of the coming Messiah (obviously Moon), and blind obedience to the directives of Moon is clearly the major "principle" of the "Church." Said one ex-Moon member: "We were taught to obey every order, including dying for Moon." The members go through a total indoctrination program, featuring continuous praying and singing, discussions, and calisthenics. The young potential convert is often stopped on the street by Moon recruiters and given warm and eager conversation along with an invitation to attend a weekend retreat. An exhausting schedule leaves no time for reflection and little for sleep. Six to eight hours of mind-numbing theology culminates in a final lecture in which the convert learns that G-d has sent Moon to save him and the world.

The member—and there are tens of thousands of them—usually gives all his possessions to the church since he needs nothing; Moon will take care of literally everything. The young people give him everything, including their minds, their bodies, their decisions, their destiny.

It is estimated that between 30 and 40 percent of the Moon members are Jewish.

Why? What makes Bernie run to the Moon? What makes him give up his body and soul?

Quotations from ex-Moon members abound: "It was like being taken care of. The people were very friendly and you really thought they did love you."

"I'll tell you what attracted me. I saw people who looked happy at a time when I felt lonely and desperate. I had no idea what to do with my life and they had a purpose."

Is this what made David Stoller, Mose I. Durst, Arthur Robins, Sheri Saeger, and thousands of Jewish Bernies become Jewish Moonies? What makes Bernie run to a church that says that the death of six million Jews was punishment for not having accepted

Jesus? What makes him happily accept a Moon "teaching" that says:

> Jesus came as the Messiah but due to the disbelief of and persecution by the people he was crucified. Since then the Jews have lost their qualification as the Chosen People and have been scattered, suffering persecution through the present day.

The Jewish Bernie is starved, literally starved for meaning in life. He runs wildly in all directions, leaping into and out of a bewildering and staggering number of isms and ideas. He swallows anything and everything in the hope that it will satisfy the cravings of his empty soul. For he *is* empty and he yearns to be filled with meaning and purpose. Who am I, he cries, and why am I? In *The Religion Situation*, edited by Donald Cutler, Professor Huston Smith tells of eight brilliant MIT science students who asked for a course in Eastern religions. They began with Eastern religious texts and then proceeded to "tantar, the kudalini, the chakras, the I Ching, karate and akido, the yang-yin macrobiotic (brown rice) diet, Gurdjieff, Meher Baba, astrology, astral bodies, auras, UFO's, tarot cards, parapsychology, witchcraft, and magic. And underlying, of course, the psychedelic drugs."

Bernie is into all of it: Transcendental Meditation of the Maharishi Mahesh Yogi, Hare Krishna (whose predominantly Jewish saffron-robed and strange-headed Krishna Consciousness people worship Lord Krishna as "the sweetest" god), Integral Yoga of the Swami Satchidananda, Zen and Tibetan Buddhism ("Zen is down-to-earth," says Philip Kapleau Roshi, who runs a Zen center in Rochester, N.Y., adding, "There is no G-d concept in Buddhism"), and, of course, Satanism.

Within a brief space of time, the following news items appeared in the press (the italics are mine):

1. New York: The Rev. Sun Myung Moon of South Korea spoke at Madison Square Garden before a packed crowd of 20,000 people. A Moon spokesman, *Marvin Schwartzman*, explained that Rev. Moon is G-d's prophet and that a central part of his theology is the doctrine that "G-d wanted Jesus Christ to find a perfect mate and have perfect children but man failed him."

2. Willamette: Local Bahai members held a meeting at Bahai Temple and then adjourned to Gillson Park for their annual picnic. *Melvin Haberman* was in charge of the afternoon's arrangements.

3. New York: The ancient ceremony of the Black Crown, a service sacred to the Kagyu order of Tibetan Buddhism, was performed for the first time in the Western world today. *Louise Baum*, a member of the Dharmadhatu or Buddhist Meditation Center, said the ceremony had particular application to today's "spiritually disturbed times."

This is Philip. Watch Philip run from Judaism. This is Marvin. Look at Marvin escape. This is Melvin. See Melvin jump over the Judaism he flees. This is Louise. She is a Jewish Tibetan.

Philip and Marvin and Melvin and Louise and Bernie after Bernie, running and running and running. The millions of them who run in all directions—and all the directions are away from Judaism. Their parents stand perplexed. Their rabbis have no answers. Their Jewish Establishment "defense" groups do not know how to defend. Bernie is running. Running from Judaism to Bridget, to Marxism, to Maoism, to One-Worldism, to Arafat, to Jesus, to the Moon, to everything that is strange. And surely the worship of strange gods that the Bible warns against was never so popular among Jewish Bernies as it is today.

Why? Where did the race begin? Who created Bernie? The Jewish Establishment devotes huge amounts of time, money, and energy to find the answer.

The puzzled shepherds of the American Jewish Community can close down their study groups and their commissions and their committees; they can put an end to the learned and expensive surveys. They can stop spending Jewish communal funds. What makes Bernie run away from Judaism? Who created the Bernie who pants after a *shiksa* or who marches for Jesus or Trotsky or Arafat or for nothing Jewish? Who created a Bernie who finds Judaism as unimportant as the color of his hair?

Why, the answer is obvious: the very same Establishment groups who are busily creating the committees, commissions, study groups, and surveys to find out the answer to these questions! Who made Bernie run away from Judaism? The American Jewish Committee, the American Jewish Congress, the B'nai B'rith, the federations on every level and in every locality, the temple rabbis, and Bernie's most intimate Establishment figures—his parents.

All of these are the criminals. All of these had a hand in the murdering of Bernie as a Jew. All of these robbed him of his heritage, of the beauties of his inheritance. All of these make Bernie run.

It was *all* the spokesmen for the American Jewish community—

the ruling clique, uniformly marching down the American road with a melting pot under their arms, beating it over and over again and shouting forth to the American Jew the Eleventh Commandment: *Thou shalt melt!*

3
The Undertaker

Who officiated at Bernie's burial? What was his mausoleum and who was his undertaker? Surely the very ones into whose care Bernie was placed so that he might grow to be a proud Jew. The temples·and their rabbis.

Throughout the country and throughout the world the Ten Days of Pentinence, 5720/1960, hung heavily over the Jewish people. There was not a rabbi who did not feel impelled to rise before his congregation and—for at least once that year—call upon them to return, to give themselves over to soul-searching, to consider the vast gulf between their own religious conduct and the high standards that they were obligated to maintain. And many were the rabbis who yearned with all their hearts to be given, if only once, a vast and towering pulpit from which to reach millions and speak to them words of Judaism.

One man had the great fortune to achieve just such a pulpit. He was a man widely known as a Jewish spiritual leader and his pulpit was unique—one of the world's great newspapers. Few men are given such an opportunity. Few men are allowed the happy privilege of rising on the awesome Days of Pentinence, and, through their pens, speaking to hundreds of thousands, to millions of readers of a distinguished publication.

Such, however, was the opportunity in the hands of Nelson Glueck, head of Hebrew Union College, the training ground for Reform Judaism. Undoubtedly the leading and best known of all Reform spiritual leaders, his article appeared in the Sunday *Magazine* supplement of the venerable *New York Times*, entitled "Book of Faith and of History."

Here was a religious leader, at the holiest period of the year, called upon to write. One might expect from him a summons to all—Jew and non-Jew alike—to think deeply of their Biblical heritage, to live once again the Bible principles of holiness, sanctity, morality, and sacrifice. Instead he faced the world, and, in rabbinical garb, destroyed the Bible.

Having gained fame as an archaeologist in the Negev desert, Glueck now turns to the question on so many lips. What do recent discoveries tell us about the Bible and its origin? Is it historically accurate? Who were its authors?

Dr. Glueck wrote (italics mine): "It is essential to bear in mind that the Bible is basically a religious, not a historical work. . . . There is therefore a vast difference between history *in* the Bible and the Bible *as* history."

Dr. Glueck was preparing the reader for the unpleasant fact that much, if not most, of the Bible is historically inaccurate. The authors, he declared, "adapted pagan myths; many of the best-known Biblical stories—the Creation, the Flood, Joseph and His Brothers—have earlier Sumerian, Assyrian, Babylonian, Ugaritic, and Egyptian counterparts."

And how is it possible for these stories to be merely transformed caricatures of the pagan peoples? How can a Divine Book be so originated? The answer by Dr. Glueck was simple. It is *not* of Divine origin.

> In Genesis, for example, at least three separate groups of writings can be distinguished. The first—in all probability the earliest writing in the Bible—was set down by anonymous scribes in Judah in the ninth century B.C. . . . [Biblical scholars tag this the "J-vah" or "J" document because of its frequent use of that form of the L-rd's name]. About a century later anonymous writers in the Northern kingdom of Israel added to the book their view of the same material. [Theirs has been termed the "E" or "Elohim" version because of their predilection for that form of G-d's name.] And still later, perhaps about 450 B.C., Judean editors intertwined both documents.

It is not my point to bemoan the fact that a Jewish religious leader destroys the very foundation of Judaism, a tragic paradox in itself.

Neither will I wearily repeat the protests of many, both Bible critics and laymen, that the discredited "J" and "E" theories not only are the grossest of hypotheses, but are riddled by contradictory

"J" words in supposed "E" documents, and vice versa. These things are clear.

It is not so much Glueck the sinner but Glueck the causer of sin that we must discuss. It is the consequences of his thinking that become important. For consider the effect of the Rabbi's words on a thinking Bernie.

Having destroyed the Divine origin of Judaism, what remains of the obligation to continue Judaism as an organized religion? If its uniqueness—the special, exclusive rituals and commandments—are indeed no longer Divine truth, then we may freely discard them and retain only the ethical or moral concepts. And, indeed, this is what Reform has done. But, of course, this is not the end. For if we are left here only with ethics, then how do we differ from other peoples and tongues and faiths? Surely atheists and agnostics and free thinkers who have no religious ties can also preach ethics and morality. What need then for a Friday night service in a temple of an established formal religion? Certainly, it becomes ludicrous to kiss a scroll which is part pagan myths, full of misplaced zeroes, and riddled with "E" and "J" documents. Such a book does not deserve any special resting place in a magnificent ark in Cincinnati or at Fifth Avenue and East 65th Street in Temple Emanu-El. At best it remains a book on a par with the New Testament, the Koran, the Rig-Veda, the writings of Rousseau, of Marx, of Ghandi. It remains, like these, just one fallible link—full of error and primitiveness—in man's climb up the ladder of civilization, and, as such, neither more nor less important (except sentimentally) than the others.

This is the inexorable, ironic consequence of Reform's destruction of the Divine origin and hence the unique truth of the Torah. Reform Judaism may have fearfully shrunk from accepting the consequences of the ridiculous spectacle of a "Book of Fraud" exalted by a fraudulent rabbi of a fraudulent temple, but surely Bernie has not.

If Reform leaders are perplexed at the lack of interest in Reform on the part of Jewish intellectuals, and if they are puzzled that the Jewish university student turns his back on them and becomes totally indifferent to all religion, the answer is clear: *They made him so*. The Jewish youngster, university student, intellectual, listen to Dr. Glueck destroy the divine foundation of Judaism, agree with him, and then—very logically—throw the entire thing into the trash box of obsolescence. They carry "progressive" Judaism to its logical conclusion: non-Judaism. Bernie is not a temple rabbi: he is too intellectually honest to give importance to a document that is neither unique nor Divine. Bernie the agnostic, the atheist, the long-distance Jewish runner from Judaism, is the flower that blooms from the seed of Glueck and all the temple rabbis like him.

In the spring of 1975, a temple in the deep South published its congregational bulletin. As it does each issue, it had a section titled "Congratulation on the Marriage of:" Among the rest were *mazal tovs* to the following happy Jewish marriages:

> Frank Canfield Hollister Jr. and Sally Ann Fraber
> Joseph Alton Kunstler and Donna Lee Hemphill
> Harry K. Wallfisch and Annette F. Faillio
> Steven M. Pollack and Peggy Ann Scott.
> And there were more . . .

The Philadelphia *Jewish Times* (one of the few independent Jewish newspapers in the United States until its takeover by the Philadelphia Federation's *Exponent*), in its October 16, 1975, issue, called Rabbi Mayer Selekman of Temple Sholom in suburban Broomall "the marrying rabbi." The point was that Selekman was ready and eager to perform intermarriages and had recently gone to Wilmington, Delaware, to co-officiate with a Protestant minister at an outdoor church wedding one Saturday. In an angry letter, the temple president, Harold Smolinsky, wrote (November 6, 1975) that the temple's board of trustees "strongly" resented the remarks and added: "We count ourselves extremely fortunate to have a rabbi who values people and sees their personal needs and happiness as his concern."

Bernie is not a fool. If his temple can congratulate the happy couple of an intermarriage and if his board of trustees can support their rabbi because he places the personal happiness of the inter-marrying Jew over that of Judaism, it is clear that: (1) there is nothing wrong with intermarriage; and (2) why should he not marry pretty Bridget and get both a *mazal tov* from his synagogue bulletin and his rabbi's presence at the happy affair?

The temple. The huge, expensive mausoleum where Bernie begins to be embalmed and buried as a Jew. The temple and its rabbi, presiding regularly over the death of young Jews. The temple rabbis. The kept theologicians who knowingly preside over fraud and grotesque jokes. The well-paid functionaries whose salaries are payments to hold their silence and to declare light, darkness and darkness, light; to give their stamp of *kashrut* on the impure meat that their temples serve up as "Judaism." The bribe-takers whose

eyes are blinded and consciences dulled by *kavod*, the honor of
sitting on the pulpit before the eyes of the congregants, and by the
comfortable salary augmented by the offerings of thankful beneficiaries of weddings, funerals, and unveilings. The false prophets
who hold their silence as Judaism is twisted, perverted, turned into
a humorless joke and who, knowing their own corruptness and
fraud of soul, rush to justify the fraud by "rabbinical" rulings that
pronounce them "good." The temple rabbis who take a Judaism of
Divinity and truth and go about Reconstructing it and Reforming
it and making a mockery of Conserving it.

The temple rabbis who took the age-old axiom of Revelation,
real Revelation, upon which is built the Divinity of Torah, and
junked it. The temple rabbis who made Judaism the product of
"wise men" (and if so, are there not wise Christians and Buddhists
and atheists?) and thus removed any sacredness and necessary reason
for observance. The temple rabbis, so many of whom do not believe
in G-d, took the real and awesome Jewish G-d of history who made
man and created all and who rewards and punishes, and exchanged
Him for a "god" who is the "spirit within man," indistinguishable
from indigestion.

They are the models of Jewish "religious" leadership we give unto
Bernie, these empty vessels whose greatest fortune is that their
congregants know even less about Judaism than they do.

These are your rabbis, O Bernie, and then they wonder why you
refuse to enter the temple over which they preside. Only they themselves know what frauds they are; only they, in their hearts, know
what a life of lies they lead; only they in the inner recesses of their
beings know the self-hate and contempt they feel for themselves
each day that they have to perform acts of faith they no longer
believe in and teach a religion that long ago they secretly began to
doubt. The temple rabbis, they created Bernie; they made Bernie
run.

In 1972, after being commissioned by Reform Judaism's Central
Conference of American Rabbis, Theodore I. Lenn and Associates
released the results of a sociological survey called *Rabbi and
Synagogue in Reform Judaism*. Though not enough Jews know
about the Lenn Report, as it has come to be known, it is more than
imperative that we take it out of the library where it was buried
and bring it to the attention of the Jewish community.

Chapter 8 of the report was titled "Religious Beliefs of Reform
Rabbis," and the first part is headed: *Belief in G-d: Traditionalists,*

Moderates, and Radicals. Based on questionnaires and interviews with Reform rabbis, the text of the chapter begins:

> There may have been a time when a study of a rabbinical group would not have included a chapter thus entitled, since it was taken for granted that everyone shared the same belief system. If that was ever true, it certainly is not so today. The data from the questionnaires and from focused interviews tell us that many rabbis are seriously questioning their own beliefs. . . .
>
> Here is how some of the self-labeling goes: "Agnostic; Atheist; Bahai in spirit, Judaic in practice; Conservative; I can't really label myself; Jew; Monotheist; Polydoxist; Reconstructionist at heart; Religious Existentialist; Theist; Theological Humanist; Traditionalist."

The highlights of the survey as stated in the report are:

Only one in ten rabbis states that he believes in G-d "in the more or less traditional sense," and of the younger rabbis (ordained 1969–71), only 3 percent do.

Some 14 percent of Reform rabbis *admit* to being either agnostics or atheists. (We may justly suspect that many more were inhibited and lacked the courage to openly admit that they, too, had doubts about the existence of G-d.)

Another 14 percent call themselves "nontraditionalist" believers; their concepts of G-d ranged over a wide field of definitions, many of them far from recognizable to those familiar with the usual Jewish concept of G-d.

Among the younger Reform rabbis, who will be leading their Jews in the future, no less than 42 percent have a radical concept in regard to belief in G-d, i.e., atheist, agnostic, nontraditional.

And so the nonbelieving rabbi is alive and well, walking with and teaching the Bernies sent to him by simple Jewish parents. Consider:

Until recently, there lived a rabbi named Martin Siegel in a 15-room suburban home in wealthy Lawrence, Long Island, one of the affluent "five towns" of the region. He was the rabbi of Temple Sinai and over a year of deeply personal psychological problems involving his wife and himself, he kept a diary which was published in 1972 under the title *Amen: The Diary of Rabbi Martin Siegel.* The entry for January 29, 1969, reads:

A young man in the confirmation class told me today he doubts whether he wants to be Jewish because he doesn't believe in G-d.

"I don't believe in G-d either," I told him. "But that has nothing to do with being Jewish."

He looked at me rather oddly. "What do you have to believe in?" he asked. "Anything?"

"Judaism is not a system of belief," I said. "Judaism is an effort to try and find some purpose and meaning in your life."

Of course, Bernie would have to be a cretin not to draw his own conclusions. And it is not only that the Jewish youngster listening to a Siegel would see in him a rabbi who does not believe in G-d. He would also, if he listened to such a "spiritual leader" long enough, hear a deeply troubled and confused person who would inculcate in his mind that Judaism itself is troubled and confused. For to the simple, ignorant Jewish youngster it stands to reason that one who is a rabbi, represents Judaism. Siegel continues a personal conception of "G-d."

A Jew must believe only what he wishes to believe, if anything. . . . For instance, it is not important whether G-d created us. Who cares if He did or didn't? It's what man himself creates and what man creates with other men and what G-d creates with us that is real and which stands behind us and in front of us.

A true Jew [sic] does not believe *in* G-d. He believes *that* G-d can be a vital force in the expression of man's life. . . . Worshiping G-d has nothing to do with believing *in* Him.

One cannot know whether all the above is the product of a truly confused mind or that of a man who has not the simple courage to say: There is no G-d and thus there is no need for Judaism, but rather let all men go out and find their happiness without creating artificial religious barriers between human beings. But he surely can know that these words, spoken to the boys in a confirmation class in Lawrence, Long Island, will not be lost on them. The rabbi of Temple Sinai will have confirmed them as the swiftest runners from Judaism on the Island . . .

The fact is that the Reform and in many cases Conservative rabbis, who harbor doubts or are convinced that there is no such thing as the traditional Jewish G-d—the One who is real, transcendental, the Creator of Man, who directs history, who is omniscient and omnipotent, who rewards and punishes—do not have the courage to come out and deny Him. They go through elaborate philosophical and intellectual gymnastics in order not to say the simple words of atheism that would make them honest men—and perhaps also men without jobs. But there are some who have broken away from Reform and Conservatism and have established "atheist" or "humanist" temples. Some still use the word G-d but make it quite clear that the word means nothing remotely like what it says.

Thus, a large advertisement that appeared in the Sunday edition of the *New York Times* on October 19, 1975, stated that it was "Announcing a new congregation for Jewish and interfaith and others in search—The Temple of Universal Judaism."

The ad announced services at the Friends (Quaker) Meeting House and said that the temple had come into being "to serve interfaith couples and families." Among its principles were: "We believe that humanity and the universe, in all their complexity and contradiction, manifest the One Living God." Translated, this means that there is no Being, independent and outside of us, Creator and Maker, known as G-d. While still lacking the courage to junk Him completely, the temple, led by Rabbi Roy Rosenberg, who has himself gained fame as one of the "marrying rabbis," had at least moved to the point where it defined G-d as being nonexistent.

At least one temple, however, appears to have made the total transition and accomplished the stupefying feat of saying that there *is* no G-d and yet building a temple and having a rabbi, committed to that proposition! It is Birmingham Temple, located in a wealthy (naturally) Detroit suburb. Founded in 1964 by eight members of the largest Detroit Reform temple at the time (with the neighborhood "changing," they decided to leave liberal theory and practice and fled to the suburbs, where they would be able to preach integration from a new temple), it was established on the principle of "free inquiry." The "rabbi" was Sherwin T. Wine, who radically reformed the Reform service, but at first retained the word "G-d"— with the congregation clearly understanding that it was being used as a symbol for the "best in man."

Soon, however, Wine and his ritual committee decided to move to a more "honest" position. If G-d meant "ideal man," then that is what should be used. Orders to that effect went out to the religious school [sic] teachers and a whole new liturgy was composed by the atheists, who dropped any mention of G-d. The *shema* and the *kaddish* were dropped and the congregation stopped praying to a

"Thou." Instead, they introduced such prayers as "Blessed be peace in the world, blessed be peace in man." The reader now said: "Let us adore the hero within us and pay rightful honor to what we must become."

Rabbi Wine stuck firmly to his atheism, saying: "If by atheist you mean a person who denies the existence of a Supreme Being existing in time and space and having the attributes of a human being [?], then I am an atheist." For this he was applauded by the Marxist-Zionist and atheist movement, Hashomer Hatzair, which, however, advised him that logic dictated his dropping the title "rabbi" and joining their group, which, for all intents and purposes, wanted what he did and which had been around for decades before his temple. Rabbi Wine did not agree and, indeed, a Society of Humanistic Judaism is now in existence and is even discussing a school which will ordain Humanistic rabbis. Indeed, these rabbis are increasingly aggressive in their assertions, as one can see from an angry letter Wine, Philip Shechter, and Daniel Friedman—humanist rabbis all—sent to the *Jewish Post and Opinion* (June 23, 1972), deploring a proposed resolution to ban rabbis from performing intermarriages. Wrote the Humanists (italics mine):

> For Jews who believe that the preservation of Jewish identity is the most important Jewish enterprise, the ban on inter-marriage is a rational restriction. However, for those Jews who do not accept this value system, the ban on intermarriage is both irrational and immoral. *We do not accept this value system.* We dissent from the belief that the primary moral obligation of every Jew is to promote and sustain Jewish identity. We are convinced that it is subversive of human dignity. . . .
>
> Individual Jews do not exist to maintain Jewish identity. Jewish identity is an ethnic and religious option available for the fulfillment of individuals. We affirm the right of individuals to marry whomever they wish to marry. . . . We are pleased to officiate at the marriage of any two people who desire our presence. . . . We hope that other rabbis will choose to do the same."

Of course, the question that every logical Bernie will ask is: Given your beliefs—and they are eminently sane and I agree with them and I care to be a Bernie and not a Jew—who needs you to officiate? Who needs a rabbi, Humanist or not? The logic is impeccable as Bernie looks at the ludicrous and mind-boggling sight of a "Judaism" that has been organized to convince Jews that they need not be Jewish!

It is important to note the reaction of the Rabbinical Synagogue Establishment to the Humanists. Wine became the subject of a bitter campaign by all the Jews who had betrayed Orthodox Judaism. The charge against Wine? That he was betraying Judaism. The *Detroit Jewish News* refused to carry the temple's schedule in its column, "Detroit Jewish Religious Services." And Rabbi Wine, a member of the Reform rabbinate's Central Conference of American Rabbis, was asked to appear before the Reform rabbinate to explain himself. The irony is delicious, though heartbreaking.

For Wine's "apostasy" and "heresy" was nothing of the kind. It was the direct result of and logical consequence of Reform Judaism, which had originally broken with traditional Judaism, its basic concepts of Revelation and a Chosen People, and which had—time after time—told Jews and Bernies: *Judaism has no dogmas.* Indeed? If true, then why the fuss over Wine? If Torah at Sinai could be dropped and the Divinity of the Talmud discarded, if the need to observe the Sabbath, eat kosher food, observe the laws of ritual purity (*mikvah*), and all the rest that Jews had held sacred for so long as an integral part of Judaism could be cast away into the trash bin—why could Wine not throw away G-d?

Wine, while hardly honest as long as he insisted on calling his "theology" Judaism and himself a rabbi, was certainly more honest than the Reform and Conservative rabbis, who, in his words, believed in "a G-d whose existence had to be saved through mental gymnastics or anti-intellectual leaps of faith" and who "was not worth having." In an article in the *Humanist* magazine (August 1975), Wine charged that Jews "have rejected the value system of the Torah—whether their guilt allows them to confess the truth or not. The real values of contemporary urbanized Jews have little or nothing to do with the ethical concepts that permeate the Torah."

Wine was striking pitilessly at the bitter nerve of truth. Both the American Jew and his temple and rabbi no longer believed in the Torah as Divine, or in a G-d that was really a G-d, and the lip service was as unreal as their hoisting high the Torah every Sabbath and saying, "And this is the Law that Moses set before the Children of Israel, by the word of G-d through Moses," and then going out to violate almost everything in that scroll. How many rabbis, temples, or congregants in the Reform and Conservative movement really believed in a G-d who hears prayers and intercedes, who

rewards and punishes according to their observance or nonobser-
vance of Torah laws? What Wine had chosen to say publicly,
frightened timid and guilt-ridden Jews in the Reform and Conservative movement who believed the same privately. Their children
—Bernies—were more honest than either they or Wine. Bernie
listened carefully, watched closely, understood what was occurring
in his Reform and Conservative environment—and chose to be
honest. He ran.

For it is not only the G-d concept that is at the heart of Judaism
as a unique and special religion and idea. Even those rabbis and
temples that may believe in a traditional concept of G-d can reject
the Torah as a divine instrument. It cannot be emphasized too
strongly that Judaism and Jewishness live and die on the question
whether they are unique, special, different from any other religion,
and most especially whether they are of Divine origin. If the Jewish
faith is not a uniquely Divine thing, it has no sanction, it has no call
on anyone, it has no right to demand allegiance from anyone. If G-d
did not create Judaism (let alone not exist), there is nothing unique
about it that calls for permanence and unflinching loyalty. If there
was not a real event at Sinai where G-d gave the Torah to the Jewish
people, Bernie has every logical right to complain about a man-made
Judaism which stands in the way of universalism and one world by
its very insistence upon using the term "Jew." And every one of the
non-Orthodox "wings of Judaism, some honestly, many less so, have
done away with Judaism as such a religion. Consider.

In 1922, a man named Mordecai M. Kaplan resigned from the
Jewish Center on Manhattan's Upper West Side and founded the
Society for the Advancement of Judaism. Thus was officially born
the Reconstructionist Movement, which today has 30 affiliated
synagogues. Kaplan decided to advance Judaism, and presumably
save Bernie, by the following definitions of G-d: "The cosmic process
that makes for man's life abundant or salvation; the Power both in
and beyond nature which moves men to seek value and meaning in
life" (see *The Future of the American Jew*, 1948, and *Sabbath
Prayer Book*, Reconstructionist Foundation, 1945). No wonder
Bernie, reading this, is driven to drink with Wine.

In his "The Meaning of G-d for the Contemporary Jew," Kaplan
was more specific, saying:

> The *modern* idea of God must reflect the democratic and
> scientific character of the only kind of Jewish civilization that
> can be viable in our day. . . . At present, the term "G-d" is

increasingly understood as a functional, not as a substantive noun, thus denoting that power in the cosmos, *incuding man*, that makes for the salvation of men and nations (italics mine).

It takes little for a thinking Bernie to thus define G-d as socialism, capitalism, free trade, ethics, or Mao Tse-tung. And Kaplan underlines this as he now describes as "divine, godly or holy, whatever impels man individually and collectively to bring about a better and happier world." (Television? Monday night football? Massage parlors?) *How* does a Jew pray to a "power in the cosmos, including man?" Kaplan says: "It [prayer] will consist of intellectual reflection on human experience seeking to identify those elements in it which are a manifestation of Divinity."

Little need be said as commentary. Bernie reads this as he reads the following description of Reconstructionism (*Jewish Week*, May 30, 1976): "Reconstructionists reject the concept of a Supernatural G-d who chooses Israel from among all the nations to serve His purpose." (Kaplan called the Chosen People concept a "futile compensatory mechanism of imagined superiority" and eliminated it on the grounds that it makes "invidious comparisons between Israel and other nations.")

> The movement does not believe the Jewish religion to be supernaturally revealed to Moses, never to be changed, nor does it accept as final the authority of the Talmud. Rather, it believes that every generation has the responsibility, the right and duty, to fashion its beliefs and practices in the light of its own ideals.

In the light of its own ideals. Bernie reads this and asks: including the honest, straightforward doing away of a G-d concept of any kind, of eliminating a Jewish People along with all national cultures? Why not? There are no longer dogmas in Judaism, including the one that says that Judaism need exist at all.

Reconstructionism, a pitiful attempt to throw away Judaism and have it too, recognizes the tragicomedy that it represents. What possible motive can it give Bernie to survive *as a Jew*? One of the spokesmen of the movement, Milton Steinberg, unable to conceive of Judaism as a religion, called it "religious culturalism" and argued for survival in terms of the social and psychological consequences of turning one's back on one's cultural origins. Assimilation, warns Steinberg, means "ceasing to be what you are" and "the deliberate throwing away of a large cultural tradition." Aside from drawing a large yawn from a Bernie who has now acquired a new cultural tradition (Bridget, Manhattan, Yale, Socialism), Steinberg's warning is dealt with by Will Herberg (*Commentary*, November 1951): "But it is surely obvious that the whole course of American history has been, for the immigrant, a ceasing to be what he was and a dissolution of the culture he had brought with him into the common stream of American life." And then Herberg hits the Reconstructionist nail on its head:

> In the Reconstructionist analysis there is no real sense of the uniqueness of Jewish existence because the concept that can alone give meaning to this uniqueness—the divine election and vocation of Israel—is either ignored or rejected.

Absolutely true. Bernie understands it and acts upon this understanding by an honest rejection of anything that gives him no reason to see it as unique. And what is true for Reconstructionism is, of course, quite as true for Reform Judaism.

From its very beginning, Reform Judaism in America rejected the concept that G-d had given the Jewish people a Torah at Sinai. Neither the Written Law (the Five Books of Moses) nor the Oral Law (the Talmud) was considered to be Divine, but rather the product of different men at different times. In the words of the Pittsburgh Platform, the Bible reflected "the primitive ideas of its own age," and "today we accept as binding only its moral laws and maintain only such ceremonials as elevate and sanctify our lives." The question is obvious: Who is to decide just what those laws are? And who has the right to decide it for today's youth? What gives the Reform rabbi the right to decide what is good? What need for a Reform rabbi? Why just the laws of the Torah that "elevate and sanctify our lives?" Why not also the laws of the New Testament, *Das Kapital*, and Buddha?

The agony that semihonest Reform rabbis and writers have felt is reflected in numerous articles, all stating the question: Why Reform Judaism? Articles that appeared in the intellectual Jewish magazine *Commentary* were legion and included: "Reform Judaism's Fresh Awareness of Religious Problems," by Eugene Borowitz (June 1950); "Reform Judaism Reappraises Its Way of Life," by Israel Knox (December 1954); and "The Dilemma of Liberal Judaism," by Emil Fackenheim (October 1960). Fackenheim has had a long, ongoing struggle within himself, as his numerous articles on the subject—all without a logical answer—attest.

The agony is nothing new. As Nathan Glazer wrote in 1951 in *American Judaism*:

> Thus, some Reform rabbis were forced by the logic of the Reform position to abandon Reform Judaism and become apostles of a religion of progress in which the distinction between religions and peoples was of no account. Felix Adler (1851–1933), son of Rabbi Samuel Adler (1809–91) of Temple Emanu-El in New York . . . could not accept a distinctive Jewish religion as valid in the contemporary world; as a result he founded the Ethical Culture Society in 1876. . . . It was one of the possible developments of Reform and not the most unreasonable one.

It is interesting to note Adler's own explanation, from the same book:

> Was I to act a lie in order to teach the truth? There was especially one passage in the Sabbath service which brought me to the point of resolution: I mean the words spoken by the officiating minister as he holds up the Pentateuch [Torah] scroll: "And this is the law which Moses set before the people of Israel." I had lately returned from abroad . . . and had become convinced that the Mosaic religion is, so to speak, a religious mosaic, and there is hardly a single stone in it which can with certainty be traced to the authorship of Moses. Was I to repeat these words? It was impossible. It was certain that they would stick in my throat.

Countless rabbis feel the same way, but lack the honesty and courage of an Adler. They remain in their well-paying pulpits, with words sticking in their throats, and privately make discreet inquiries to officials at the Federation of Jewish Philanthropies concerning psychiatric help. Rabbi Martin Siegel (who by now has escaped Lawrence and gone on to Columbia, Maryland, to run an interfaith center along with a Catholic nun, a Protestant minister, and a Jesuit priest, all of whom help intermarrying couples overcome their "guilt") wrote in his diary:

> Why am I a rabbi? I don't know. How did I become a rabbi? I'm not sure. . . . What is the rabbi? Who is the rabbi? What is the rabbi supposed to be? Why am I the rabbi? Through a

decade as a practicing rabbi, first as a chaplain in the Marine Corps, then in Wheeling, West Virginia, and now in Long Island, the questions have never gone away.

One could feel sad for the lost and confused rabbi if one did not think of all the lost and confused Bernies he helped to drive away by his own confusion.

Adler was not the only honest Reform rabbi who packed his bags and left. At Temple Israel in Boston, one of the most prestigious temples in the United States, two successive rabbis left because they could not accept Judaism as a distinctive religion. Solomon Schindler left the pulpit to become a spokesman for Edward Bellamy's national socialism, and his successor, Charles Fleischer, left to establish a community church in Boston. To quote Glazer: "If what Judaism had to say was only what rational man inspired by a desire for justice and progress could accept, then why Judaism?" It is one of the few statements before which Bernie is prepared to bow his head and murmur Amen.

And so, today, Reform rabbis are torn apart in their frantic effort to escape from the dilemma of a Divine Judaism, in which they do not believe, versus a nondivine Judaism, which is irrelevant. They are increasingly unable to accept a G-d who really is not, but who is necessary for Jewish survival. In the words of Fackenheim: "The present fashionable combination of disbelief in an existing G-d with the active perpetuation of a religion as a 'useful' or 'wholesome' illusion is both intolerable dishonesty and, from a religious stand-point, blasphemy." They cannot escape from the intellectual imperative that Fackenheim, in one of his innumerable essays on the subject—that say so much about his own dilemma, inasmuch as he so brilliantly poses the problem, but never the solution—put this way (*Commentary*, December 1951):

> If revelation must go, with it must go any possible religious justification for the existence of the Jewish people. In the absence of a binding commandment supernaturally revealed to a particular people, it makes as little sense to have a Mosaic religion for the Jewish people today as, say, a Platonic religion for the modern Greek nation. . . .
>
> We cannot have it both ways; either Judaism is unique as a divine revelation to the Jewish people or Judaism emerges as gradually evolving from, and in interpenetration with, surrounding cultures, making a contribution no doubt, but a con-

tribution which has, at least in good part, been absorbed by non-Jews. . . . If, then, revelation is impossible, only one religion remains tenable in the end: the religion of humanity, expressed in what one might call a "bible of mankind," a compendium of what is best in world literature and art.

This, of course, is precisely what Bernie would say, and while Reform and Conservative theologians and rabbis agonize over it, Bernie does not. He simply discards Judaism with barely a second thought. He chooses, not even a *religion* of humanity, but simply humanity. Or nothing. Or whatever he wants. And that of course may have little or nothing to do with ethics or what is "best" in moral and ethical literature and art (which is of course what Fackenheim means). For who is to say that ethics—the kind that we approve of—is truth? Given no revelation and no certainty; given perhaps, no G-d, man is free to decide the truth for himself. Therefore, who gives anyone the right to hang an Adolf Eichmann? Who says that truth decrees goodness or helping the poor and lifting up the oppressed? Who says that there is an ultimate standard of human conduct? Who are the rabbis—or anybody—to pontificate and moralize?

The rabbis of the temple, if they are prepared to think honestly, or at all, sit in an intellectual sweat. And desperately seek refuge for their own personal psychic stability and peace of mind. They may seek it in evasive, long-winded, impossible-to-understand language, either the flowery prose of a Heschel or the impossible language of a Kaplan. Or they may make fraudulent use of rhetoric and definitions that are deliberately unclear. Suddenly we have not G-d but "G-d *ideas*; progressive revelation; religious genius"—all full of religious sound and fury and signifying hypocrisy and evasion.

Faced with their own liberal, modern ideas, they cannot escape a Rabbi Wine's rapierlike thrust that Jews in modern times simply do not accept the Torah value systems. And if not that, and if the Torah is really a mixture of myths, legends, taboos, superstitions and ethnic chauvinism—how to deal with it?

Within the Reform movement there thus arise two trends, both refusing, in the end, to be honest. On the one hand, more of the young rabbis are moving inexorably to the road of Adler, Schindler, and Fleischer, the road to self-destruction of Judaism and its assimilation into the world of general "ethical monotheism." Thus, in the Spring/Summer 1975 issue of *Brief*, a publication of the American

Council for Judaism, Rabbi Michael P. Le Burkien wrote in response to criticism of a previous article of his:

> My anonymous critic claims to believe in the G-d of Abraham. I do not. That particular bearded G-d sat on a throne. He was anthropomorphic, vindictive, intensely territorial and He opposed intermarriage. In short, He was a ethnocentric male chauvinist.

Obviously, that kind of G-d and His Torah—which is found in the ark of every Reform synagogue in the United States—is an unappealing thing, and Rabbi Le Burkien is well on his way to joining all the Bernies whom he will manage to "educate" on the way out—to Bridget. Indeed, but for the grace of whatever Jewish girl he happened, by chance, to marry, we might have the newest of Jewish madnesses, a rabbi whose *rebbitsin* is a genuine Bridget *shiksa*.

The propagation of the Bernie species is carried on in hundreds of Reform temples whose rabbis, whether or not they openly speak as Le Burkien or privately believe it, are riddled with doubts. Any such rabbi will not and cannot give over to the child a feeling of certainty that Judaism is *truth*. One who does not believe in something cannot convince another person for very long, if at all, and children are the most difficult to deceive. Indeed, it is *impossible* for one to deceive a child for long; he has a natural intuition that perceives truth or falsehood, he can sense fraud in the words, the motions, the very atmosphere of the adult—rabbi, teacher, or parent. The Reform rabbi cannot transmit that which he is not sure of, and Bernie senses it, absorbs it, and runs away.

Le Burkien is part of a large and growing group of Reform rabbis who have organized a caucus within the Reform rabbinate known as the Association for a Progressive Reform Judaism (APRJ). The immediate impetus for the birth of the group was a desperate attempt by Reform leaders to stem the incredible phenomenon of rabbis performing intermarriages and accepting the tidal wave of Jewish disappearance. According to the Lenn report, no less than 41 percent of the nation's Reform rabbis officiated at mixed marriages, a fact that was so astounding that the *New York Times* made it a featured story (June 15, 1972).

The Reform rabbis might attempt to disguise their actions with high and lofty motives. Thus, "It will help to combat the defection of many of our people who are being lost to Judaism because of the spiritual insensibility of so many of our colleagues," said a letter sent by Reform Rabbi David Eichorn to 89 rabbis, each of whom had indicated that he was prepared to or had already performed intermarriages. The list was circulated both to give these rabbis a boost in morale ("look at how many others do it, too") as well as to enable them to recommend colleagues to intermarrying couples in different areas. Or the statement by Rabbi Charles Shulman: "The rabbi's refusal to officiate will have no bearing on their intentions but may only serve to create an image in their eyes of a harsh and unyielding religion."

This is the image that these rabbis would like to present to their fellow rabbis, to Jews, and to themselves: that their motives in performing mixed marriages stem from their desire to save Jews, that it is a consciously thought-out decision for the good of the Jewish people. In reality, it is a decision based on a desperate realization that the ranks of Reform Judaism are being decimated by intermarriage and here is a way to "keep them." A second real reason, quite as important, is the question: "What is good for the rabbi?" As more and more Jewish parents begin to accept the intermarriage of their children, they now cause serious problems for the rabbi who refuses to officiate.

Thus, it has long been the practice of Jewish newspapers to carry announcements of engagement and wedding announcements of mixed couples. One of the best was the one that appeared in the *Jewish Herald-Voice* of Houston, Texas, replete with a large picture of a blue-eyed, blonde bride. It read: "Mr. and Mrs. James E. Shannon, Gulfport, Mississippi, announce the engagement of their daughter, Carolyn Marie, to Gustave Alexander Saper, the son of Mr. and Mrs. O. F. Ingargiola of Pass Christian, and the late Edgar Goldberg Saper of Houston. . . . She is the granddaughter of Col. and Mrs. Eugene Wink of Gulfport." It is not every Jewish Bernie who can marry a Mississippi colonel's granddaughter.

In any event, when one paper, the *Baltimore Jewish Times*, announced in 1975 that it would no longer carry such items, a veritable storm broke. Wrote one Herbert Fink, "Your policy smacks of bigotry!" Mrs. Louis Crystal fumed, "Who do you think you are? What right have you to decide whose engagement you will announce? It certainly is none of your business whose children marry whom. It's okay for you to advertise nonkosher eating houses. In this week's *Times* you have 34. . . . If that is not being a hypocrite, I don't know what it is." *Touché!* The *Times*, stung into answering the charge, revealed its own bankruptcy: "Clearly, the

threat of intermarriage to the perpetuation of Judaism has been the
one issue—not dietary laws—that all three major rabbinical bodies
have recognized as the most dangerous facing American Jewry."
The failure to understand that the new "unimportance" of *kashrut*
and other Jewish laws that once made Judaism unique is precisely
what now makes Judaism itself unimportant to young Jews and
sends them into intermarriage, this failure is the hallmark of the
Jewish Establishment.

The growing acceptance of intermarriage is a sociological factor
among Jews. Most Jewish parents—nonobservant and ignorant of
most of Judaism themselves—were opposed to intermarriage for
much the same reason that they insisted on planning grandiose Bar
Mitzvahs. It was hardly love of Judaism, but rather the sense of
social status and what the neighbors would say. In the case of the
Bar Mitzvah, what would neighbors say and what kind of an
inferior social status would it imply if a Bar Mitzvah "orgy" was not
planned? In the case of intermarriage, it was not so much the caring
about Judaism but the *shame* at what the community would say,
that made the prospect such a terrible thing. Today, with so many
of the "neighbors" having the same problem, the shame recedes and
efforts are made to rationalize it away and even make it a positive
thing. In the face of this development, Reform rabbis—who, like
the *Baltimore Jewish Times*, accept non-*kashrut*, eating it, and who
violate a thousand other Jewish injunctions—face an angry and
dangerous community which increasingly insists that hypocrisy is
fine with them as long as it does not interfere with their lives, but a
refusal to marry Bernie to Bridget, when the rabbi's wife behaves
for all the world like the *shiksa*, will not be tolerated.

As more and more Reform rabbis succumbed (as in so many other
things) to community pressure, the Reform movement, trying to
overcome a century of image that portrayed it as something less than
really Jewish, condemned intermarriage at its 1973 convention in
Atlanta. While a ban on intermarriage is hardly a startling thing
for a rabbi, it did serve as a rallying cry for the radical rabbis in the
APRJ. In September 1974, the group's president, Prof. Eugene
Mihaly, who is on the faculty of the Hebrew Union College,
Reform's major training school for rabbis, decried the tendency in
Reform Judaism to "restrict the freedom which Reform Judaism
came into being to promote and preserve." Mihaly had hit on a vital
and most sensitive point. What he was saying was that Reform
Judaism itself had come into being by overthrowing Jewish dogmas
and beliefs that had been sacred for centuries. It had done so by

proclaiming that each generation had the right to decide what it saw as being the proper "Jewish" way. How, then, did the Reform movement now dare to impose discipline and dogma on other Jews? Reform, in the eyes of these rabbis, was becoming Orthodox.

In August 1975 the APRJ, now grown to nearly 150 rabbis, decided to launch an ambitious educational program as well as a publication. It vowed to fight against a "closed, ethnic, parochial, and national Jewish existence" and it guaranteed to pull Bernie to universalism—and Bridget.

On the other hand, a second group within Reform hoped to meet the challenge to their intellect not by moving to assimilation, but by moving to "tradition."

Thus we find a whole host of items: In Evanston, Illinois, the Free Synagogue has decided to bring back the second day of Rosh Hashana (Reform generally decides to observe only one day); a new *Shabbat Manual* has been introduced by Rabbi Gunther Plaut; an article in *Time* magazine (November 26, 1974) tells of more temples using *yarmulkes* and experimenting with kosher food. What is the meaning of all this? Is there a genuine return to Judaism and will the young be influenced? Hardly.

The experimentation at Reform's rabbinical training school, Hebrew Union College in Cincinnati, is just that: Experimentation. It is a *personal* search on the part of the young rabbis to escape from the clear bankruptcy of Reform Judaism, just as the experimentation in certain temples is a frantic search for something that will make Judaism "relevant." Once they attempted to bring jazz and rock-and-roll bands into the Friday evening services. That passed with no visible change in a properly cynical and disgusted Bernie, who prefers his music in discotheques. The "return" to ritual is no different except that it shows an increasing desperation on the part of the same Reform rabbis who, in great measure, consider themselves agnostics, atheists, or radically nontraditional. That this is true can be seen from a series of articles that appeared in the *Jewish Post and Opinion* in January 1975.

From second-year student Sam Rothberg: "When I go to services I enjoy going to an Orthodox place. It's a totally free experience. You can do what you want." Of course. "Free experience. Do what you want." This is the theme that over and over again pervades the comments of the Reform "returners to tradition." A total failure to understand the very essence of Judaism; a massive ignorance of the foundation of foundations of Judaism, *which is the precise opposite of "Do what you want,"* which contradicts in every way the pagan, un-Jewish Reform that does indeed preach "Do what you want."

The acceptance of the yoke of heaven: this is Orthodox Judaism. The total submerging of the human will to G-d. The rabbis of the Talmud saying: "Make His will thine, so that He will agree to do your will." The rabbis saying: "There is no freedom except through the stone tablets of Sinai." The Torah declaring: "If thou shalt walk in my statutes it will be good and if not, it will be bad." The rabbis telling us: "Let not a man say: I cannot abide pork and therefore shall not eat it, but rather, I enjoy pork but what am I to do when my Father in Heaven has forbidden it!"

For the Reform "returners to ritual" at Hebrew Union College, there is no understanding of the need to bow the head and bend the will. *They* remain the deciders; *they* choose what they desire; the rituals are a game, a fad, a passing fancy. Neither the Reform rabbis nor Bernie will be saved by such a "Judaism."

Lee Lifschitz, a fourth-year student, tells us that what a Jew observes is "purely a personal thing of what turns you on—what makes you feel good." Obviously, then, a great many Jews are observing the "Jewish ritual" of sex and drugs . . .

Senior Bruce Adams likes ritual because "it's fun, but I don't feel commanded to do it. We keep kosher at home purely for identity reasons." Fun. Bernie finds his fun in other things—Bridget. Is he less of a Jew for it?

For Rabbi Kenneth Erlich, assistant dean, "Ritual is poetry." (And what if one prefers Alan Ginsberg or Le Roi Jones?). Erlich is also specific about his likes and dislikes. The theology behind Kol Nidre is "abhorrent"; the *mikvah* "I really dislike"; "I'm still struggling with certain things like the *bris* [circumcision], which is definitely the product of a male-oriented society."

Eli Herscher would like to put on the *tefillin* (phylacteries) but has problems with the prayers. "I realized that I'd have trouble saying them and that would associate me with certain concepts like a personal G-d [read: a G-d who is real, to whom one prays, who directs history] which I have trouble accepting."

Not from such paragons of confusion will salvation come, nor from the vaunted return to ritual per se, absolutely missing the point of Judaism: a real, personal, omnipotent, and omniscient G-d who revealed Himself at Sinai and *commanded* the Torah.

The tragedy of the Reform rabbinate stems from the bankruptcy of the Reform ideology. It has failed to give the rabbi a meaning for being Jewish. It graduates people who are abysmally ignorant of hard-core Judaism: the Torah with the essential commentaries in the original Hebrew and the Talmud and the basic commentaries. There may not be ten young Reform rabbis in America whose Talmudic knowledge is the equivalent of that of a yeshiva high school student, and the bitter joke is that the Reform rabbi may be able to tell you about the sociological environment of the Talmudic scholars but not what they said. Indeed, as I said earlier, the greatest blessing that has been vouchsafed these rabbis is that their congregants know even less than they do.

It is the ignorance of the rabbi that drives him into sermons whose content is so heavily political and social. Not because he cares more for the oppressed than the Orthodox—the rallies for Soviet Jewry and Israel are heavily weighted to Orthodox youth—but because he has little to say about *Jewish* scholarship. The book review is not social commentary but a lifesaver for the rabbi who cannot review the Talmud. How apt are the words of David Daiches, son of the famous scholar and rabbi of Edinburgh, Scotland, Salis Daiches. Writing in *Commentary* (February 1951), Daiches said: "I object to the term "rabbi" being used generally as the Jewish equivalent of minister, a practice that deprives it of the nobility and grandeur that invested the title when it was confined to those who had achieved the hard discipline of obtaining the proper ordination [smicha]."

And their throwing themselves into every non-Jewish cause available is also a product of barren, sterile Reform Judaism. The head of the Reform movement, Maurice Eisendrath, who supported the Black militant demand that synagogues pay "reparations"; the head of the American Jewish Congress and president of the Reform rabbinate, Arthur Lelyveld, who boasts unceasingly of having his arm broken in a march for Civil Rights in Mississippi; Rabbi Stephen Jacobs, the Los Angeles rabbi who used his 1976 Rosh Hashana sermon to condemn Jews for thinking too much about themselves; Rabbi Richard Sternberger, Reform official who spent five days in a Mississippi jail fighting for Black voting rights and who has been spending time aiding Mexican-Americans in their lettuce boycott.

The question arises: Are there no Jewish problems that demand these rabbis' time? Soviet Jewry, Syrian Jewry, Israel, Jewish urban poor—these are things that the Reform rabbis cannot find time for. The reason? There is a deep self-hatred at work here, with the rabbi *needing* to touch upon issues that give him a reason for being. And if the issues are universal enough so that Judaism can take one more step down the road to assimilation and integration into "humanity," this will lift his own burden of confusion that much more.

Poor Bernie! The poor Bernie who is exposed to the temple rabbis, who is expected to acquire knowledge and identity from men who have neither, and who only succeed in imparting their own confusion and reason for *not* being to the Jewish youngster, who soon decides what he will be when he grows up: a non-Jewish adult.

Confusion? By the carload! A special liturgy committee, set up by the New York Federation of Reform Synagogues, met on September 12, 1976, to eliminate "sexist" terminology from the prayer book. I quote from the *New York Times* item (italics mine):

> *Cecile Fallon*, moderator of yesterday's meeting and regional administrator of *Catholic Charities Community Life Center* in Patchogue, L.I., described the task force as "made up of well-educated, hard-working female congregants who wish to change things from within because *we want our daughters to remain Jewish.*
>
> "They will not work for a community and pray, using a liturgy that systematically excludes them," she said.
>
> *Mrs. Fallon, who is Jewish and married to a Roman Catholic,* thanked the college for its facilities.

It is, of course, clear that Ms. Fallon's daughter's gravest obstacle in wanting to remain Jewish is the terminology of the prayer book and not the fact that she has a Catholic father.

Or:

> But now along comes an item specifically designed for the observant Jew who may want to combine prayer with a subliminal reminder of America's 200th anniversary: a Bicentennial "Yankee Tallit [*talles*]."
>
> A new company calling itself the Yankee Tallit Works is offering a *tallit* made of lightweight kettlecloth denim, braided *atarah*, orange decorative stitching, and natural-color fringing. A spokesman . . . noted that the *tallit*, a matching *kippah* and appropriate *tallit* bags has "a uniquely American design." It was also designed, he said, to attract younger people "who believe that prayer should and could be a less formal experience without having to deviate from tradition or *halacha*. . . ."
>
> The first "Yankee Tallit" was presented to Rabbi Alexander

Schindler. . . . Schindler, upon trying on the new Tallit, said it "is an exciting idea that should appeal to the young American Jew."

Of course. There is little doubt that the thing that has caused young Jews to cease praying in temples has been the lack of a Yankee Tallit . . .

Or the reaction of one of America's leading Reform rabbis, Jacob Weinstein, to the advice of a Denver Orthodox rabbi to young Jews to refuse the "first date" with a non-Jew. Wrote Weinstein:

> Why should we start to build walls around ourselves . . .? Is it not time for the more rational forces among us to resist this traumatic recidivism? To bar them [young Jews] from interfaith or even interracial experience is an admission on our part of uncertainty about our own values. . . . Better to take the losses attendant on the exercise of freedom than accept the gain of a superimposed caution.

Why build walls indeed? Bernie agrees and the first wall that he knocks down is the one closest to him—that of Judaism.

Or the words of Rabbi Arthur Lelyveld attacking the 137th Psalm for its "primitive exaltation of force" and its "revolting anathema" against the Babylonians. Says Lelyveld: "The brutalities in our tradition must be seen as human failure. They are there because of the fact that our tradition preserves the good and the bad."

It takes little perception to understand what Bernie's reaction to *that* is. If something is bad, get rid of it. If the tradition does not allow it, get rid of the whole tradition. Why not take all traditions, get rid of *all* the bad, and put all the good into *one* tradition? Eminently sound questions, and Lelyveld has not the courage to ask them or the knowledge to answer them.

Of course, intermarriage can only evolve in one way as far as the temple rabbis are concerned. It will, of necessity, become accepted and approved. Thus, Rabbi David Eichorn scoffs at the high inter-marriage rate figures and says that he cannot "believe" they are so high. And Rabbi Nathan Perlman, Rabbi Emeritus at Temple Emanu-El in Manhattan, emerges with the following fascinating comment: "Jews have fought for years to mix freely in our society and intermarriage is the result. *I have nothing against intermarriage if the family is to be a Jewish one"* (italics mine). And so we arrive at the ultimate in the theater of the Jewish Absurd. It is all right not to be Jewish as long as you are Jewish. The *halachic* rule that a Jew is someone born of a Jewish mother or a convert according to the proper *halachic* procedures, is cast into limbo, with people defining Jews in every and any way they care to. Suddenly there looms the awesome spectre of a de facto split in the Jewish people—two nations—as the traditionalists fear to accept a person as "Jewish" because of the total breakdown of the term.

And Rabbi Everett Gendler, subconsciously echoing the hopes of so many confused Jews who would welcome the emergence of a way to escape from Judaism into a universal faith, sees the hope in the growth of intermarriage. Says Gendler: (*Response,* Winter 1969–70):

> There is indeed . . . "the possibility that a new religion is in the making." It may be, if it develops, the new Judaism or the re-Judaized Christianity or the new cosmic humanism or ??? As we consider soberly, not hysterically, the circumstances of its emergence . . . how, then, can we do other than relate supportively to such a development?

The travesty leads even the *American Jewish Yearbook* to conclude in the 1973 lead article that Reform Judaism faces "serious problems of an erosion of its strength through intermarriage and lack of strong theological commitment."

Bernie cannot find help as a Jew from the rabbi, his gravedigger. Said Reform Jewish thinker Jacob Petuchowski, sadly: "We have reached the stage where we no longer have standards" (*Jewish Post and Opinion,* January 17, 1975). It took Petuchowski many years to discover it. Bernie was quicker. He knew it by Bar Mitzvah time.

And then, there is Conservative Judaism—the most anarchistic, undefinable, and Jewish jungle of them all.

One of the leading Conservative laymen, Julian Freeman of Indianapolis, said in 1955 (in *Conservative Judaism,* by Marshall Sklare):

> What further complicates the matter is that ten different Conservative rabbis will have ten different ideas of Conservative Judaism. I speak from personal experience when I tell you that in interviewing approximately ten Conservative rabbis who were candidates for our pulpit, each and every one of them had a different slant on Conservative Judaism.

This frank statement by a leader of the Conservative movement is an echo of many others:

> [In Conservatism] one can never be quite certain that he is speaking for anybody but himself. Conservative Judaism has nowhere been defined. . . . One searches . . . for even a trace of an attempt to deal with fundamentals. . . . These essential considerations seem either to have been overlooked because of the pressure of more "practical" affairs, or to have been studiously avoided because of excessive politeness.

It is a clear fact. Unlike Orthodoxy, which has a clear ideology: real Revelation from Sinai, a Chosen People, Divine sanction for the Written and Oral Law, interpretation strictly within the framework of the divine *halacha*; unlike Reform, which has a definite rejection of Revelation and the Chosen People and which is free to do with laws, customs, and the like what it wishes—Conservatism is neither here nor there. It is the proverbial Jew whom Elijah mocked, saying: "How long do you intend to halt between two opinions?" Conservatism, an ideological-less movement, wallows about in anarchy, its problems camouflaged by a superficial growth in synagogues (usually called centers) and a growth in superficial members. But if ever there was a parallel to the time of the Judges— "In those days there was no king in Israel; each man did what was right in his own eyes"—it is with the Conservative movement.

Does the Conservative movement accept Revelation as a historical fact that actually happened in exactly the way the Torah describes it? Does it believe that the Torah it raises high in the centers each Saturday morning to the words "And this is the Law that Moses set before the Children of Israel" is that really? Are the laws of the Torah and the Talmud divine? The questions are unanswerable because the Conservative movement is not a movement. It is a combination of centers, each going pretty much at the religious pace it chooses, each doing what is best for its members in *their* eyes. When one *knows* that a heavy percentage of the rabbis in the centers are graduates of Orthodox yeshivas who took the Conservative pulpit because there was no Orthodox one available or because this was a better-paying one (and that tells a great deal about the rabbi and how much greatness we can expect him to give our children), and when one adds to this the fact that Mordecai Kaplan and Reconstructionism began as a group with Conservatism, with

Kaplan teaching his entire adult life at Conservatism's Jewish Theological Seminary, the jungle becomes impossible.

The worst of religious fraud occurs in Conservative ideological circles, as an immense game is played about the Law Committee's charade, pretending to rule on modern-day problems in obedience to *halacha*. Conservative rabbi Arthur Hertzberg, president of the American Jewish Congress, in an address to Conservatism's Rabbinical Assembly in May 1975, earned the following news report from the *Jewish Post and Opinion*:

HALACHIC DECISIONS CALLED PLAY-ACTING

Grossingers, N.Y.—The view from a top American rabbi that Conservative Judaism is eclectic and that many of Conservative Judaism's *halachic* decisions are play-acting brought no response from the rabbis attending the Rabbinical Assembly's 75th annual convention here.

The "lack of response" is not explained. Is silence to be considered an admission of guilt?

Hertzberg specifically pointed to the *"halachic"* decision by the Conservative Law Committee that eating dairy food out of non-kosher dishes in a restaurant is permissible. He flatly said that this "cannot be defended *halachically*, as most of us do." The AJC president called upon the Conservative rabbis to cease the charade and admit that "we are living with *post-halachic* Judaism."

Similar Conservative Law Committee decisions have ruled that electricity may be used on the Sabbath and travel by car to the synagogue is permitted. No serious effort has been made to justify these decisions as *halachically* permissible.

No group struggles more nervously than Conservative Judaism with the problem of ideology and belief precisely because every Conservative leader knows that if Revelation cannot somehow be defended and admitted to, there is no essential difference between Reform and Conservatism. And so, all kinds of theological gymnastics are resorted to.

The concept of Revelation, as Jews always knew it, is not seriously accepted by Conservative rabbis today. In 1975 the editor of the quarterly *Conservative Judaism*, Rabbi Stephen Lerner, published the results of questionnaires sent out to a number of Conservative rabbis. In his own words, "Virtually all the symposiasts shared a nonfundamentalist approach to Revelation and acknowledge the changing nature of Jewish law while granting the importance of *halacha.*" Noting the fear of Lerner's hesitancy to be honest enough to say clearly that the rabbis rejected the concept of Torah from Divine Sinai (taking refuge instead in "nonfundamentalist approach"), we also see that the Jewish Law becomes something which was never Divine but nevertheless "important" to be kept within some kind of *halachic* order. Why?

Because Conservatism was originally founded in Germany as "historical Judaism," recognizing the importance of keeping hold of a rich past and *if* it is not necessary to drop it, to preserve as much of it as possible. What emerges is a kind of nostalgic (some would say parochial) affection for a magnificent antique that has no real utility but it is valuable for its memories. What is postulated is perhaps a kind of *bubbe-zayde* religion. We know that the old folks are senile and speak nonsense, but we would never dream of putting them away by euthanasia.

Revelation is brilliantly accepted and rejected at one and the same time by one of Conservatism's leading thinkers, Robert Gordis, in his *A Faith for Moderns* (1971):

> The Bible uses physical terms to describe man's experience of G-d's Revelation, because there are no other terms to use. . . . In sum, the description of Revelation is always a metaphor, because poetry, endowed with overtones, is capable of implying more than it sets forth. Its truth lies precisely in its nuances."

Nu, Bernie, "nuances." What did he say? Was there an actual Revelation where Jews heard G-d speak, or not? Gordis continues:

> It is clear that Revelation may be conceived of literally, allegorically, or mystically, but for the religious spirit it remains a sine qua non, the source from which the sense of G-d and the knowledge of His will flow to man.

Nu, Bernie, was there a Revelation? Answer me literally, allegorically, or mystically. What can one say to such deliberate confusion of words that masks a confusion of soul? The Conservative movement tends to produce poets of Confusion. One sympathetic viewer of Abraham Heschel, Conservatism's prize thinker, wrote: "A reader insensitive to Heschel's use of language might easily believe that he is throwing up a barrage of words, talking or even lulling himself into belief in G-d." Thus Jacob Petruchowski in *Commentary*, May, 1958.

Of course Conservative Judaism has quietly buried Revelation (like a thief in the night, lest it be branded Reform). Thus it is hardly surprising to read an interview with Rabbi David Graubert, president of the Bet Din, the ecclesiastical court for Conservative Judaism in the Middle West. Graubard is obviously more than an ordinary Conservative rabbi in some lonesome center. He is, if not a lawgiver, a law decider, a member of the Rabbinical Assembly's Law Committee. And says Graubart (in the *Jewish Post and Opinion*, October 25, 1974): "If we tell our children all of the Bible is divinely ordained, it can be a shock for them when they get to college and study evolution; however, if we tell them early what we think is true, what they learn later won't shatter those concepts." In a word, teach your child that the Bible is part myth now, lest someone else tell him later. One sees that Bernie will be doing well at Rabbi Graubart's center.

Graubert does perform the *mitzvah* of putting on *tefillin*, (phylacteries) despite the fact that "he has found no evidence that what we take as the command in the Bible to put on *tefillin* meant any such thing . . . nor is there any evidence that Jews did put on *tefillin* at that time."

Why does he put it on? For the same reason he eats kosher food: "Because it preserves the identity of Judaism." To which, of course, any normal Bernie blessed with the barest of common sense would look up and ask: What is so important about preserving the identity of Judaism?

And Rabbi Aaron Blumenthal, a leading Conservative rabbi, could say in the *Jewish Herald-Voice of Houston* in September, 1975: "Too many of us look upon the Bible, the Talmud, and the Codes as the last word on all matters. They are not . . ." And if they are not, surely Bernie has every right to choose for himself what is the last word—and from any source, not necessarily Jewish.

The charade that is the Conservative Law Committee is seen in its method of reaching solutions. In the words of Sklare:

> Matters reached an impasse in the early 1940s and a new approach finally emerged. Essentially what it involved was that in some instances legal decisions would be rendered outside of the boundaries of what would be considered a liberal interpretation of Jewish Law.
>
> During the 1950s and 60s, sharply divergent opinions were encountered on almost every *halachic* problem in the Rabbinical Assembly. Important *halachic* opinions of the body's Committee on Jewish Law and Standards were seldom

unanimous. . . . The result was that in an effort to achieve a workable approach to liberalization, Conservative rabbis were accorded the privilege of following the minority opinion if they were so inclined.

Of course, it reeks of fraud. Leave aside the great and weighty questions that the Law Commission ponders. What does a Conservative Jew or rabbi do in his *everyday* life? When there is a question concerning the Sabbath or *kashrut* or any one of a thousand things that can arise, to whom does the Conservative rabbi turn for an answer? Since the Law Commission has not yet ruled, does he turn to Jewish precedent—the Talmud, the Code of Jewish Law? Of course not. He decides *according to his own taste*, since he possesses neither the ability to research the law nor the desire to. The vaunted "faithfulness to tradition" and insistence that Conservatism is its inheritor is the worst kind of fraud, lacking even the dishonesty of the Reform.

A parable is told of a king who was once riding along the road, when he passed a farm where, on the side of the barn, was painted a number of targets. To the king's astonishment, there was an arrow in each and every bull's-eye. The king went over to the farmer and asked him how he had grown to be such an incredible archer. "Very simple," replied the farmer. "First I shoot an arrow, and after it hits somewhere I paint a circle around it."

The same is true with Conservatism. Its rabbis and leaders first decide what they want to decide. Then they rationalize it with "*halacha*." Not for nothing do we have each and every Conservative rabbi doing what he wishes, and a movement that can have in it fugitives from Orthodoxy as well as Mordecai Kaplan and Robert Gordis; rabbis who adhere to every religious rule (because they were born Orthodox) and those who do not wear *yarmulkes* and violate many of the Sabbath requirements; synagogues where most of the service is traditional and synagogues with organ music. Such a "Judaism" has nothing in common with *halacha*, and any attempt to claim otherwise is mere lack of courage and honesty.

What makes the entire thing a sham is the basic fact about Conservative Judaism, that it is not the rabbis and not the theology which set the tone but the *individual centers themselves*. In the words of Clarence Gross, an official of a Conservative center:

I take my rabbi's spiritual advice. . . . I will listen to his teaching for my personal edification; but when it comes to determining the religious character of my congregation . . . I reserve the right to ask my rabbi to implement the general feeling of myself and those other members of the congregation who with me express them, even though they might run counter to what my rabbi personally feels.

This is the crux of Conservatism. The individual synagogue is the heart of the movement and it could not care less what the Religious Commission Law and Standard says. Of course Conservatism plays games with the *halacha*, and of course the Commission's "historic" decision to allow driving an automobile on the Sabbath was, in the words of a Conservative rabbi, David Novak, "an enactment having no basis whatsoever in the *halacha.*" But the reason for the Commission's decision was more telling than anything else. It ruled as it did because in practice there was not a Conservative worshiper at a Conservative synagogue who did *not* ride anyhow! The worshiper did not care *what* the Commission ruled, and the Commission—and Conservative Judaism—was faced with the ludicrous situation of being rabbi/general without armies. The Conservative decision was a collapse before *practical* necessity, as it has been on a dozen issues. No one waited for official sanction to introduce late Friday night services, mixed pews, marrying a *kohen* to a divorcee. When *duchening*, the blessing of the congregation by the *kohanim* (priests), was ended in Conservative synagogues, when microphones were used on the Sabbath, no one asked, for the simple reason that had the rabbi objected the congregants would have gotten another rabbi.

The central truth about Conservatism remains: It is a body that came into being not because of ideology but because of *sociology*. It was not rabbis or religious creed that rocketed Conservatism to the quantitative heights of today, but the social developments after World War II. The move to the suburbs placed Jews in the position of needing a synagogue, and Conservatism, of which they knew little or nothing except that it was "between" Orthodoxy and Reform, was the lucky winner of the pragmatic heart of the American Jew. The Conservative Jew is not more religious than the Reform one. His observance level is woefully weak, and if not for the children and their Bar and Bat Mitzvahs, one wonders just what would be left of a Conservative movement. There really are no Conservative Jews, only Conservative rabbis, and half of these are Orthodox ones who looked for greener pastures.

The Jew in the Conservative center may observe more rituals but he does not observe more *mitzvahs*. Some time ago, Reform Rabbi Prof. Petuchowsky tried to say that Reform Jews also observe many commandments. In *Heirs of the Pharisees* (1970), he stated: "If a Reform Jew loves his neighbor he is observing one of the commandments. If he refrains from murder, adultery, theft, he is observing. . . . There is no need to keep count of all the commandments that a Reform Jew does observe."

The same claim is made for Conservative Jews, only more so. And the answer to both is the same: *Neither the Reform nor the Conservative Jew* observes any *mitzvot*, commandments. For the essence, the very nature of the commandment is that one does it because he is *commanded* to. The Jew in the Conservative center on Long Island does not light candles because she was *commanded* to. Everything that the center observes is *agreed* to by the congregation. It is a democratic thing, their "thing." Should women be counted toward a quorum? Vote. Shall we introduce this or that, shall we reintroduce the practice of *duchening*, the priestly blessing of the congregation? Congregation B'nai Emunah of St. Louis *decided* to. This is not Judaism; when Goldberg *decides for himself* to pray, he is instead practicing Goldbergism. When the Conservative Jewish Center of Long Island *decides* to introduce a ritual, it is practicing self-worship. When the "official" Conservative movement deigns to introduce a law or custom, *it* is not practicing Judaism. It is only when the center, the rabbi, the body, bends its will, tells its Bernie that it is G-d who ordains the action and commands the law, that Judaism is in play. It is only when there is a bowing before the heavenly kingdom and the instilling in oneself of the *yirat shamayim*, the fear of heaven, that Bernie will stop running.

He may go to services until his Bar Mitzvah; he may join the United Synagogue Youth; he may take a trip to Israel with them or spend a summer in their Camp Ramah. But until he does things because G-d commands them, his chances of turning into a Bernie are awesomely good.

One can see the failure of Conservatism in what should be its proudest achievement, the Solomon Schechter Day Schools. They are growing, true, but the difference between them and the yeshiva schools is enormous. That difference lies in the latter's belief in Divine Torah and the awe of heaven they possess. The Schechter children, in the end, become Jewish prep school students. They are candidates for Bernieism, par excellence.

Julian Freedman saw the Bernies in his own movement and said:

> No amount of talk will dissipate the fact that there is confusion throughout the movement. Some people insist on saying "Don't bring it up in public—time will help out." Well, the Conservative movement is about fifty years old. Some of us are getting pretty well along in life, and we want a scheme for living today.

The alternative of course, is death. Death to Bernie as a Jew.

4
My Son, the Bernie

Once, too many years ago, I was a young rabbi of a suburban synagogue on Long Island. The vast majority of the congregation's members were refugees from Brooklyn, for even then there were neighborhoods that were beginning to die out, though Jewish organizations were too busy to notice. The members—to a man (and woman)—were nonobservant Jews, people who sent their children to Hebrew school so that they might become Bar Mitzvah and acquire enough Jewish "culture" to keep them from marrying Bridget. It was not an easy time for the new suburbanites, for the mortgage-heavy homes were beautiful on the outside but quite empty on the inside (the poor husband's two jobs did not bring in enough to buy furnishings, too). One of the Sisterhood luminaries, who used to look suspiciously at any "fanatical" deviations on my part, looked even more suspiciously at my "heresy" when I told her that she could speak on the telephone as she sat *shivah* for the ghost of her father.

It was an interesting community and one of the most interesting people there was one whom I will call Rudnick. Rudnick was a tall, thin, bony chap with graying hair and a cynical outlook on religion, which he enjoyed but never made the mistake of taking too seriously. He transgressed every commandment—religiously—and fasting on Yom Kippur never really lasted beyond the fourth hour of the day with him. Total sanctification of the Sabbath was not for Rudnick; neither was abstinence from the delicacies of a ham sandwich.

But with all that, Rudnick had one religious claim to fame that, as far as my own personal experience is concerned, is unequaled. Rudnick the Sabbath desecrator, Rudnick the *trayfnyak* (eater of nonkosher food), Rudnick the sinner—had the hugest Hanukkah menorah I have ever seen in my life. Not only was it the biggest but, while all ordinary Hanukkah observers kept theirs in their windows, Rudnick had his eight-foot candelabra on his front lawn.

I remember the first time I saw that phenomenon. It was a cold, clear night, the kind that enabled the huge object to blaze with light (Rudnick used oil to light his lawn decoration). I stood in awe in front of the blazing giant with Rudnick standing by, his face lit by a hugely satisfied grin.

"Tell me, Rudnick," I said. "Tell me frankly. You are not the kind of a man that one would call religious. I don't count on you for services and, to be frank, I passed you by as you walked into the Chinese restaurant last Friday night." Rudnick shifted his feet a little uncomfortably and stared at the top of his menorah. "In the face of all that, Rudnick, tell me. Why the menorah?"

Rudnick looked at me and thought for a long time. Then, putting his arm around me, he turned away from the menorah so that we faced the street and the houses on the other side. House after house was lit up like a Christmas tree—because it was that season and the neighborhood was the classic Jewish-Italian one that we once knew. From every house, strings of brightly colored lights went off and on in an artistic display of Sicilian talent, and complicatedly decorated trees could be seen inside, through the picture windows.

"You see that, Rabbi?" Rudnick asked again, only this time his voice was not as mellow as before and when I glanced at his face, his smile was gone, replaced by a strange firmness about the jaw.

"Rabbi, the first year I moved in here, I was the only Jew on the block and those neighbors of mine lit their Christmas decorations to beat the band. I made up my mind that no *goy* was going to have a better holiday than me—that's why the menorah!"

Rudnick, Rudnick. I never forgot him. Nor his eight-foot menorah. Nor his Judaism.

I often think of Rudnick. I think of him mostly at special moments of religious experience. I think of Rudnick when, on the eve of Sabbath, with the sun setting and the shadows of night approaching, the men of the congregation murmur: "*Yedid nefesh, Av ha'rachaman* . . . Companion of my soul, merciful Father, draw near thy servant unto Thy will; let Thy servant fly swiftly as a deer to prostrate himself before Thy glory. . . . Glorious and magnificent One, light of the world, my soul is ill with its craving for Thee; I beseech Thee, O L-rd, heal it by granting it the sweetness of Thy splendor . . ."

I think of Rudnick on the High Holidays, in the little synagogue where people who come to pray were there but yesterday. People who need no guide to show them to a seat that has been reserved for them from last year and which sighs in exquisite ecstasy as its cold wooden bones become warmed at last by the twice-a-year familiar backside. In this little *shul* where people believe in G-d, I think of Rudnick as I speak the words of the poet in the prayer-book: "The soul belongs to Thee, the body is Thy work; O spare Thy creation. . . . Gracious and Merciful, Pardon Thou our great guilt."

Or: "As clay in the hands of the potter, who expands or contracts it at will, so are we in Thy hand, O gracious G-d. Heed Thy covenant with us and hearken not to the accuser . . ."

Or as the shadows of night envelop the fading day of Yom Kippur, and the congregation, clothed in simple white, stands before the open ark, hungry and weary from a tiring and enervating fast, and calls forth to its Father in Heaven: "Have mercy upon the entire community of Yeshurun—Israel; forgive and pardon their iniquity; help us our G-d who saves. . . . We are Thy flock and Thou our shepherd, we are Thy vineyard and Thou our keeper. . . . Our Father, our King, we have sinned before you . . ."

Rudnick may have an eight-foot Hanukkah menorah on his lawn, but he will never write a poem of love to G-d. Because he does not believe in Him. And that is the source of Rudnick's sickness and of that of all the Rudnicks large and small. And how sad it is. What makes Rudnick a Jew? Clearly, only the non-Jew. Rudnick is that proverbial, stiffnecked person whose Jewishness is totally negative, totally lacking in any positive reason, totally devoid of anything in its own right, but which flares up every so often because he must show the *goy* that he also has something.

What is that something? Rudnick neither knows nor cares. But no one will be able to say that he has something and Rudnick does not. There are a hundred variations on the Rudnick-Judaism. There is the Herzl whose Jewishness consisted of and existed solely because of anti-Semitism. There is the Soviet Jew who would have assimilated long ago but for the fact that the Russians insisted that his identity card carry the annotation *"Yevrei-*Jew." These are the Jews who have remained Jews because of the *goy*. That which they were not prepared to accept from the Jew, they cling to because of the *goy*.

It is not a very healthy kind of Judaism and its practitioners are not very healthy Jews. But they exist in the millions, and certainly in the form of the multitude of Jews who join the suburban temples for the completely negative reason that some Jewish identity must be retained so that the apple of their eye will come home with a Shirley rather than a Mary.

Why? Why should it bother them so? They would have great difficulty in telling you. But one thing is certain. They do *not* want a *shiksa* for a daughter-in-law. Not because they believe in G-d; not because they believe in Judasim; not because their lives are tied with yearning to the beauty of an exclusive Jewishness and its *mitzvot*. Not the beauty of the Jew but the presence of the *goy*— that is the sum and substance of Rudnick-Judasim. Not for Rudnick is the yearning for communion with G-d or the need to "prostrate himself before Thy glory." Not for Rudnick is the soul made "ill with craving for Thee." Not for Rudnick the deep awe and love for the One who is our shepherd while we are His flock, our watchman while we are His vineyard. Not for him the humility and yearning of the Jew who cries, "The soul belongs to Thee and the body is Your handiwork." No, Rudnick lights a Hanukkah *menorah* and dedicates it to the *goy* across the street.

Rudnick is not merely a person; he is a concept. He is so many of the six million American Jews. He is Bernie's father and mother. He brought his Jewish son into the world and, daily, digs his grave.

The rabbis of the Talmud discuss whether the generation is influenced by its leader or whether the leader is influenced by the generation into which he is born. It seems clear that both interact and that each influences and is influenced. If the Jewish Establishment influenced and led the American Jew, so did the American Jew know what he was getting and like what he got—and deserved. More. In great measure, the American Jew *demands* the kind of life-style that creates Bernie. The American Jews, father and mother of Bernie, are also senior partners in the production: What Makes Bernie Run?

If one were to look at the "religious" map of American Jewry and at the cold statistics that are regularly handed out by the American Jewish religious establishment, he would be greatly impressed. It is beyond dispute that temples and centers have sprung up in every far-flung part of the United States. There is little doubt that there are more Bar Mitzvahs per square inch of catering than ever before. It is indisputable that temples are bigger than ever before and that Sisterhoods, Men's Clubs, and American Jewish Congress tours to Israel are booming.

None of it has anything to do with religion. The "Judaism" that exists in America today, in the Conservative, Reform, and Reconstructionist sector, deals with sociology, not theology. The people who attend the temples are practitioners of Jewish folklore, not believers in G-d and surely not committed to His Torah. Consider the modern temple and Jewish center.

The temple, that was created to give G-d a place on earth on condition that He know exactly what His place is. The temple, where man thinks up G-d rather than admit that He made him. The temple, where the Jew can create any kind of religion that he cares to and call it Judasim. The temple, where things too difficult are junked and where from the Board of Directors shall come forth Torah and the voice of the L-rd from the approving Sisterhood membership. The temple, run by men whose ignorance of Judaism is exceeded only by their arrogant insistence on spouting it. The temple, where Bernie visits "G-d" and meets "Judaism" and flees from it in horror. The temples: they created Bernie, they made Bernie run.

The overwhelming truth about the American Jewish temple/center is that it came into being to please man and not G-d. It is not a place of awe where the Jew comes to bend his neck beneath the yoke of the *mitzvot*, the commandments. He, the American Jew, decides what "commandments" he will "obey," and, of course, that very thing is what changes Judaism into "Goldbergism" or whatever happens to be the name of the American Jew who has become his own lawgiver.

The American Jew threw away the Orthodoxy—the authentic Judaism—of centuries because it was too embarrassing and too uncomfortable. He wanted an *American* Judaism; he wanted a *convenient* Judasim; he wanted a *comfortable* Judaism; he wanted a Judaism that was not *too* Judaistic.

It was not the rabbis who created the "boom" in temples and centers. It was not theology that suddenly inspired the American Jew, parent of Bernie. The explosion of what passes for religion in Judaism was a sociological phenomenon that is a direct product of the unique American Jew, Bernie's parents, the ones who had such a share in driving their Jewish *naches* away from Judaism's embrace into the waiting arms of Bridget.

The parents, the good Jewish parents. The loving Jewish mother who took off her golden nose rings and made a Golden Calf which she worships avidly. The Golden Calf called "success" and "money" and "making it" and "my-son-the-doctor." The Golden Calf of material success before which she burns incense and for which she

threw the G-d of Jewish values into the trash cans of medieval ob-
scurantism. The Jewish father whose values are those of the
garment center and the racetrack and bagels and lox on Sunday
morning before taking the family out to the Chinese restaurant on
Sunday afternoon. The Jewish father who tries to think like a
Gentile, dress like a Gentile, act like a Gentile, drink like a Gentile,
and curse like a Gentile, and then demand that his son marry a
"nice Jewish girl."

The Jewish parents whose credo is upward and upward in wealth
and status and who created a comfortable Judaism that would ac-
commodate their needs. Who moved to the suburbs and created a
suburban Judaism and a suburban G-d, ethical and cultured and
nice—a vaguely Jewish Santa Claus. Who turned down the Orthodox synagogue of their parents, grandparents, and generations beyond because it was too Jewish and too out of step with modern
times and too difficult and too outmoded and not compatible with
the new pagan-Jewish life-style they were creating. Who turned
either to the Reform that gave them both status (how familiar their
Christian friends would find it if ever they stopped by) as well as
license (one could be almost anything and do the same in that incredible anarchy known as Reform) or—better still—to that new
and upcoming movement known as "Conservatism." How many
Jewish refugees from Brooklyn and the Bronx arrived in their new
status symbols in Massapequa to find themselves surrounded by
strange natives known generally as goyim with large tribal groupings called Protestants? How many Jews, in panic, fearing that
their son would come home with a Mary rather than a Shirley,
banded together to build a quick temple or Jewish center to save
their precious ones? How many of them who did not know a Jewish
concept from a Catholic catechism decided to adopt Conservatism
because "Orthodox is too old-fashioned" and "Reform is too much
like a church"? And how amazed was the minuscule, unimportant
Conservative movement to be suddenly besieged with requests for
Conservative rabbis who did not exist!

And how many Conservative temples were suddenly hiring Orthodox rabbis who prostituted themselves before the Long Island god
of gold? And how true it is that it was not the Conservative "movement" that built all the new temples that suddenly sprouted and
made them so prominent, but the ordinary, ignorant Jews who
bought a temple just as they bought any other commodity they
needed and who set the terms of the deal. The American Jew cannot
distinguish between Conservatism and Reform because they have

no definition. Because they were created not in the image of Judaism but in the image of the American Jew.

Marshall Sklare, the leading American Jewish sociologist of the Conservative movement, discussed the concept of Conservatism in the mind of the average Jew who claims that this is what he follows. In his classic work, *Conservative Judaism*, published in 1955, Sklare lists the replies of Bernie's parents when asked the simple question: "What do you mean when you say you are Conservative?" Consider the following definitions:

> . . . I keep a kosher home as far as possible and I light [Sabbath] candles. But when I go out I eat all sorts of things I don't have at home. To me that's Conservative.
>
> We are not as strict as the rabbi would like us to be but we keep all the festivals. . . . We always have a big Seder and we don't have any bread during Passover. During the war I decided not to buy kosher meat any more. . . . But . . . I could never buy pork or serve butter with meat at meals.
>
> . . . I don't keep a kosher home but I am a 100 percent Jew at heart. I don't run to synagogue but I wouldn't do anything to harm the Jewish people.
>
> I believe . . . there should be a certain amount of old and new customs. I don't like to walk into the synagogue feeling I'm in a church and take my hat off, and everything in English.
>
> I wouldn't say I was religious—and I wouldn't say I was Reformed. . . . I don't believe in going into temple and then coming out and riding.

As Sklare points out, the respondents saw their movement as "a halfway house" between Reform and Orthodoxy." He proves this by a few more replies:

> Well, sort of not Orthodox but more Orthodox than Reform. . . . I'm not 100 percent Orthodox and of course I'm not Reformed—I'm just in between.
> . . . I guess you'd call it the middle of the road . . .

Out of this towering intellectual babel, a distinctive pattern emerges. Conservatism is "in between." The American Jew eschews ideology for pragmatism. He knows and cares nothing about theology, ideology, or intellectual honesty. He needs a religion and picks the one that combines ease and lack of guilt feelings. He chooses the one that is not as difficult as Orthodoxy and not as "Gentile" as Reform. And we would do well to pause and consider the roots of Conservatism's growth after World War II and thus understand the irreligious mishmash from which it—and Bernie—grew.

The end of World War II saw an American Jewry that was still preponderantly inner-urban, Eastern seaboard. The vast majority lived in "Jewish" neighborhoods where, whether they observed commandments or not, they were part of a permanent Jewish environment. Jews were the great majority in those areas and the synagogue (invariably Orthodox) on almost every block, along with the kosher butcher store, the public school that was 90 percent Jewish, the totality of the Jewish atmosphere, made the reality of being Jewish a thing that never left the Jew.

But World War II changed the economic and social habits of a nation and those of the Jews even more than most others. The economic boom that emerged from the pent-up wealth that could not be spent during the austere, ration-filled war years burst forth and a great migration took place from the inner cities to the outer parts and the suburbs. From Brownsville and Flatbush in Brooklyn, from the Grand Concourse and Fordham Road in the Bronx, from Manhattan's Lower East and Upper West Sides, the story was the same—Jews streaming to the Long Island and Westchester suburbs. It was, geographically, a journey of tens of miles, but socially —an awesome change.

Suddenly, far from being the majority in the warm, familiar neighborhood, the Jew of Long Island (and all the Long Islands of America) found himself to be a distinct and clearly visible minority. When Christmas came to Freeport, *it was Christmas*, and no one could miss it! When Bernie went to school he found himself with strangely named children—John, Tommy, Kevin. Worse, far worse from the point of view of the suddenly worried parents, Bernie also had classmates named Kathy and Rosemary Anne and Bridget. And worst of all, he did not merely go to *school* with Gentiles, he played with them, brought them home, and asked if he could go in their houses.

Most of the young adult Jewish parents who had come into suburbia were people who had rarely attended synagogue in the old, inner-city neighborhoods. Their Jewishness had ended after a Bar Mitzvah that was meaningless and distasteful, and the tragedy was that the European Jewish parent had insisted on building synagogues rather than yeshivas, trusting in the *melamed* (private teacher) to fill his child with enough Jewishness to overcome the American assimilation. And so, when the young Jewish parents migrated to the suburbs, the thought of a synagogue was generally both out of sight and out of mind.

Reality now intruded. Clearly, something had to be done, lest Bernie carry his friendship with Bridget too far. And yet another problem had arisen: *Them*. The Gentiles. The suburbs were dotted with churches of all kinds, Catholic and Protestant of varied descriptions. In the suburbs it was clear that people not only had churches but worshiped in them. Surely, there was something suspiciously un-American about an individual—let alone an entire group—that did not have a House of G-d.

The Jewish families who met in the new areas to discuss the situation generally agreed that what was needed was a Jewish institution that would serve as a religious sanctuary but, more important, also as a "center" where Bernies and Shirleys could meet. The roots of the institution that arose in suburb after suburb thus had nothing to do with G-d or religion. The need to keep Bernie from Bridget, to infuse him with some "culture," as well as the necessity of having a Jewish address and spokesman to the outside Gentile world, were the factors that gave rise to the new suburban temple.

And how did the Jew choose the affiliation of his new edifice? While many areas did opt for Reform temples, the vast majority decided upon "Conservatism." Neither ideology nor theology played a part in this choice, since the average Jew had not the slightest knowledge of any ideology that Conservatism might or might not have. The suburban Jew knew only that he did *not want* Orthodoxy with its dual liabilities: the foreign and ghetto connotation on the one hand and, on the other, the demanding and difficult Judaism that he did not wish to be burdened with.

For the American Jew, one and two generations from the immigrant, there was a definite purpose to life: Enjoy. He wished to be successful, wealthy, and happy. He wanted to enjoy the material things, the good life that was available to him in this world. The symbols of success and happiness—the home in the suburbs, the automobile (two?), the status—these were the important things to him, and everything he did was aimed at achieving them and not jeopardizing them. The Jew, who had been the most religious and spiritual of men, now became "this-worldly," a successful materialist, one of the best of them. Orthodoxy, which meant a special, separate, parochial, demanding, particularist life collided with the Jew's desire to assimilate, integrate, mix, climb the ladder, enjoy life with as few taboos as possible. No, Orthodoxy was clearly no way of behavior for a Jew on the way up.

Reform, on the other hand, was too "Gentile." The average Jew, raised in the nostalgic atmosphere of an Eastern European-rooted home, did not have the courage to make as great a break with Judaism and practice as he might have wished. To be sure, in theory, there was not the slightest difference between those Jews who built Reform temples and the others who opted for Conservatism. Both were as ignorant of Judaism and both believed in as little as the other. But there remained the psychological block about Reform ("too much like a church"), and the same Jew who violated the Sabbath with impunity found it impossible to pray with his head uncovered.

There was neither logic nor intellect involved as the suburban Jews chose to build their Jewish community centers as Conservative "temples." It was all based on ignorance and pragmatism, a feeling that Orthodoxy is too Jewish, Reform not Jewish enough, and—as some Jewish Goldilocks fantasy—Conservatism was found to be "just right" ...

The American Jew suffers from an advanced case of national amnesia. He is not sure who he is. And his "temples" and "centers" reflect this confusion and anarchy.

It is not the rabbinical association or the individual rabbis who control the temples and centers. It is not the theology or the ideology. There is no religious discipline or authority. Since the temple was conceived and brought into this world by the individual, ignorant, and confused lay Jews, they are the ones who set the tone, lay down the policy, and are the authorities for the law.

The temple, for the Jew in America, serves a need, just as any other item does. If one needs to travel, he buys an automobile. If he desires recreation, he buys golf clubs. If his wife feels cold, she purchases a mink coat. The temple and center are no different. They were built not out of conviction or *commandment*, but rather because of a utilitarian need. The suburban Jew needs a tax shelter for his money and a Bernie shelter to save his child from Bridget; he wants a factory that produces Bar Mitzvahs; he wants a social and recreation framework—for these he bought the temple and rabbi. As long as they fulfill his needs and will, he is content, but the moment they become too religious (or not religious enough, as he decides), he then makes it quite clear who controls things, who is the real authority.

For the rabbi is essentially an employee and though the courtesy game is played so that he can save face and *act* as the spiritual leader, he is, in fact, still not more than an employee. The words of Clarence Gross still ring true: ". . . I reserve the right to ask my rabbi to implement the general feeling of myself and those other members of the congregation."

Of course. "And Man made the temple in his own image." What the Sabbath policy of the temple or center shall be, is ultimately decided not by a Code of Jewish Law, rabbi, or rabbinical body, but by whatever the members of that particular "religious" institution decide, and all the Conservative claims of "evolving the *halacha*" ring hollow in the valley of reality.

There is a general understanding among members as to just what they are prepared to accept from the rabbi. He is given a certain latitude, but let him go beyond it at his peril. There is a kind of unfunny game that is played when the rabbi is hired. He is free to be, personally, whatever he cares to be, and oddly enough, many congregations prefer a rabbi who is pious, presumably on the theory that he takes on their sins and fulfills their commandments for them. He is even expected to censure the congregation from time to time—both for his own peace of mind and for their own good— but the censure should never go beyond the bounds of theory and should never touch certain subjects.

Consider the description that appeared in the *New York Times* this year of the hiring of a rabbi by a Conservative temple on Long Island, the Jewish Community Center of West Hempstead:

> The religious conviction of the prospective rabbi was also left unresolved. Frank Wexler, a retired high school principal and a former president of the congregation, said the new rabbi must show "a greater willingness to change than our late rabbi did."

"The religious conviction of the rabbi was left unresolved." When Judaism was Judaism, did the question ever arise? Was "religious conviction" a problem? What rabbi did not have it, and a uniform kind at that? The problem here is that he may, indeed, have it— and the kind that the center does not want. It is the congregation that decides on the "proper" religious conviction and it is not Judaism that is being practiced here but something akin to "West Hempsteadism." And what is the foundation of this religion?

Change. Change in the direction of whatever the members desire. And Mr. Wexler makes it clear that the rabbi must be willing to accept that change.

It is of interest to ask what makes the members of the selection or search committee capable of choosing a rabbi. They have but the vaguest idea of Talmud or *halacha* and certainly cannot test the rabbi's competency in Jewish law and scholarship. For all they know, he may be a gross ignoramus and they could never tell the difference. But their own Jewish incompetency is irrelevant because they are not choosing a rabbi on that basis. They are not seeking a scholar; they are not looking for a *halachic* expert who will assert the authority of the law. They want a good speaker who will entertain them; a charming man who will represent the "Jewish community" in the eyes of the Gentiles; someone to hold their hands at funerals and *shiva* calls (and just prior to that in the hospital); and a glorified baby-sitter for their children. They do *not* want someone who will try to impose religion on them. They do not want someone who will influence their children too much and thus cause "conflict" in the home between what Judaism teaches and what the parents practice. They want a "safe" rabbi.

The *Times* article continues:

> The congregation is not looking for a man who will install a *mechitza* [the partition that separates men from women in all traditional synagogues]. But we're also not looking for a rabbi who will give women *aliyahs* [calling the congregant up to render a blessing before the Toran is read]. *I don't think we are ready for that.*

The question in the mind of the speaker (one Mervin J. Pelton, CPA and chairman of the search committee) is not whether this is in accordance with or contrary to Jewish tradition, but whether *we*, the congregation, the givers of the law in West Hempstead, the authorities on Judaism for ourselves, are *ready for it*. When we are, we will have it.

Just as mixed pews—clearly a violation of *halacha* that nevertheless exists in every Conservative center—came about without the slightest pretense at *halachic* justification because the Jews and *especially the women demanded it*, so too with all other questions. When the congregation votes to have change, it will be and the rabbi's choice is to go along or get along his way. If the Conservative movement ever gathered up the courage to ban something that the vast majority of its members wanted, it would find that the temples either became independent or joined the Reform movement. Conservatism would be left with a theological seminary to which students would never gravitate since they would never be assured pulpits.

The *Times* article concludes:

> "I think we should be looking for a rabbi who will be willing to move forward when we are ready," said Joseph Alcabes, an engineer.
> "Sure, but what is forward?" asked Mr. Rader.

The story of the American Jewish Conservative and Reform movements, a study in confusion, anarchy, and irreligiosity. In the words of an Orthodox-descended Conservative rabbi, Samuel Rosenblatt, as quoted by Sklare:

> In the eyes of the layman, Conservative Judaism stands for the right to be *mchalel Shabbat* [a Sabbath desecrator] and to eat *trayyfot* [forbidden foods]. . . . When I tell them that Conservative Judaism believes in *Shmirat Shabbat* [Sabbath observance] and in *kashrut*, they think that I am talking out of my hat.

Certainly. Because if they believed otherwise, they would have never chosen to be "Conservative" in the first place. Religion in America is a shopping center. One needs religion? He chooses from all the models. Truth? Revelation? Ideology? Who cares? The American Jew is just looking for a good-looking religion that will get him where *he* wants to go.

The rabbi who knows the charade that is being unfolded here and the indignities that both he and Judaism are being subjected to, is not to be pitied. Knowing all this, he opts for the status and the salary that is his if he "plays the game," accepts the ultimate authority of the congregation, and shuts his eyes to what goes on about him. If one is prepared to watch Bernie after Bernie arise and, knowing that any attempt to give him real Judaism and thus indeed create conflict in the home can cost the rabbi his job, decides to bury principles and accept the situation; if one is prepared to sit before a search committee and hear some ignorant lout tell him what is expected of him—then the "job" of rabbi will be a sweet one. But it will then have turned into a job instead of a calling. And the rabbi will have gained suburbia and lost his soul. That so many rabbis do it, says a great deal about the kind of spiritual leadership American temples have. It goes far to explain what makes Bernies run.

There exists a mutual contempt society that grows between fraudulent rabbi and fraudulent temple. Each knows the "game" that is being played; each knows that the other knows it; each has nothing but contempt for the other; each must continue to play the game because there is a mutual need for the partner in contempt.

The temple stands in the suburbs, an expensive "House of Leaving Judaism." If it is an old joke—this Edifice Complex—it is nevertheless true. Temple Israel, for decades situated on Poplar and Montgomery Streets in Memphis, announced in 1972 that "after much agonizing" it was moving to "the fringes of the city." (Could the agony have been the usual liberal one that precedes the junking of comfortable theory that calls for integration everywhere but your own neighborhood?) In any event, if there was agony, there may or may not have been ecstasy as the Brotherhood President informed the members that the initial estimate of the cost of the new building was $3.5 million.

I recall speaking in a huge, multimillion-dollar temple in Syracuse, New York. After taking me for a tour of the place, the rabbi told me that the costs had exceeded the original estimates. The members had come to him with a suggestion to cut expenses. The first suggestion? The religious school . . .

The Templeites may believe that size of structure can compensate for tinyness of religious substance. Or it may be necessary to show the Gentile how magnificent is our House of Worship (for the naive Gentile really does believe that this is what a Jewish church is). And so one reads the following Page 1 (!) news item in *Post and Opinion* (December 8, 1972):

> What could be the largest menorah in the United States embellishes the foyer of Temple Emanuel in Grand Rapids, Michigan, and during Hanukkah is moved to the altar where the lights are kindled each night despite its 600-pound weight. . . . It is 8 feet long and a little over 4 feet high.

There is more than a little symbolism to this American Jewish worship of hugeness, and especially the grandiose Hanukkah, an

American Jewish phenomenon. If Yom Kippur is our most solemn holiday, Purim our most joyous, Passover our most intense, and Shavuot our most neglected, then surely Hanukkah is our most ironic.

When one considers the huge neglect and desecration of the truly major Biblical holidays, not to mention the basic Sabbath, one is stupefied to see the universal observance of Hanukkah. Not even the devoutest Hassid can outdo the suburbanite when it comes to the Feast of Lights. In the temple, for weeks in advance, little Maccabees, Judah and Judith alike, dramatically declaim in preparation for the obligatory play. Picture windows that frame the supper table where bacon is being eaten, are decorated with the hanging letters "Happy Hanukkah," and the electric menorah glares defiantly at the Gentile. And the ignorance and confusion of the American Jew is underlined with irony.

The American Jew listens with deep pride to the heroic Maccabee deeds and a shiver of *naches* runs up his spine. He listens to the story of Jews who chose death rather than eat ham, were killed rather than desecrate the Sabbath. His rabbi speaks of nobility and courage and martyrdom. Only while Bernie listens, inside him a little voice asks: What are we celebrating? What is so noble about the Maccabees? They were crazy! I think bacon and eggs are delicious and so do my parents, and what madness possesses a man to die rather than let bacon pass his lips? I think Sabbath prohibitions are archaic and nonsensical, and why in the world should I praise someone who died lest he violate them? Why should I, who was taught by my rabbi that the Bible is not divine but a mixture of myths, make a big deal of some people who, ignorantly, thought it was the word of G-d? Why should I praise Jews—the Maccabees—who tried to impose Judaism (Orthodoxy) on other Jews and who killed a Jew who ate pork?

Hanukkah. In Bernie's logical mind it is all one great mistake. But such is the illogic and madness of this "Judaism" that nothing matters and everything is possible. Conservative Temple Israel in Stroudsburg, Pennsylvania, and the Conservative congregation in Geneva, New York, need rabbis. There are no Conservative ones available at the moment ("Sorry, gentlemen, but they're on order") and thus they hire Steven Westman and Joshua Goldstein, who happen to be Reform. What in the world does it matter? There is no basic difference, anyhow, and the congregants will decide, in any event, on the kind of Judaism that is appropriate for them. It is no surprise, therefore, that we read in *Post and Opinion*, April 2, 1976:

> The number of Reform rabbis in Conservative congregations continued to grow as Conservative congregations announced their willingness to accept Reform rabbis. The situation developed after more Reform rabbis were being ordained than there were openings for them in Reform congregations."

The religious law of supply and demand. When the supply of Reform rabbis exceeds the demand of Reform temples, they become Conservative—because the whole thing is irrelevant, anyhow.

The temple service. The frantic drive to find some magic formula to convince Bernie to attend. The Orthodox have no problem. Their synagogues, (*shuls*, they insist on calling them to this day, to the intense embarassment of other Jews), are filled with youngsters who do not stop attending after Bar Mitzvah or marriage, for the simple reason that they believe that they are performing the *commandment* of praying to a real G-d. But what can Jews who do not really believe it, do to convince their children that a "good Jew" goes to temple?

> You'll have to attend a Reform Sabbath eve service where the two rabbis of the congregation and a Hassidic [sic] rabbi dance on the pulpit and where a religious school orchestra is thumping out rock music to Jewish songs and where the clapping and stomping are almost frenzied by the worshipers, to get the picture at the Indianapolis Hebrew Congregation.

Thus the opening paragraph of "The Editor's Chair" (*Post and Opinion*, February 27, 1976). The depth of desperation of the American Jew. Rock and roll will not save Reform or the Bernie it destroys. As a one-time "kicks" kind of thing, it will attract the youngster—not for G-d, but for the beat. But afterwards, Bernie knows that there is a better rock band at the local discotheque, and as he grows still older he grows contemptuous of the rabbi who is less capable of influencing Jews than Elvis Presley.

One of the myths that the Reform and Conservative movements attempt to propagate is that they saved American Judaism from extinction. Thus, the argument goes, had there been no Conservatism and Reform, the Jew would have ended up with no religion and what he has now is better than nothing. Leaving aside the

theological argument whether half a falsehood is better than nothing, the argument is historically false.

Reform and Conservatism did not "save" Jews. It was not they
who built the temples and the centers. Those thousands of new Reform and Conservative edifices arose because the conditions of the
time dictated them. It was the American Jew, who, had he stayed in
Brooklyn, might not have built anything or found it necessary,
for his social and sociological needs, to have a religious institution.
What would have happened had there been no such thing as Conservatism and Reform to legitimize the bastard Judaism that the
suburbs produced? What if the only Judaism and the only rabbis
had been Orthodox? The answer is clear: *With no choice, Bernie's
parents would have been compelled to choose authentic Judaism
and Bernie would have been created a Jew.* Far from saving American Jews, Conservatism and Reform allowed them the luxury of
legitimacy in that insane hodgepodge they created. The suburban
Jew built a house, brought a swine into it, and was able to find a
"rabbi" to certify it kosher.

How Conservatism has saved Judaism! How it has succeeded in
imparting Jewish observance to American Jews who otherwise would
have ceased keeping the Jewish tradition! In the words of Marshall
Sklare (in *The Jewish Community in America*, 1974):

> The available evidence suggests that the Conservative strategy
> of liberalization, innovation, and beautification has been a
> failure . . . the majority of Conservative Jews do not follow
> even the most basic Sabbath observances. To cite the example
> of Conservative-dominated Providence, Rhode Island, only 12
> percent of those who designate themselves as "Conservative"
> attend services once a week or more. And what is even more
> serious, attendance at Sabbath worship declines with each gen-
> eration; while some 21 percent of the first generation attend,
> only 2 percent of the third do so.

Of course, Sklare mercifully spares us figures on how many Conservative Jews abide by the Sabbath prohibitions enumerated in the
Talmud and Code of Law. Never would a group of Jews be closer
to unanimity. He continues:

> *Kashrut* is yet another area of observance that constitutes a
> problem. . . . Only 37 percent of Conservative households in
> Providence buy kosher meat. Furthermore, in only 27 percent

of the households are separate dishes utilized. And true to the pattern . . . observance declines in each generation.

For understandable reasons the Conservative elite have avoided publicizing the painful evidence. . . . And Conservatism's failure in the area of the suprasocial [read: religious] is heightened by its brilliant achievements in the social arena: its success in building synagogues, in promoting organizational loyalty, and in achieving primacy on the American Jewish religious scene.

Brilliant achievement? There is surely nothing brilliant about Conservatism's leap to Number 1 on the religious hit parade. Precisely because it had no religious philosophy and allowed every synagogue to do what it wished, it was able to gather in every and all type of suburbanite. It saved no one, not even itself.

And, again, Sklare writes, this time in an article "Jewish Religion and Ethnicity at the Bicentennial" (Midstream, November 1975), concerning the hundredth anniversary of Reform Judaism's Union of American Hebrew Congregations (1973):

And overall there was a feeling of malaise, a vague sense of ill-being and depression. Perhaps the most obvious sign of Reform's feeling that something had gone wrong was the fact that instead of issuing anniversary volumes extolling Reform achievements, it felt compelled to call upon social scientists to diagnose its condition and to recommend a course of treatment.

The American Jew is spiritually sick, of that there is no doubt. But to expect help from the Reform and Conservative religious invalids? Doctors of divinity, heal thyselves . . .

Bernie's parents bought their temple and their rabbi and proceeded to create Judaism and G-d in their own image. The garment center knew exactly how to cut a suit to fit . . .

Judaism, but not too much. If Bernie was sent to that vast cultural wasteland known as the "religious" or "Hebrew" school which he so despised, it was not so much that he might become religious as that he might acquire "culture" (at least enough to let him babble the proper words on the great day of Bar Mitzvah initiation rites). If he came home and mentioned something about Sabbath observance or a ban on ham and bacon, his parents smiled and told him that "we aren't sending you there for that" or "you don't have to listen to everything the teacher says." They played games with Bernie and thought that they could deceive him, never realizing, in their own stupidity, that it would not work. They created a fraud and thought that they could foist it on their Bernie. They created a Judaism that was created in their own image—a Cohenism or a Goldbergism or a Schwartzism—and tried to pretend that it was Judaism. They defrauded themselves because it suited them, and thought that Bernie would grow up to be as fraudulent, hypocritical, and materialistic as they. But he did not. What had made Sammy run did not affect Bernie.

They thought that Judaism was a faucet that could be turned on and off at will. They wanted to give up the uncomfortable and the inconvenient things, but still keep the "important" things, like marrying a Shirley. Bernie was honest. He took the whole thing and junked it. He turned on the faucet all the way and Judaism spilled out, in toto. He married Bridget to the wailing of his parents who shrieked to one and all: *"Where did we go wrong???"*

Where did they go wrong? Where did they go right?

The American Jew has no religion, if by religion we mean the traditional, time-honored Judaism of awe of the Almighty and happy bowing to His will. The American Jew has a folklore; his Jewishness is made up of ethnic bits and pieces and is derived, so to speak, from two Prime Causes. Were I a Talmudic sage I might phrase it: "On two things does the modern Jew stand—on *goyim* and on *cholent.*" Let me explain.

The goy; the Gentile. The phenomenon of the Jew who is Jewish because the Gentile made him so has already been discussed. If today there are millions of Jews who have not opted to assimilate and disappear, it is because their efforts to do so came to an abrupt and ignominious halt. Many a Jew wanted it; it was the *Gentile* who said No! Had the Gentile agreed, there would have been mass spiritual suicide, with Jews eagerly and enthusiastically opting for Jim and Kathy and Bridget and Tom. But the Gentile refused, and an Enlightenment and Emancipation rapidly degenerated into the Ku Klux Klan and Christian Frontiers and German-American Bund —and into the horror of the Holocaust.

Who can say how much the Holocaust contributed in its terrible way to a strengthening of American Jewish identity? The Jew in America was horror-stricken to see what the Gentile could do to "him" in the twentieth century. Auschwitz was an unimaginable trauma for an American Jew who wanted badly to believe that the persecution of 20 centuries was merely a product of religious bigotry and ignorance. The Germans were clearly not ignorant and Hitler and the Nazis were clearly not religious—and nevertheless *it* happened. The Gentile, in the form of the Holocaust, made Bernie's father and mother Jews to a greater extent than they would have ever been; it also gave them an Israel and made them "Zionists."

For Israel, too, owes its birth to a Holocaust that created Jewish refugees from former solid citizens of Europe and led to shock, bitterness, and fear among Jews who demanded that a Jewish State be created where *it* would never happen again. Indeed, in the inner recesses of the American Jew's mind, Israel became and remains an insurance policy for which he pays premiums in the form of UJA and Israel Bonds checks. And if the *goy* is the father of irrational American "Judaism," the mother is *cholent*.

For millions of Jews who had left the Judaism of tradition and Torah, becoming members of the New Judaism, the intellectual contradictions and objections were muted by *cholent*. I do not speak of *cholent* that cooked away all Friday night in the oven and that emerged with its potatoes and beans, hot and more than filling. I am speaking of all the *cholent* that remained as warm nostalgic memories in the minds of countless Jews. I speak of the nostalgia that passed for Judaism and that kept the Jewish dreamers from breaking with their people.

Millions of Jews remained Jews because they were raised in truly Jewish homes. Imbedded in their memories were their own experiences and early lives. They had seen and lived a real Sabbath in their parents' or grandparents' homes; they remembered the Kiddush wine cup and the two challas; they remembered the real Passover Seder; they remembered the packed Orthodox *shul* where people went to *daven*, not to "pray"; they remembered the Jewishness of the Old Judaism and so they moved on to New Judaism, but could never bring themselves to face the contradictions and absurdities that would force them to drop it entirely. They had to remain Jews because of the grip that nostalgia had upon them. Because of *cholent* . . .

The Gentile and nostalgia, these were the building bricks of the peculiar American Judaism. And from it came forth the bits and pieces that, after all the other difficult and uncomfortable things were discarded, remained to make up the fabric of that Judaism. Israel—supplying a vicarious pride in seeing tough Jews so that the anti-Semite will be deterred and the Gentile's image of the Jew be changed for the better. Kaddish and Yahrtzeit—the prayers for the dead that stem from some lingering ancestor worship that

makes the Chinese brand pale into insignificance. The Bar Mitzvah
—without which there might not be temples or prayers. Jewish
food, Jewish jokes, Jewish books, (or books by Jews) but *not* any
that deal with scholarship, law, and heritage. Jewish "heroes"—
vague pride in Albert Einstein and Jonas Salk and a Nobel Prize
winner who is nominally Jewish and in Sandy Koufax. Jewish
"villains"—nervousness if a publicized white-collar criminal is *too*
Jewish, lest it reflects on "us." These are the things that comprise
American Jewishness. And, of course, the unceasing round of Jewish
organizational meetings—B'nai Brith, Haddassah, Sisterhood, UJA
breakfast, Little League, Scouts—with their breathtaking array of
bazaars, rummage sales, canasta and bridge clubs, Las Vegas nights,
theater parties, and infinitum ad nauseam. This is American "Judaism"; the average American Jew has never opened a Bible, let
alone studied it or finished it. A Jewish book for him is *Portnoy*;
never was there a religious group more ignorant of its own heritage.
The Jew wrote the Bible; Jimmy Carter studies it.

The confusion, superficiality, and emptiness of this "Judaism" are
staggering. It is replete with contradiction, irrelevancies, and absurdities. What is Judaism? Of course, Israel. And in Dallas, Texas,
Jewry learns that "Sunday, November 7, is Hadassah Fund-Raising
Day at Burger King!" With 10 percent of all sales given to the
Jewish State's main hospital, Dallas Jews were urged to rush down
to the nonkosher restaurant and "enjoy a terrific meal and help
make November 7 an eventful one for Hadassah." Only American
Judaism is capable of placing a nonkosher hamburger at the dis-
posal of the Jewish State. One can begin to understand a Bernie who
might ask: "Mother Hadassah, what is Jewish about that state?"

Does it really matter? *Kashrut* has long since taken a back seat to
just food, any food, as long as it is "Jewish." Thus in the American
Jewish suburb, the "Mr. and Mrs. Club" advertises for its Jewish
function: "Beer, cider, and setups will be provided, with a mid-
night lox and bagel buffet. There will be a special award for the
most authentically dressed couple." What is Jewish about this affair?
Why, they served bagels and lox . .

When Conservative Judaism fails and Reform is bankrupt, we
can always depend on Culinary Judaism. An old story used to tell
of the thoroughly assimilated Jew who was asked, "Isn't there *anything* Jewish about you that remains?" "Yes," he said, "I am still
afraid of dogs." The American Jew has overcome that, too. For
him, who has thrown away everything else, there still remains a
"cholent Judaism." He still eats "Jewish food," a product of

nostalgia and Bernie's grandmother. Of course, Jewish food does not have to be kosher, and we emerge with the sublimest advertisement of them all: You don't have to be kosher to eat Jewish. Kosher-style delicatessens are the Conservative and Reform restaurant versions of their temples. Thus Norman Friedman, in an article on "Jewish Popular Culture in Contemporary America" (*Judaism*, Summer 1975), writes of a Beverly Hills eatery:

> Nate 'n Al's is a superstar deli, renowned for its celebrity clientele—Milton Berle (Nova Scotia salmon and *fresh* hot tongue), Shecky Greene (corned beef), Joey Bishop (salami and eggs). . . . *All hams come from Poland and Sweden but "we bake them"* . . . (my italics)

Judaism is alive and eating well in Beverly Hills. Indeed, it is not only nostalgic food—that which comes from the "old home"— that can be called Jewish, but American Jews, true to their new trend of conversion of Gentiles, have succeeded in proselytizing an entire *group* of pagans: Chinese restaurant people. There is no truer evidence that one is passing through a Jewish neighborhood than the sudden proliferation of Chinese restaurants. This too, is Judaism . . .

What else is American Judaism? *Fiddler on the Roof*, where the American Jew can smile at the prototype of *zayde* and *bubbe*, knowing that he can leave them at the theater. *Fiddler*, where the nervous American parent who is terrified of Bridget learns soothingly that Zayde Tevya had the same problem.

And the books! All the books that are "Jewish." In his *Diary*, Rabbi Martin Siegel writes:

> April 4: Tonight was the night for the Sermon of the Year, the great crowd-pleaser, the drawing card. I spoke about Philip Roth's novel, *Portnoy's Complaint*. . . . The turnout was staggering. I saw faces I hadn't seen since last Yom Kippur.

Yes, this too is Judaism in America.

And using a Yiddish phrase—that is *very* Jewish. And if one is used on television, all the Jews achieve something akin to a minor Victory at Entebbe. Part of Jewishness in suburbia is enjoying life, or at least being so busy as to give the impression of it. The Jewish woman who has led the drive to emasculate not only her husband but her religion leads a frenetic life rushing about here and there, seeking to find some meaning that was lost when she opted for the Golden Calf. She joins organization after organization and attends luncheon after luncheon and helps charity after charity (with her *time*)—not because of any special love for people or out of any call of humanity and social service. *The American Jewish woman is bored*, bored unto death, and the organization for her becomes not a means, but an end in itself. Materialism has become a monkey on her back and she is addicted. The family/style page of the *New York Times*, June 6, 1975, carried a story headed: "They Held a Morning Party to Learn to Apply Makeup." It began as follows:

> Scarsdale, N.Y.—Linda Englander got up early the other morning, saw her two older children off to grammar school, and parked the baby with a neighbor. . . . This was no ordinary suburban kaffeeklatsch. The party was called a beauty show and its show-and-tell star was Ann Thompson, a sales director for Mary Kaye Cosmetics. . . . Promptly at 9:30 A.M. the six women arrived. . . . Mrs. Thompson asked the women to take their makeup off. "My false eyelashes, too?" asked Jaye Seedler. . . . "I've never used a mask," commented Shirley Golub. . . . "It gives you a nice color," said Carol Greenhouse. . . .

The bored, vapid, and frustrated American Jewess.

And what else is the American Jew? The liberal fighter for integration in Mississippi (but *not* Forest Hills). Do we grow angry at Bernie for fighting for all causes in the world except his own? Consider from whom he learned.

The Great Neck (Long Island) *Record* of May 25, 1967, carried the following article under the heading "Stokely Was Here Sunday":

> Although unable to make Friday's speaking engagement at Great Neck North High School, Stokely Carmichael, former head of SNCC, did appear Sunday at the home of Mr. and Mrs. Seymour Lichtenstein, 144 Kings Point Road, under the sponsorship of the Great Neck Committee for Human Rights. Here he is shown addressing a crowd in the Lichtenstein living room. Standing alongside of him is Moe Tendler, counsel to CORE. This was a fund-raising event. Admission was $5 per person. It was announced that the Lichtensteins gave $5,000, their children gave $25, and the Great Neck Forum donated $1,000. The total collection was estimated to have reached the expected

goal of $10,000, to be evenly divided between SNCC, CORE, and Dr. Martin Luther King's Southern Christian Leadership Council.

Let it be noted that the date was May 25, 1967, less than two weeks before the outbreak of the Six Day War. Arab mobs were pouring into the streets shouting about throwing the Jews into the sea. All over the world, Jews were fearfully praying against the prospect that Israel might go under. They were frantically attempting to raise Jewish money to prevent another Holocaust. And other Jews were in Great Neck raising money for Stokely, who repaid them on August 27 of that year by appearing before the Organization of Arab Students at Ann Arbor, Michigan, and saying that he and other Black militants were ready "to take up arms and die if necessary to help the Arabs free Palestine."

There were so many Great Necks and so many Jews like those who gathered to applaud and smile as the little Lichtensteins gave $25 to the anti-Semite. (One wonders where the little ones are today.)

The American Jew, product of the *goy* and of *cholent*, whose Judaism is nostalgia, ethics, the memory of the Holocaust, and the UJA. But what of his child? What of Bernie?

What happens when a child is born free and unencumbered with memories? And what happens when a young Jew is raised in an environment where, for the time being, history has allowed him never to know any meaningful anti-Semitism? What happens when he roams campuses filled with (pretty and handsome) Gentiles, freedom-filled neighborhoods and workplaces, a world of his own that is apparently uninhabited by hatred of the Jew? What happens when a whole generation grows up that does not know the *goy*? What happens? Why, the obvious. Not being forced to be a Jew, he does not remain one; not consciously, not actively, not caringly.

And what happens when a young Jew arises who does not know *cholent*? Who comes from a home where Judaism lives only in the nostalgic mind of the parents but which is never practiced? Who never saw the *shul* but only knows the mausoleum that passes for a temple? Who never tasted the Kiddush wine or searched for *chametz* on Passover eve? Who never saw a *sukkah* and never danced on Simchas Torah? Who never smelled the *cholent*! He has no nostalgia; he remembers nothing warm and tender that pricks his conscience and makes him ashamed of letting go. He has no *cholent* to make him forego the *shiksa*. And when one has neither *goyim* to beat him and force him to be Jewish nor *cholent* to prod him into nostalgic reminiscences, he has no reason to be Jewish and so he leaves.

He leaves and runs to Bridget and there is nothing to stop him. The American Jew saw Liberalism and proclaimed it good.

Liberalism believes in man's opportunity to gain personal happiness and peace of mind. It cannot understand why two people who are compatible and who love each other should be separated because of rituals, creeds, religions that are antiquated and the product of men to begin with. Dr. Saul Hofstein proposed a solution to the problem of intermarriage. The report of his wisdom was carried by the Jewish Telegraphic Agency: "He urged parents to explain to their children at an early age that the child's marriage outside the faith would make the parents unhappy." Indeed. "Bernie, I know you love Bridget and that she is beautiful, wealthy, intelligent, kind, and liberal. But marrying her would make Daddy unhappy." One can see how such an argument will have a profound impact on Bernie; Bernie wants to be happy, and Bridget makes him ecstatic. If Mother and Father find her difficult to take, he can advise them to take a Milltown but he will surely not give up a Bridget.

The parent, intellectually confused and torn between the logic of liberalism and the *cholent* gut-feeling of Judaism, pathetically attempts to argue with Bernie. Since the parents' lives also revolve around the goal of "happiness," they naturally gravitate to that immediately, seeking to persuade their Jewish son that differences in religion will lead to marital discord, divorce, and unhappiness. Bernie, stars in his eyes, is less than impressed. With his Bridget, he can conquer the world. His parents take out all the arguments that they heard in the rabbi's adult education class: you owe it to your people to stay Jewish; you owe it to your ancestors to stay Jewish; you owe it to us to stay Jewish; you owe it . . . Bernie is convinced he owes nothing to anyone. He has been taught liberalism well. He is a human being, an individual, and all artificial ties are reactionary and antiquated concepts. Bernie owes only one allegiance —to his own happiness, and that is Bridget.

The Jewish Establishment, basically responsible for the Bernies, has long since given up the struggle. They are conceding the impossibility of preventing intermarriage. And conceding, implicitly, their own bankruptcy. Thus they aid the parent and, indeed, push the parent into doing the same. They create a new ethic and response to intermarriage—an acceptance, an understanding that is yet another retreat before assimilation. The parents, who need no urging, follow their lead. Though in the marrow of their bones they know that their Bernie has committed the worst possible form of treachery to his people, the kind that even *they* can sense, they are helpless to stop him and have grown too weak to choose a Judaism they do not really believe in, over their child. Their response is: "I would make every effort to show him the error of his way. Then I'd accept the situation but I'd be brokenhearted."

One mother, whose child converted to Christianity, went further. She was not prepared to merely be brokenhearted. She thought long and hard about who caused her son to run and how it came about. In the December 26, 1975, issue of the *Baltimore Jewish Times*, she wrote a tragic but incisive analysis which she called: "Why Has My Son Joined a Monastery?"

> It's still unbelievable . . . visiting our 24-year-old son who, three months earlier, had became a postulant in an Episcopal monastery. How utterly impossible, yet all too true, that Ken aspires to become a monk!
>
> We sat motionless on the hard wooden benches listening to the monastic choir. It seemed to us like a fantasy and reality simultaneously, but reassuring to hear some of the same prayers we are familiar with from our own temple, reinforcing our knowledge that each of us has the same G-d. We wondered how we could sit there without screaming our protest as we watched our son bow before the figure of Jesus and cross himself. With almost superhuman control, we survived the short service and silently followed the others out of the room. . . .
>
> After a time, a parent's intense guilt complex may subside, but I doubt that mine will ever vanish. I am to blame for many commissions and omissions, and belatedly I realize that overwhelming love is not in itself sufficient to give a child. How much more beneficial it would have been to have set a Jewish example for him to follow!
>
> I blush with shame as I confess that I was especially proud of being a Reform Jewess and how I looked down on the more observant Jews, especially those Orthodox sporting long beards. How silly I considered many Jewish customs, as being out of step with the times. If only I could live my life over, my foremost desire would be to have my sons acquire a fine Jewish education, for my son's defection has transformed me from a barely observant Jewess to one with deep Orthodox feelings

inside. I find the resultant enrichment of my soul from all the suffering I endured partial compensation for all the trauma. I have discovered that the most gigantic hurdles are not insurmountable when one has an abiding faith in G-d, for only He made it possible for one to accept the unthinkable. Let nothing prevent your giving your children a truly Jewish environment so they won't grow up ignorant of the customs and beauty of our religion. Go with your children to temple on Saturday mornings so that they may be exposed to their traditional heritage. How much more important than a rejuvenation at the beauty shop, a shopping spree, a tennis game, or a few extra hours of sleep!

The words are hardly typical. Those who make Bernie run are, usually, hardly contrite, humble, or honest. Rather, the arrogance of Bernie's murderers is stupefying. All of them—sleek Jewish Establishment organizations and their portly leaders; the million-dollar temple/mausoleums; the temple rabbi/functionaries; the pitiful and hapless parents. All those whose yardstick was "What will the Gentile say?" and who proceeded to tailor their "Judaism" to fit not the Jew, but the Gentile; all those spiritual schizophrenics who did not know whether they were Jews or not, fish or fowl, meat or milk; all these now point their accusing fingers at Bernie and shout indignantly: "Why are you such a bad Jew? Why are you a traitor to your people? Why can't you marry a nice Jewish girl, like your mother? Why do you want to marry a *shiksa?*"

The hypocrisy is nauseating and amusing at the same time, but Bernie listens and finds nothing humorous in it. "Why do I want to marry Bridget? Why not? What is a nice Jewish girl like my mother? One who desecrates the Sabbath like my mother? So does Bridget. One who eats nonkosher food like dear Mom? So does Bridget. One who comes to synagogue three times a year to parade about in our version of the Easter parade? Bridget has the real thing."

Of course, what Bernie is really saying—no, crying out—is: "Tell me, someone. Why should I be a Jew? Why is it important to be a Jew? What difference does it make? Why not knock down the barriers between religions, nations, and groups once and for all? What is there to Judaism that is so unique and special that I should adhere to it faithfully and marry within my faith? Why be a Jew???

5
Hello, Columbus; Goodbye, Zayde

In June 1973, Albert E. Arent rose to address a plenary luncheon session of the National Jewish Community Relations Advisory Council at the Washington, D.C., Hilton. The topic of his speech was: "Let Us Restore the Balance: Democratic Pluralism and Creative Jewish Living."

The luncheon was graced by hundreds of distinguished and respectable delegates from every part of the United States, for NJCRAC is the apparatus for clearance, coordination, and joint policy on domestic affairs for the Jewish community. Here are gathered all the famous and near-famous Jewish national organizations, the American Jewish Committee, B'nai B'rith and its Anti-Defamation League, American Jewish Congress, National Council of Jewish Women, and more and more. Added to these are some hundred state, county, and local Jewish community relations councils and federations from coast to coast, so that the result is a mighty umbrella group that claims to speak on all domestic issues for the American Jewish community.

As the Council of Jewish Federations and Welfare Funds wrote in a 1966 report: "Federations and welfare funds increasingly have become the Jewish community's "central address" . . . to consider problems which concern Jews as a community." They *are* the American Jewish community in the eyes of the Gentile and Jewish communities, and Al Arent, chairman of NJCRAC for the past three years was acknowledging a gift, inscribed with the words, "In affectionate appreciation of distinguished service." And this is what the distinguished chairman said (italics mine):

When, a year or two ago, I heard bright, committed Jewish college students declare on the floor of the national convention. "We are not Americans, we are Jews," in the context of a debate about American Mideast policy, I was shocked but put it down to youthful hotheadedness. But how often since have I heard Jews . . . address themselves to political, social, and economic issues in terms almost as exclusively parochial, asking over and over again, "What is the *Jewish* dimension in this issue?"

American democratic pluralism is unique in this world . . . this pluralism has two aspects: first, the concept of *individual* participation in an *integrated* society seeking its own perfection through the progressive elimination of want and the cultivation of true *equality*; second, the concept of creative group living—groups interacting, their actions fueled by their own needs and impulses, *but always within the bounds of the common national interest.*

This pluralism finds its fullest realization in the achievement by all groups of an optimal balance between integration in the general society and the maintenance of a separate distinctiveness. . . .

We are *American Jews*—and thanks to American pluralism that is far different from being Jews *in* America. Our ties to our Jewish *heritage* and our *affinities* with our fellow Jews everywhere commingle comfortably with our *United States nationality.* We can be whole as Jews and whole as Americans and there is no conflict within us.

But of late in our American society this balance of integration and distinctiveness has grown increasingly skewed toward separateness and away from integration, toward a preoccupation with more parochial group concerns and away from the concerns of the society as a whole. I find this disquieting and even dangerous. . . .

Is it not time for the American Jewish community to assume its traditional role in the forefront of the common endeavor to advance equal opportunity, equal rights, and equal justice for all Americans? Can we not serve our country and *Jewish interests* best by involving ourselves actively in the pursuit of social justice, joining hands with other groups dedicated to the same cause . . . ? *The foremost obligation of the Jewish community remains the preservation of American democratic*

pluralism. It is only within the context of our unceasing efforts
to maintain an economically sound and morally just American
society that we can begin to arrange our *other priorities.*

I have quoted at some length from Mr. Arent's speech because
it is a representative expression of the Jewish Establishment's position on the purpose of American Jewish life and the ways to achieve
it. They, above all, go far to explain what and who makes Bernie
run.

The concept of Judaism that had kept Jews staunchly Jewish
throughout history, and the only kind that could conceivably allow
them to survive as an honest minority in the midst of a massive
majority sea, was the one that was based on twin pillars of *exclusiveness,* one national and the other religious. On the one hand, the
Jew believed that he was part of a Jewish *nation,* not "grouping,"
and not merely bound to other Jews by "common ties," "affinities,"
or simply "common descent." A Jewish nation meant that the Jew,
in the midst of an *involuntary exile,* lived as a separate nation
among other nations, different not only in name but also in destiny.
A Jewish nation implied separateness, division, and parochial, overriding interests. It meant that Jews looked upon the countries into
which they had been thrust as temporary shelters with the hope and
obligation to go home to the Land of Israel at the first possible opportunity, a categorical imperative.

On the other hand, there was the *religious* pillar, itself based on
a special, different, exclusive quality that was far different from
mere ritual differences. Judaism spoke of a religion that was Divine
in the actual and literal sense of the word, having been actually
and literally revealed to all the Jewish people standing at Mount
Sinai. It meant that they had been given a *Torah*—a Written and
Oral Law—that had come from G-d Himself and that its concepts
and ordinances were Divine and immutable. It meant that Jews
were a special, *Chosen* People, different and *apart* from all the
others, and that they had to cling to a life-style which was not only
important per se but which also called for the opposite of integration with the nations. A Chosen People, in a Chosen State, building
a special, Chosen Society—this was the Jewish concept that had
kept Jews alive—*as Jews.* This was the concept that gave meaning
to and reason for remaining Jews and not just "human beings."
This was why Bernie was such a rarity in the days before the
Emancipation of the eighteenth and nineteenth centuries. This
kept Bernie home, far from the race for Bridget.

The "Judaism" that emerged from Emancipation and Enlightenment was, as described by Arent, a "Judaism" tailored to insure Jewish safety, physical survival, and social, political, and economic equality. Above all, it is aimed at the overriding Jewish goal, the one that takes precedence over all others—the overcoming and elimination of anti-Semitism.

The Jew of the United States arrived from Europe with a long memory and deep traumas. He remembered century after century of persecution, pogroms, Crusades, Inquisitions, Jew-hatred in all its forms. Here at last, he thought, was a country in which all of this could be eliminated. And so the Jewish Establishment—with the eager approval of the vast majority of American Jews—embarked on a determined policy to eliminate Jew-hatred and guarantee for themselves an equal, happy life, free of fear and persecution.

The solution to Jew-hatred and persecution became the Melting Pot.

Allow me to quote briefly from my book *Never Again!*:

> Melt! This was the new Categorical Imperative. Melt! This was the way to assimilate properly and with honor. . . . Melting meant the blurring of the distinctions. Melting was the great egalitarian credo of the American Jew:
>
> Hear O Israel, America is our G-d; America is the land of One.
>
> In the Melting Pot, all stewed together. In the Melting Pot there was an indivisibility that forever hid the Jew as a distinct entity to be attacked. . . . Melt! This was the way to abolish Jew-hatred.

In his *Zion in America* (1974), Henry Feingold recalls:

> Israel Zangwill's play *The Melting Pot* became immensely popular among the "uptowners" [the German Jewish Establishment in America]. It proposed a solution. The sooner the new [Russian Jewish] immigrants would give up their cultural characteristics and melt into the undifferentiated mass, the sooner anti-Semitism would disappear.

It was *not* a desire to totally assimilate by giving up Jewishness completely. The Jews who wished *that* were not part of the Jewish Establishment, since they wanted no part of anything Jewish, Establishment or not. What the Jewish Establishment wanted, and still wants, is to have its cake and eat it, too. To integrate, yet somehow to be vaguely "Jewish" in such a way that one does not "betray" his people. The Reform German-American Jewish Establishment, after all, *did* have temples, did have a "Judaism," did have institutions. The point is that they had melted enough so as to lose the "grating" Jewishness that prevented them from being comfortably American.

The Melting Pot was *the* Jewish weapon in all this. And in order to melt, one had to create a religion that was not so intense, not so separatist; one had to junk the idea of a Jewish *nation* as it had always been known and make it clear that American Jews were a group bound to other Jews by "affinities." America was their country and Israel was a deeply loved, historically connected land that Jews supported but certainly did not look upon as their "home." They had, too, to discard a religion that was too separatist, with too many nationalist connotations of Zion and Return, a religion that spoke of Revelation and a Chosen People, a religion that was too divisive and too parochial. And though they used the terms "Jews" and "people," they never really meant them in the basic sense of those terms. They had to live the kind of a life that did not give reason to the Gentile to think that Jews were less American than others—and certainly not more Jewish than American. Above all, their Jewishness had to be compatible with the American lifestyle, with the latter being the dominant aspect of their lives and the "Jewishness" becoming an *additional*, supplementary value.

And so the Jew placed his trust and his energies in such things as Liberalism and Education and Equality and Democracy and Secularism and Love and Public Relations. These were the ingredients of the Melting Pot. If America could be a land where all these things existed and where there were no barriers between peoples and races and colors and creeds, then Jews would be safe and secure. And if the stewing of the Melting Pot, which would dissolve differences, also demanded that meaningful Jewish distinctiveness be dropped, then that was the price that had to be paid.

The Jewish affinity for the Melting Pot lay, therefore, in the strategic need to build a safe society, free of anti-Semitism. Eventually, however, as the Jew leaped into the pot and did indeed melt; as he lost his knowledge of Jewish tradition and mingled with Gentiles freely; as he became an equal American and a pale, carbon copy of a Jew—*he began to believe in it.* He was now no longer a Jew who *used* Liberalism or Secularism tactically; he now *became* a liberal. He really believed that to melt and to knock down the barriers between peoples was the correct ideological way of life. The Jew who originally wanted Liberalism to save himself, after decades of experiencing and living it as a life-style, began to believe in it for its own sake and began to disappear as a real Jew.

Let us therefore review what Arent is saying—and *echoing*, for he speaks for the vast majority of Jewish Establishment leaders. First, he raises high the banner of "democratic pluralism," which he interprets as the Jew, in his *individual* life, participating in an integrated society, being an American exactly like all others and sharing their life-style and aspirations, while at the same time recognizing "creative group living" but within the bounds of the "common national interest." This enables us to "commingle comfortably" our Jewish "heritage" and "affinities" with our *American nationality*.

Unfortunately, words, which were once used precisely to give the most exact kind of definition, have long ceased to be used that way. Phrases and expressions are either deliberately or ignorantly garbled and interchanged with concepts meaning something quite different. And though the Melting Pot has become an unfashionable concept (thanks not so much to a growth in *Jewish* identity as in Black Power rejection of it), what Arent terms "democratic pluralism" means the same thing. For "democratic" or "cultural" pluralism certainly does not imply what it did in Europe with such people as Simon Dubnow and his "Diaspora Nationalism." There, the Jew was indeed a nation, living in, let us say, Poland, and sharing *to an extent* the common life of the nation, but essentially existing as a separate group with his own schools, language, and destiny. That is not what Arent wishes.

In the words of Oscar Janowsky (*The American Jew: A Reappraisal*, 1972):

> Cultural pluralism may mean *no more* than the existence in a free society of a variety of linguistic, intellectual, spiritual, and social subgroups who are part of an all-encompassing milieu but who maintain their singular institutions *in addition* to those shared with the population as a whole. . . . In the case of Jews, these relate to the experiences of a long history, the Hebrew and Yiddish languages, distinctive folkways, symbols, traditions, and customs, a sense of kinship with Jews in other parts of the world, and concern with the Jewish cultural center in Israel. We must underscore, however, that these

distinctive Jewish cultural interests are *additional* to the all-embracing American cultural pattern with which the American Jews are identified. . . . The English language is his idiom, American history, literature, and ideals are his cultural values as they are the values of other Americans. His unique Jewish cultural assets are *additional* or *supplementary* to the all-embracing American cultural pattern (italics mine).

Of course, this is so. And this is the kind of "Judaism" that Arent wishes. To be basically an *American*, for that is his nationality, and at the same time to *comfortably* commingle a "Jewishness" that he calls "heritage" and "affinities" with other Jews. What is a "heritage"? Shared history? Shared food menus? A belief in a vague "G-d"? What are "affinities"? Jews all over the world who are brothers, or only cousins, and distant at that?

The dream is to be an *American*, and the Jewishness—whatever that may mean—is decidedly secondary, in addition to, and merely supplementary to the main thing. This *is* the Melting Pot; it is really assimilation, of a kind that is more dishonest than the real thing.

And, of course, it is an illusion. Any honest Bernie knows that democratic pluralism cannot be "comfortable" for Judaism; that there must be conflict between Jewish interests and those of the population as a whole, and that, most of all, there is the question: Why cling to a narrow creed that can threaten, *by its very nature*, the interests of a higher number of people, of human beings? Why not be an American without a hyphen? More, why not be a human being? When there is a conflict between a Jewish value and liberal, American values, what takes precedence? And if the Jewish one, why?

Arent is a Jew by "heritage" and "affinity," but is not really Jewish. His call for social justice and getting involved with the liberal needs of others reflects his need, which stems from fear of anti-Semitism that may arise if we do not melt, and also a *deep-felt belief in liberalism that transcends Judaism!* Arent may pay lip service to Judaism, but his heart and mind lie elsewhere. He is a man whose values, ideas, and ideals have been shaped not in Jewish schools or in Jewish books, but in Gentile American ones. He is first an American, first a liberal, first an individual who integrates, and then—only long afterwards—a Jew, with the kind of comfortable Judaism that commingles with his Gentile concepts.

Bernie is much more honest. He knows that there are irrevocable differences between Judaism and liberalism, unless one wishes to make from Judaism an ethical creed that he already possesses without temple or dues or Bar Miztvah orgy. He knows that the kind of Judaism that Arent preaches is irrelevant at best, and too often in the way of progress toward knocking down barriers between races, creeds, and peoples. Bernie does not need democratic pluralism. He does not need to melt. He wishes to *dissolve* and disappear as a Jew and remain only Bernie, human being.

Arent calls upon Jews to do "social justice." In the words of Charles Liebman (*The Ambivalent American Jew*, 1973):

> The difficulty is that because social action can become a way of life, by commanding the total involvement of an individual, it cuts across institutional boundaries and makes particularistic religious preoccupation seem trivial. . . . Once a Jew finds religious expression outside his institutional framework, he is less likely to return to his traditional camp. . . .
>
> Social action is superficially compatible with Jewish law but its life-style is not. One can—but one does not—drop out of a freedom march because it is taking place on the Sabbath or Yom Kippur. One does not measure the risk of arrest in a Southern prison in terms of the availability of kosher food. . . . *Most importantly, a young couple, after working together and developing a mutual dependence, do not resist love and marriage because one is a Jew and the other is a Gentile* (italics mine).

Indeed not; Bernie marries Bridget in the highest concept of social justice.

Arent is uncomfortable with unadulterated Judaism; that is both his problem and that of the Jewish Establishment. It is embarassing, it divides him from the Gentile, and above all he does not believe in it. He is uncomfortable with Zionism and Israel, if the truth must be known, and his lip service to it is one that must be paid since Israel is beloved by masses of the American Jewish community. He grows angry with the too few young Jews who place their Jewishness over all else. They know that Arentism, Pluralism, Melting Potism, is an impossible thing. One cannot fool all of the Bernies all of the time. In the end, they reject the approach of Arent and the Jewish Establishment—a Judaism that is *prayer*, neither meat nor dairy, neither fish nor fowl—and decide to be honest. One either becomes a totally committed Jew or a Bernie. Thanks to the Jewish Establishment, the vast majority of young Jews have opted, in some degree or another, for the latter choice.

How did American Jewry get this way? How did an American Jewish Establishment arise that was able to make Bernie run?

Legend has it that the first of Columbus' crew to spy the New World was a Marrano, a secret Spanish Jew. What is certainly true is that after the New World was discovered, millions of Jews were able to spy it, feel it, yearn for it, and move heaven and earth to get to it.

It is true that the yearning to move to America was shared by Poles and Germans and Swedes and Italians and Irish, but for the Jew the hope was a different one. For all the rest, America was a dream; for the Jew, it was almost a *need*. For others it was an escape from poverty and economic and social misery, an opportunity to climb the ladder of success. For the Jew—groaning under all the misery of others but also on the rack of hatred, pogroms, and humiliation as a Jew—the New World was a desperate hope of escape, of freedom, of life itself. And so, from the teeming cities and the poor *shtetls*, they came. From the Russian Empire, from Poland, from Galicia, from Lithuania, from Eastern Europe's cauldron of Jew-hatred they came. From the cauldron to the melting pot.

The Jew came to America with his clothing on his back and his Judaism in his pack. It was the kind of Judaism he had lived from birth, from the childhood *cheder* (religious school) to the totality of Jewish communal life—a Sabbath that was real; kosher food; prayers; blessings; the *mikvah* for family purity. The Jew who came from Eastern Europe during the great migrations between 1880 and 1920 was a *Jewish* Jew.

The Jew took his Jewishness with him into the streets and the sweatshops where he began the long process of becoming an American. He looked forward to the great American dream, to making a life for his son that would be better than the one into which he was born. He dreamed of his son's being a fine American and a good Jew. And that son, gladly and eagerly, gave unto Caesar what was his and then informed his Jewish G-d that He would have to be satisfied with ten cents on the dollar.

The son didn't want to run away totally from his Jewish heritage, but only reach an accommodation with it, to live and let live. One thing above all haunted him—the fear of anti-Semitism. He felt compelled to do everything to prevent it from harming him in this land, including the *Americanization of his Jewishness.*

Subconsciously, the new American Jew of Eastern Europe, one step from the Old World and not sure how firm his step in this one was, moved in the direction of all his Emancipated cousins in Western Europe. He knew that as the price of his admission into the Great American Dream he would have to pay part of his strict, parochial, separate Jewish identity. He was ready if all the other nationalities and groups that composed America would also melt and anti-Semitism and danger to his existence would dissolve with them, so that he would be guaranteed the equality and security he so badly wanted.

And the Jews of Eastern Europe did not arrive in a total Jewish vacuum. They found many other Jews who had arrived before them and who had succeeded in organizing their own community and in building their own lives. These Jews were, for the most part, what might be called the Second Aliyah, the second wave of Jewish immigation, the predominantly German Jews who had begun to arrive in 1825, achieved a measure of flood from 1836 to 1880, and by the latter year totally dominated the American Jewish community, both quantitatively and qualitatively. (The First Aliyah were mostly Sephardic Jews who combined an aristocracy with an ability to assimilate into the young American colonies. Except for some individuals, they did not, as a community, shape subsequent American Jewish life.)

It was the German Jews who set the tone for American Jewish life. They had brought to the New World not only themselves but also many ideas which were the products of the Emancipation and Enlightenment their European brethren were so busily pursuing. All of this added up to the Melting Pot philosophy, so that they could build an equal, happy life, free from anti-Semitism. Consequently they created the same kind of emasculated Judaism that the German-Jewish community in the Old Country had created, a Judaism that totally eliminated its own national concepts and that "modified" the religious aspects so that Revelation and Chosenness were safely buried.

The power and thrust of the German Jews was such that, except for a handful of Orthodox synagogues, it was the Reform temple that dominated the American Jewish scene until almost the beginning of the twentieth century. American Reform Judaism at first organized such temples as Har Sinai (Baltimore), Emanu-El

(New York), and Sinai (Chicago), each time calling upon a Reform rabbi from Germany to take the pulpit. The first Reform temple was the one in Charleston, South Carolina, whose statement of principles read (my italics):

> They subscribe to nothing of rabbinical interpretation or rabbinical doctrines. They are their own teachers, drawing their knowledge from the Bible and following only the laws of Moses, *and those only as far as they can be adapted to the institutions of the Society in which they live and enjoy the blessings of liberty.*

Bernie was being conceived.

In 1869, two prominent Reform rabbis, immigrants from Germany, David Einhorn and Samuel Hirsch, met with a number of other Eastern Seaboard rabbis in Philadelphia to lay down the clear Reform line on whether Jews were still a nation. The conference concluded unequivocally that "the Messianic aim of Israel is not the restoration of the old Jewish state . . . but the union of all the children of G-d." Bernie was beginning to show signs of life.

The Reform ideology was succinctly outlined in a platform adopted at a special conference in Pittsburgh in November 1885. Under the chairmanship of the dominant figures, Isaac Mayer Wise and Temple Emanu-El's Kaufmann Kohler, Reform ruled that: "We consider ourselves no longer a nation but a religious community, and expect, therefore, neither a return to Palestine . . . nor the restoration of any of the laws concerning the Jewish State." With the rise of political Zionism, Wise, at the convention of the Reform rabbinate the same year the first World Zionist Congress was held (1897), denounced the new movement as a "nationality swindle" since "we are Jews by religion only." The convention thereupon resolved that "we totally disapprove of any attempt for the establishment of a Jewish state. Such attempts show a misunderstanding of Israel's mission . . . [which] has been expanded to the promotion among the whole human race of the broad and universalistic religion first proclaimed by the Jewish prophets." If one put his hand to the stomach of the American Jewish community, he could easily feel Bernie kicking.

What is most important about the 1897 Reform opposition to Jewish nationalism was the reason given after the ideological one, for it is this reason that was the real cause of Reform anguish:

Such attempts do not benefit but infinitely harm our Jewish brethren where they are still persecuted by confirming the assertion of their enemies that they are foreigners in the countries in which they are at home and of which they are everywhere the most loyal and patriotic citizens.

The fear and insecurity of "What will the Gentile say?" oozes from every pore of the paragraph; the real fear was hardly for "our Jewish brethren" but for themselves—the American Jews—and the impact Zionism would have upon *them*.

The struggle to make sure that Jewish nationalism's "poison" not infect the American Jewish scene was a long and bitter one, with Reform Jewish leadership and the secular Jewish Establishment, which it dominated, leading a long struggle against Zionism. It was only the advent of Hitler and the Holocaust that forced a change in the bitterly negative attitude of most of the Establishment leaders.

For many decades the most prestigious of the American Jewish Establishment groups was the American Jewish Committee. Founded in 1906 by the wealthiest American Jews, its major goal was "to prevent infringement of the civil and religious rights of Jews and to alleviate the consequences of persecution." In this role, it not only fended off Gentile anti-Semitism but fought any Jewish move that it considered dangerous to Jewish liberty, equality, and happiness. When the Balfour Declaration gave Zionism its most famous achievement, a promise by the British government to aid in the establishment of a Jewish National Home, the vast majority of the AJC was aghast. Naomi Cohen in *Not Free to Desist* (1972) reports that they "flatly rejected the aspiration of Jewish statehood, subscribing to the anti-Zionist position enunciated by Reform Judaism: "America is our Palestine, Washington our Jerusalem," and "felt that to affirm a separate Jewish nationality would endanger the rights secured by Jews throughout the emancipated world."

It was Hitler, not Jews, who made the American Jewish Committee drop its bitter anti-Zionism. But even after the State of Israel came into being, the fear of the Gentile caused the AJC, in its declaration supporting the creation of the state, to add: "Citizens of the United States are Americans and citizens of Israel are Israelis; *this we affirm with all its implications*" (my italics). Twice, in 1950 and again in 1960, when Israel's Prime Minister David Ben

Gurion asserted that Jews had an obligation to come live in Israel, AJC leader Jacob Blaustein protested. (In 1960, Ben Gurion said that Jews living outside the Land of Israel are as those who have no Divinity—a quotation from the Talmud—and that Jews of the Western states face "the kiss of death, a slow and imperceptible decline into the abyss of assimilation.") In return for a guarantee of economic and financial aid, Blaustein won from Ben Gurion a statement to the effect that the Jews of the exile have no G-d *unless they live in America.* Blaustein underlined his intent by emphasizing that "to American Jews, America is home. . . . There, they share its fruits and its destiny." Ben Gurion, in a note to Blaustein in 1963, calmed him by writing: "Don't be afraid of dual loyalty. Every human being has many loyalties."

But Blaustein and the Jewish Establishment were terrified of dual loyalty charges by the Gentiles, and the efforts to dilute the national aspect of Judaism, begun in Europe at the time of Napoleon, continue to this day in the American "Judaism" that was founded in the New World.

There are those who argue that things have changed and that the unanimous support for Israel we see in the Jewish Establishment shows that Jewish nationalism has revived among the Jewish leaders. This is manifestly not true.

To be sure, there has been a change in the Jewish community in the sense that Jews today will accept the idea of a Jewish "people." But this is not a meaningful change in the substantive sense of the term. The concept of a Jewish "people" is really a concept of Americans of Jewish national descent, very much like that of those who came as immigrants from all over Europe and who are today Swedish-Americans, Polish-Americans, Italian-Americans, and the like. It certainly does not in any way imply to the Jew that he is a foreigner in the United States. No matter what his subconscious, gut feelings about the reality of anti-Semitism, the most "Jewish" of the Establishment groups looks upon the United States as the home of the American Jew (Jewish-American?). The American Jewish Establishment—at best—has love for Israel, takes pride in it, works to support it, but sees its own destiny in America. The national concept of Judaism which always existed until the Emancipation—*that there is a Jewish nation that is apart from those nations into which the Jewish one has been exiled; that the home of the Jewish nation is only the Land of Israel, and that until then there is a need for the Jew to be separate and apart and parochial*—that concept which kept generations of young Jews from becoming

Bernies is totally rejected by the Jewish Establishment. And thus Bernie was born.

The attitude toward Israel becomes important to understand. For most of the Jewish Establishment, until Hitler's Holocaust, a Jewish State was not something greatly to be desired. Whether there was outright opposition to the concept from the vehemently anti-Zionist Reform-rabbi-led American Council for Judaism or the slightly milder anti-Zionist American Jewish Committee, or whether the opposition assumed "non-Zionist" form (B'nai B'rith), a Jewish State was not a thing most Jewish leaders in America wanted. And even the minority "Zionists" were Zionists in the sense of the classic Jewish joke: A Zionist is one Jew who raises money from a second Jew to send a third Jew to Zion.

American Zionists are more properly "*friends* of Zion," or lovers and *supporters* of Zionism. The American Jewish Congress' Stephen Weiss, who was the leading American Zionist, surely had no intention of living there; neither did any major American Zionist leader ever emigrate to Israel before the age of Social Security or thereabouts. Haddassah women raise their money for Israel but their children for America.

For many of the American Jewish leaders, the State of Israel is a fact of life that they accept, but with increasing impatience concerning its primacy in the life of the average American Jew. Thus, Reform Rabbi Balfour Brickner could call Israel "the G-d we currently worship," at the same time participating in a symposium in March 1974 calling for less of an emphasis on Aliyah (emigration) and, instead, settle for a "lend-lease" of American children to study for a year in Israel. At the same conclave, Conservative Rabbi Wolfe Kellman called for the closing down of the Israeli Aliyah Centers in America and letting those who really want to go, get there themselves. Clearly, Kellman has no such intention, and his fellow Conservative Rabbi Jacob Neusner said so quite clearly in a letter to the *Post and Opinion* (January 19, 1973): "I have no intention of settling in the State of Israel and I do not want my children to."

The real attitude of the Jewish Establishment and the American Jewish parent of Bernie is seen in the June 1976 exhibit "Cultural Pluralism—America's Gift to Jewish History" that was opened in New York in the presence of 300 Jewish leaders. Said Dr. Saul Padover, in describing this as a "Jewish Golden Age": "The American gift to Jewish history consists of the enormous opportunity that the United States gave the Jewish people." Clearly, here we have a

Jewish "people" who have no intention of being that. Their home is America; they are American citizens; they are grateful for the opportunity to be equal to all others; and they do not want anything to change. What they call "people" is really culture; there is no concern here of separate nation but rather of some kind of historical descent and common experiences that have a common meaning to those called "Jews."

The classic words of former Supreme Court Justice Louis Brandeis are always quoted by American "Zionists" as proof that there is no conflict between being an American and a Zionist. Their more important value lies in the definition they gave "Zionism," symbolizing the change from a Judaism which saw the Jewish people as a separate and distinct *nation*, whose home was only Israel, to a new, vapid concept:

> Every American Jew who aids in advancing the Jewish settlement in Palestine, though he feels that neither he nor his descendants will ever live there, will likewise be a better man and a better American for doing so.

A better *American*. This is not Jewish nationalism. This is not Zionism. This is "love of Israel, the Old Country"; this is Friends-of-the-State-of-Israelism. It is manifestly not the powerful separatist and parochial nationalism which alone can have the effect of making Bernie realize that there is a Jewish *difference* that transcends bagels and lox.

It is this rejection of the pillar of Jewish nationalism that sees the American Jewish Establishment fanatically committed to a refusal to even consider the thought that anti-Semitism might reach awesome physical proportions in America in the manner that it did in the Old World. The refusal is a sharp, hysterical one that says much about the groups who "protest too much."

On May 26, 1972, there appeared on the Op-Ed page of the *New York Times* my article, "A Call For Mass Emigration to Israel." The gist of it was that not only could it happen again, but the American climate was one in which the groundwork was being laid for a possible repetition of brutal, physical anti-Semitism. The reaction was instantaneous and more than a little frenetic. Morris Abram, honorary president of the American Jewish Committee, immediately replied (June 2, 1972) to say that the article was "absurd," "pure fantasy and the expression of a deep, personal and pathological anxiety." He trotted out the polls that purported to show "a dramatic decrease in anti-Semitism." He cited the Jewish people's "unquestioned allegiance and loyalty" to the United States (though nowhere in the article did I question it or even mention it, since Jewish attitudes toward Gentiles have nothing to do, in the end, with theirs toward Jews). Curiously, Harry Golden, in his reply to me (Letter to the Editor, June 12) also touched on this nonpoint by writing the following astounding paragraph:

> To the question of where my loyalties would be if America went to war with Israel, I would answer that the day America declares war on Israel I will commit suicide so the Republic will be safe.

The weekly *Jewish Journal* of Brooklyn, in an editorial, "Speak For Yourself, Meir," saw "no analogy between pre-Hitler Germany and the present-day United States," and added: "This is our land. . . . Everything we hold dear is here. Why should we foresake this land?" Abraham Heschel, venerable mystic of Conservative Judaism, attacked the "hysteria" inherent in the call. Rabbi Marc Tanenbaum, National Director of the Interreligious Affairs Department of the American Jewish Committee, called it a "bizarre outburst" and said that American Jewish life, "reads like an unmitigated success story." Rabbi William Berkowitz, President of the New York Board of Rabbis, said that " as American Jews the demands of the hour should not cause us to give up on America." Over and over again the theme was the same: America is our land and we will not leave. It cannot happen here.

Suddenly, however, other voices began to be heard. Eli Wiesel, one of the Jewish literary gods, also wrote an Op-Ed page article in 1974 in which he stated: "I admit it sadly. I feel threatened. For the first time in many years I feel that I am in danger."

And Nathan Glazer, prestigious sociologist, wrote an article for *Commentary* which he called "The Exposed American Jew." In it he wrote of a possible anti-Semitic outburst in economic and social terms because of the growth of quotas—as well as because of a possible backlash in the event of a clash in policies between Israel and the United States.

While these statements were a little more difficult to attack, since both Glazer and Wiesel are respectable figures, Rabbi Brickner, Director of the Department of Interreligious Activities of the Reform movement's Union of American Hebrew Congregations, scoffed at the warnings of anti-Semitism and said, "America 1975 is not Germany 1933"; while Phineas Stone, writing in the Federation of Jewish Philanthropies-dominated *Jewish Week*, called Glazer's fears "hastily and wrongly reasoned," saying that "it should be possible to make America safe for all its religious, cultural, and ethnic groups, the Jews included, if we join together to uphold democratic principles."

The refusal to want to see a possibility of anti-Semitism destroying the American Jewish community stems from the basic fact that the Jewish Establishment sees itself as American first and wants badly to believe that the good life and happy society it has attained will be permanent. It has truly evolved into a Jewish form that believes in liberal, integrated, assimilated society as the ideal way of life.

Nevertheless, the facts are there for those who wish to see them, to learn what the reality and the future are.

We have lived in America over the last 25 years with an illusion of the steady decline and eventual disappearance of serious Jew-hatred. That illusion was nurtured by a quarter century of unparalleled affluence and comfort. When people's stomachs are filled and their cravings satisfied, they do not cease to hate Jews, but they have no time or need to indulge their emotions. Simultaneously, it was a period when the guilt of Auschwitz hung heavy over Gentiles. It was difficult to articulate Jew-hatred in an era when the world still smelled the gas and the burning flesh in the crematoria. Not that the Jew was suddenly accepted; it was simply not possible to speak openly of nonacceptance.

Both of these obstacles to Jew-hatred are no longer with us. The first disappeared in the end of the American monopoly on world wealth and production and trade. The economic honeymoon is over, and people who have lived the good life for so long are far more dangerous than others when they are suddenly called upon to sacrifice and give it up. They will sooner turn savage and brutal and follow those demagogues who promise to "restore their days as of old." And Auschwitz is also buried. Buried in the aftermath of the Six Day War that was such a blessing to the Jew-hater, for it allowed him to cast off the albatross of guilt that he had worn for 25 years. Suddenly the Jew was no longer oppressed; now he "oppressed" the Arabs. Now he was the "aggressor." Now he could be attacked and threatened and villified and hated, with no more guilt.

And America at this moment, freed of restraint and obstacle to Jew-hatred, sinks into a deep and terrible crisis. America is undergoing a psychological crisis of massive proportions, in which for the first time the basic concepts of the nation are questioned and people have lost faith in their nation and its destiny; in which faith in the very democratic process is undermined as politicians are unanimously mistrusted and held in contempt. America is undergoing a social crisis that sees long-held and sacred concepts questioned, doubted, and attacked. The American becomes a confused, uprooted person who has lost his moorings, desperate for assurances and security.

And while America is undergoing this political crisis, the Soviets are suddenly emerging, after years of military inferiority, to achieve parity or perhaps superiority in many areas of technical and military weaponry. Suddenly, not only NATO, Western Europe, and the Free World look nervously at an awesome offensive military build-up, but serious questions arise concerning the security of the United States. Worried and frightened Americans will surely ask the questions concerning who supposedly led the fight for disarmament and for military cuts.

And America is also undergoing a profound economic crisis, one that may be inherent in the present American and world system— one that comes on the heels of a social and psychological change in the American, that has made him a slave to materialism and incapable of giving up the "good life" to which he has become so addicted. The American is not prepared to make the kind of adjustment that may see his living standards drastically reduced while at the same time American power and prestige in the world fade. He is faced with a growing military threat to his country and a socioeconomic threat to his own personal life. Of such things are born the envy, jealousy, bitterness, frustration, and fear of the lost and desperate. And the lost and the desperate turn viciously on the nearest and most plausible scapegoat. That scapegoat will be the Jew. It is the Jew who is most visible. It is the Jew who is "wealthy," who is liberal, who is in the forefront of busing and integration and all the things that disturb the average white American. It is the Jew who is the eternal target for the discontented and the malcontents. The widely heralded "populism" of our time is nothing more than a popular selfishness, made up of "outs" who want "in." The Fascists and Nazis received their base support from such "populists," too.

The humorless joke that is constantly repeated that polls "prove" that Gentiles approve of Jews has become almost obscenely dishonest. One recalls the famous B'nai B'rith poll in 1967 "proving" that there was almost no anti-Semitism to be found among Blacks. Polls that ask people sensitive and "dangerous" questions such as their feelings for Jews are almost guaranteed to give untruthful answers. As far as the constitutional guarantees that men like Brickner and Stone revel in, let it be clearly stated that Weimar Germany had its constitution (framed by a Jew); it had a Jewish foreign minister (Walter Rathanau) 50 years before Kissinger; it had a Socialist government; and it was meaningless. A constitution is a scrap of paper when the people refuse to give it life.

No, the United States in 1977 is not Germany 1933. But it is terribly similar to Germany 1928. Those who do not *wish* to see it are to be pitied because of what awaits them, and they are to be condemned for what they do to others.

The seeds of the European Jewish assimilation of the nineteenth century have borne fruit that is eaten happily in America. The Jewish *nation* no longer exists for the vast majority of the Establishment; in its place has emerged a "people" (read: "of common descent") with a flavoring of religion. In a study by Charles Liebman (*Dispersion and Unity* 10, 1970) it became clear that the overwhelming majority of Conservative and Reform leaders agreed with the statement: "While there must be warm fraternal relations between Jews of the U.S.A. and Israel, the center of American Jewish life must be American Judaism." Certainly, the Polish-American would say that his "warm and fraternal" relations with Poland do not make him a Pole, and his child looks upon Poland as something increasingly unimportant. Why should the Jew be different?

There is growing evidence that Jewish leaders are beginning to deemphasize almost total concentration on Israel and are beginning to speak increasingly in terms of "dual centers" of Judaism, the State of Israel and the Diaspora. The reason: they really wish to remain in America and really see themselves as American Jews. There is also a gnawing fear that few like to speak about.

In his article *"The Centrality of Israel"* in *Judaism* magazine, 1976, Chaim Waxman writes about the negative reaction that the Yom Kippur War had on many American Jews:

> The consistency between loyalty to America and pro-Israel sentiment was no longer clearly present and there are indications that there was a decline in pro-Israel sentiment. Since the primary source of identification for most American Jews is with America, it is understandable that many of those who

define the situation as one in which they must choose between loyalty to America and loyalty to Israel would choose the former.

The fact is that there is a gnawing feeling that perhaps Israel may not survive and that perhaps we had best reconsider how *we* should survive. Indeed, the primacy of Jewish survival in America can lead the American Jew to come face to face with the need to modify even his "Zionism" or Friends-of-Israelism. Having watered down the concept of Jewish nationalism to one in which the Jew is first an American and has no need to live in Israel, the Jewish Establishment is increasingly pushed into a position in which it says "we are friends of Israel but even friendship has its limits."

In 1974, the then Chairman of the Conference of Presidents of Major American Jewish Organizations, Rabbi Israel Miller, arrived in Israel. In a statement to the press he pledged that, in the event of crisis for Israel, "American Jewry will climb the barricades." I put it that not only will that not come to pass, but that added to the growing inevitable isolation of Israel, as enemies, neutrals, and "allies" stand to the other side, there may well emerge the ultimate tragedy and shame—the failure of the American Jewish community to stand by Israel at its moment of truth.

Let us begin by understanding that the United States is well on its way to disengaging itself from the position of "ally of Israel." Even if foolish Israelis and the impossible American Jewish leaders really believed that American policy would stroll arm in arm with that of Israel until the end of days, there were those few who understood from the beginning that this was not true. The fact is that U.S. policy was never in line with that of Israel. At best, when the status quo was kept for six years after the Six Day War, Washington was calm simply because it was not pressured to pressure Israel into concessions. But from the outset, the United States was committed to not allowing Israel to keep any (aside from unimportant areas) of the land liberated in 1967. The Rogers Plan, which embodies this American Middle East axiom, was in itself only an affirmation of a policy statement made by Lyndon Johnson immediately after the Six Day War.

The Yom Kippur War was a success for the Arabs precisely as they planned it, in that it shattered the freeze, broke the status quo, and frightened the United States into beginning the job of choking Israel into retreat. I will not go into the history of the errors, retreats, and confusion on the part of the Israelis since the

Yom Kippur War. Suffice it to say that the United States has clearly moved to a point where it has forced Israel to make concessions the latter never wanted to make and which it had vowed it would never make. Those concessions are not nearly enough for Washington, which is now in the process of freeing itself from the refusal to recognize a "Palestine people" and its unwillingness to sit with the PLO. The demands by the United States will include territorial retreat and Israel's sitting with the PLO, demands that will cross the limits of any Israeli government's ability or willingness to accept. At that moment, the confrontation between the United States and Israel will be a real and serious one. The pressure will be open and ugly and the recriminations bitter. At that point, American and Israeli interests will clearly and dangerously differ and American Jews will have to take a stand: Israeli interests or American ones? What will happen? When the moment of the barricades has arrived, who will go up on them? Who will ascend the barricades of Rabbi Miller and who will stand within its lofty and dangerous place? Will the American Jewish groups, the B'nai B'rith and Sisterhood of Suburbia watch the menacing scenario and choose Israeli interests over American ones?

When America tells Israel: The "Palestinians" have a right to their own land and you yourselves have recognized a "Palestinian" people. The "Palestinians" must be given the right to elect their own leaders, and if they choose the PLO, so be it. The "Palestinians" have the right to their own state, and if they wish to create one between Israel and Jordan, you cannot stop them. The "Palestinians" and the PLO have indicated that they recognize Israel by their willingness to sit with you at Geneva or by their statement that they are willing to postpone their ultimate aim of a "democratic, secular Palestine" until some future time.

Therefore, you must sit with them and prepare to give up all the lands conquered in 1967, including the Sinai, the Golan, the Gaza Strip, and the West Bank. Therefore, you must allow a "Palestine" to be set up immediately and we and the Soviets will guarantee your boundaries. Therefore you must do this because we will not allow you to risk a war and our involvement in it. Nor will we jeopardize our oil; nor will we lose our potential Arab business market; nor will we allow the Russians to take influence in the Middle East because we remain stigmatized by the label "Ally of Israel." Therefore, if you are not prepared to do this we will cease our military and economic support for you . . .

When America talks this way to Israel and Israel knows that the

Arabs are liars and committed to the destruction of a Jewish State of any size or shape. When Israel will protest that it cannot and will not allow the enemy to return to the 1967 borders where he stood a scant 15 miles from Tel Aviv and on the edge of the new city of Jerusalem, and back to the Golan Heights where he shelled the Jewish settlements below for 19 years, and to the Sinai where Egyptian air bases will be five minutes from Israel's cities. When Israel finally says no and there is a definitive split and Israel and America part company . . .

With whom will the American Jews go? When the split causes an outcry on the part of the Jew-haters and Jew-dislikers, and Israel's "intransigence" causes the American Jewish position to weaken and become insecure, what will the American Jew do? As it becomes excruciatingly difficult and then impossible to back both American and Israeli interests as the American people see it, will Rabbi Miller and the Jewish leaders and the American Jews climb those promised barricades?

I fear not. In fact, I fear the very opposite. I fear that the American Jews, prompted by a large segment of their leaders, will fearfully urge Israel to make "every effort" to be conciliatory, to be flexible, to be compromising, to "take a chance" for peace. To do anything but jeopardize the American Jewish community by leaving it open to that most frightening of charges, "dual loyalty." To save the American Jewish community from having to choose between Israeli and American interests, and to save the American Jew from a situation that will see anti-Semitism given an opportunity to rear its head in earnest.

For years, whenever the question of dual loyalty arose, the American Jew scoffed at the possibility. And when the questioner persisted and spoke of the possibility of a war in which America and Israel were on different sides, the Jewish answer was always an impatient: "Such a thing could never happen." But such a thing *is* beginning to happen, at least in the political arena, and the American Jew will be faced with a decision that he will have to make.

I fear that he will reject the barricades and choose his own immediate, narrow interests.

The American Jewish Establishment carefully followed the lead of Europe's enlightened and emancipated modern Jews in burying the traditional Jewish concept of a nation, separate and apart from all others. Similarly, just as the Old World saw emancipated Jews emasculate not only the national but also the *religious* character of Judaism, so, too, did the New World gain its modernized, Americanized version of "religion."

We have seen how the first Reform temple in Charleston decided that it would follow only those Jewish laws that "can be adapted to the institutions of the (American) Society in which they live and enjoy the blessings of liberty." The tone was set for American "Judaism." The effort undertaken was to make it as compatible as possible with America and to change those things that were at variance with integration and joining the American mainstream.

In 1883 the first class of Reform rabbis was graduated from the Hebrew Union College in Cincinnati. Their ordination was to take place as the highlight of the convention of the Reform Union of the American Hebrew Congregations, and a sumptuous banquet was arranged at the famed resort, the Highland House. Among the delegates were some who still observed *kashrut*, and one of the graduates, David Philipson, wrote to describe the event:

> Terrific excitement ensued when two rabbis rose from their seats and rushed from the room. Shrimp [a nonkosher seafood that is *trayfa* or nonkosher] had been placed before them as the opening course of the elaborate menu. . . . The Highland House dinner came to be known as the *trayfa* banquet.

Unkind commentators would add that it symbolized the emasculated Judaism of America, the *trayfa* Judaism.

Is there any wonder that Bernie can be found at McDonald's with Bridget? The nonspecialness of Judaism is underlined by the junking of kosher food laws. Why not do the same with laws against intermarriage? At least the Orthodox Jew who opposes it does so because he wishes to keep alive a Judaism that is different and unique, that is from Sinai. At least he can point to a Divine injunction against intermarriage. But from the mouth of those who discarded the Divinity of the law, and to whom the only "uniqueness" of Judaism is its "ethics," the anger at Bernie for marrying Bridget sounds little short of racist.

In his *Diary*, Rabbi Martin Siegel writes:

> June 7: I conducted a Bar Mitzvah this morning. At the reception afterward one of the . . . boy's relatives . . . became upset because bacon was served with the hors d'oeuvres.
>
> "What kind of *shul* is this?" he complained to me.
>
> "We're very broad-minded," I said. "We allow the caterer a free hand."

Only a fool would think that Bernie is too big a fool not to hear this and not to run away from Sinai, holding his nose.

The Columbus Platform of Reform Judaism (1937) stated: "Reform Judaism recognizes the principle of progressive development in religion." Translated, this means that Judaism could be "progressively developed" into whatever one wished. Bernie clearly could agree with that and carry it to its logical conclusion: Judaism could reach the point where it was no longer needed.

With no pillars of exclusiveness—with no unique nation or religion, with nothing to make it important to be a Jew rather than a human being—of course Bernie disappeared in growing numbers. The American Jewish Establishment, driven by fear of the Gentile and the need to establish a safe haven, created a Judasim that has no reason for being. It not only buried Bernie, but it did other things for which it will never be forgiven.

From the beginning, fear of "What will the Gentiles say?" pervaded the lives of the Jewish Establishment in America. They carefully watched what Jews did, to make sure that the statement or the act would not "rock the boat" and cause unnecessary problems in the truly lovely and comfortable world they had carved out for themselves.

It is impossible to exaggerate the extent of this nervousness and insecurity that lay behind the seemingly secure and poised American Jewish Establishment. Every major decision was subconsciously measured by the eternal yardstick of "What will the Gentiles say?" And the crimes against *Jews* and the "Jewish anti-Semitism" that emerged can never be fully measured.

The eternal imperatives—"All Jews are responsible one for the other; thou shalt not stand by thy brother's blood"—these cardinal principles of Judaism were violated time after time because of the fear on the part of the Jewish Establishment of what this might do to their own standing in the eyes of the Gentiles. It was, of course, a consideration not limited to American Jewry.

The older, Sephardi community of France had won citizenship in 1790 by disassociating themselves from the later-arrived Ashkenazi Jews, whom they described as "lowborn" in contradistinction to their status as "wellborn" and "productive." Nevertheless, the disease did not pass over the American Jewish scene.

When the pogroms and May Laws crashed down upon the heads of the Jews in the Russian Empire in 1881, a migration of vast proportions erupted. Jews, fleeing for their physical and economic lives, swarmed into border towns such as Brody, on the Russian-

Austrian Galician border. It soon became clear that what was occurring was not an isolated and temporary phenomenon, and the initial response of the American German Jewish Establishment was one of panic at the thought of all of these penniless, backward refugees reaching the American shores.

Rabbi Max Lilienthal suggested in 1881 that the stream of emigration of helpless refugees be diverted to Palestine, not because he was a Zionist (he was quite opposed to the idea), but because he feared the creation of a problem that would arise with the influx of so many Jews. Jacob Schiff, one of the barons of the Jewish Establishment, actually sailed to Europe to plead with Jewish leaders to direct the immigrants away from America. And the B'nai B'rith instructed their European representative, Nissim Behar, that "the continued influx of Russian and Romanian Jewry would jeopardize the Jewish position in America." The problem of Russian Jewry, they insisted, would have to be solved in Russia.

Irving Aaron Mandel studied the attitude of the American Jewish Establishment toward the East European Jews. In an article in *American Jewish Archives* VII (1950), he writes that "the State of New York had passed restrictive immigration laws and the *American Jewish Israelite* (edited by Reform leader Isaac Mayer Wise) suggested the use of these laws by immigration authorities to return some 200 indigent Russian refugees who were about to arrive on the steamer *California*."

The influx of literally hundreds of thousands of East European Jews in a brief space of time was a critical thing for the German Jewish Establishment in the United States, as Stephen Birmingham tells us in his classic book *"Our Crowd"* (1967). Crowded into tenements on the Lower East Side of Manhattan where crime, violence, and filth added to their "grievous lack of qualities," the Russian Jews were spoken of in the German-Jewish press as " a piece of Oriental antiquity in the midst of an ever-Progressive Occidental civilization." The *American Hebrew* queried: "Are we waiting for the natural process of assimilation between Orientalism and Americanism? This may never take place." The *Hebrew Standard* wrote: "The thoroughly acclimated American Jew . . . has no religious, social, or intellectual sympathies with them. He is closer to the Christian sentiment around him than to the Judaism of these miserable darkened [sic] Hebrews."

At first the United Hebrew Charities and the Baron de Hirsch Fund attempted to persuade the Russian Jews to settle outside of New York. New Jersey and the Catskill Mountains, with their "country air" were touted as being of great benefit. It was no use. There were too many and the only hope was to Americanize them so that they could assimilate as quickly as possible and not be an embarrassment to their German-Jewish cousins. The East Side settlement houses that were set up were essentially defense efforts on the part of the German Jews. Birmingham writes:

> Money was given largely but grudgingly, not out of the great religious principle of *tzedaka*, or charity on its highest plane, given out of pure loving-kindness, but out of a hard, bitter sense of resentment, embarrassment, and worry over what the neighbors would think.

It was the kind of thinking, Birmingham relates, that caused the dowager Mrs. Solomon Loeb to warn her children and grandchildren not to push or hurry for the exit on a train or "people will think you are a pushy Jew." It was the eternal yardstick: What will the Gentile say?

The period of the rise of Hitler to power in Germany in the 1930s provided another tragic lesson in what both fear of the Gentile's reaction and the emasculation of Jewish national feeling could do to the imperative of "Do not stand by thy brother's blood."

In anger and frustration over the Nazis' increasing persecution of Jews, a number of Jewish individuals and groups called for a boycott of German goods and products. Clearly there were two sides to this suggestion, pro and con, but just as true is the fact that the old yardstick was present here, too:

> A further consideration was the threat of increasing anti-Semitism at home. An effective boycott meant publicity and publicity meant noise. A public Jewish outcry could help no one, warned prominent (even sympathetic) non-Jews. . . . It would only evoke public antagonism, arouse popular prejudice, and squelch any discreet negotiations in progress.

So reported Naomi Cohen, author of *Not Free to Desist*. The American Jewish Committee, with this among its major considerations, opposed the boycott.

Even worse was the attitude of the AJC and other prominent Jews in the fight over relaxation of immigration quotas as Hitler was intensifying his campaign against the Jews. The terrified Jews of Germany and Central Europe desperately attempted to flee the coming fury. The great hope was that the United States—the great humanitarian nation—would relax the rigorous quotas that it had imposed on immigration. Strong opposition to any such change came from many civic and labor groups who, for various reasons, feared an influx of immigrants. In the words of Ms. Cohen:

> Warned by Washington officials that relaxing the immigration requirements might increase anti-Semitism in the United States, the Committee deliberately advised friends in Congress against proposals for open hearings.

According to Arthur Morse, author of the best-selling *While Six Million Died*, Undersecretary of State Sumner Welles had said: "It was my very strong impression that the responsible leaders among American Jews would be the first to urge that no change in the present quota for German Jews be made." Morse adds that "Welles was correct in stating that some American Jews opposed changes in the quota. There was fear among a small but influential segment of Jewry that increased immigration might aggravate domestic anti-Semitism."

Similarly, the American Jewish Committee and other anti- and non-Zionist groups did little more than pay lip service to efforts to get Jews into Palestine. The Committee, says Ms. Cohen, "could not agree that it was the sole haven lest that be construed as arguing that only in a Jewish homeland was Jewish survival possible." (Cyrus Adler of the Committee commented in 1933 that Hitler would be pleased no end if all the Jews of Germany left for Palestine).

And it was this same fear on the part of all the major Jewish groups that led to the heinous and unforgivable crime of Jewish silence as the war broke out and Jews were exterminated by the thousands, *daily*.

Warnings that action on the part of the Allies to help the Jews might, in some unspecified way, "hinder the war effort" and President Franklin Roosevelt's warning to Stephen Wise, head of the American Jewish Congress, not to turn it into a "Jewish war" lest it provoke anti-Semitism, says Morse, "placed those American Jews who wished to take direct action in an awkward position. If they fought for more vigorous policies toward their own brethren their own patriotism might be impugned." And of course, anti-Semitism might threaten *them*. For the good of American Jewry, European Jewry was allowed to go under with only sterile tokens of protest.

It is by now part of the historical record that American Jewish leadership knew as early as the latter part of 1942 that what was happening in Eastern Europe was no longer "persecution" but sheer genocide, nothing less than a Holocaust. One need read only the painful essay by Haim Greenberg, "Bankruptcy," (*The Jewish Frontier*, Feb. 1943) to learn that the facts of the gas chambers and crematoria were clearly known as early as three years and four million Jews before the end. The Jewish oligarchy was seized by a deadly paralysis and a moral numbness that led them to watch haplessly and quietly as a third of the Jewish people was slaughtered.

All of this was a natural and inevitable consequence of the Jewish Establishment policy of the destruction of the uniqueness of Judaism and Jewishness. It was a natural consequence of the Melting Pot.

The Jewish Establishment is undaunted. It either cannot see or refuses to see that intermingling, integration, and undisciplined freedom are disastrous for Jewry. It refuses to see that only a voluntary separation and total Jewish involvement can save Bernie. It does not wish to know that demanding the dismantling of barriers between groups *must* lead to Bernie marrying Bridget.

In 1877, the Jewish banker Joseph Seligman attempted to gain admittance into the famous Grand Union Hotel in Saratoga. He was barred. Seligman fumed over the refusal of the Gentile to allow him to mingle with him, eat nonkosher food with him, violate his Sabbath with him, and introduce his Bernie to him. Jewish groups joined in condemning the Gentile for refusing to allow Jews to assimilate.

It became the first of a long struggle by Jewish "defense" groups such as the B'nai B'rith Anti-Defamation League, American Jewish Committee, and American Jewish Congress, to insure that hotels, country clubs, golf clubs, and private clubs of all kinds take in Jews. Invariably Jewish bodies have won admittance and to that extent Jewish souls have been lost.

Jewish liberalism fought to the Jewish death the right of Bernie to become a member with Bridget's father. No Gentile club or hotel was spared the righteous liberal Jewish Establishment wrath. The climax was clearly the protests by Jewish Establishment groups over the membership of President Carter's Attorney General-elect, Griffin Bell, in all-Christian clubs. They won the day; Bell had to resign his memberships and liberalism had triumphed. But the final bitter laugh was on the Jewish liberals. In a kind of tragically delicious irony, Carter demanded that his legal counsel Robert

Lipshutz resign from his *all-Jewish* club and the poor Atlanta Jew went on nationwide television to tell America that such clubs were un-American. It was the ultimate in logic. That which the Jewish Establishment demanded for Gentiles—liberalism—was now demanded of them. The Jewish Establishment was told: "Either eat your cake or have it; it cannot be both ways."

Beneath it all lies a fearful belief that it can indeed happen again —in America. Every time the Jewish Establishment succeeds in calming the Jew—and itself—there erupts a Spiro Agnew (who, but for the grace of Heaven, would have been the President of the United States). And Jews sit fearfully and listen and watch as he appears on national network television to explain how Jews control the Congress and the communications media. And it is all followed by a coordinated barrage of Establishment protests and statements to the press, *all* including the reassuring and anaesthitizing statement: "It is clear that Agnew is not representative of the American people." And neither is General Brown, or the others who, increasingly, make statements that make Jews shudder and quietly ask themselves: "Again?"

"American Jews strike me as being continually on the defensive against anti-Semitism," said David Daiches in *Commentary* in February 1951:

> They have continually to prove that they are good Americans first, and Jews afterwards, and the obvious way of doing that is to join in the general "democratic" chorus that nobody really differs from anybody else, that all religions are equally true, that Jewish worship is really just the same as Christian worship, that a rabbi can appropriately preach in a church and a Christian minister in a "temple," and that a common ignorance of the Bible and of theology can unite everybody.

It was and is to make sure that Christians understand that Jews are essentially decent, good people without horns and tails, that the whole "goodwill" or "interfaith" program was set up. For the Jew, traumatized by a history of suffering and persecution, wants to believe that people no longer hate him, that he is loved. And so, we get interfaith. To make Jews be loved and to prove that all men are basically similar. *Interfaith.*

Thou shalt melt, thou shalt integrate, thou shalt amalgamate, thou shalt be an American as all others. The Establishment rabbis beat the drums for interfaith, enthusiastically exchanging pulpits with ministers, in a frantic effort to prove to Christian and Jew alike that there is essentially no difference between them. They were partially successful—the Christians were not convinced, but the Jews were.

On February 11, 1975, Ronald Sobel, rabbi of the prestigious Reform cathedral, Emanu-El of Fifth Avenue in Manhattan, exchanged pulpits with Monsignor James Rigney, rector of St. Patrick's Cathedral, some 20 blocks down the Avenue. (Cynics at the temple commented that few people noticed the difference.) The occasion was a masterstroke by the B'nai B'rith Anti-Defamation League, which had conceived the idea and convinced the two cathedrals and the Roman Catholic Archdiocese of New York to participate. The idea, in turn, was the brainchild of the ADL's department of intercultural affairs, which deals with the Catholic Church (for some reason there is a second department in the ADL, that of interreligious cooperation, which handles Protestantism), and was yet another round in that combination of tragedy and waste know as Interfaith. Here are some of the highlights of the day:

When Rabbi Sobel introduced Monsignor Rigney, he said: "I am Ronald, your brother; welcome James, to this House of G-d."

In his speech at St. Patrick's, Rabbi Sobel said:

> It is recorded in the twenty-second chapter of the Gospel according to Matthew that one day a man approached Jesus to inquire which is the greatest commandment in the law. And Jesus answered him by quoting from the religious literature of his people, from the sixth chapter of the Book of Deuteronomy, "And thou shalt love the L-rd, thy G-d, with all thy heart . . ." This is the first and greatest of the commandments, said Jesus. Then he turned to the Hebrew Bible again and quoted from the nineteenth chapter of the Book of Leviticus. "And thou shalt love thy neighbor as thyself."

Moses said it. Jesus said it. It is now for us, both Christian and Jew, to live it—the life of love upon a foundation of justice.

Benjamin Epstein, head of the ADL, later said:

> We are turning away from the dark past to a future bright with the promise that our children and theirs will not be blighted,

as we and our ancestors have been, by religious hatred and bigotry.

In yet another part of his sermon on the mount of St. Patrick's, Rabbi Sobel said:

> We who are Jews will have to demonstrate our concern for the hungry masses in Asia and Africa and South America who are not our coreligionists. . . . You who are Christians will have to be concerned for the spiritual plight of the Jews in the Soviet Union."

Leaving aside the fact that Emanu-El, for half a century, until prodded by Jewish militants, did indeed show concern for all the non-Jewish masses of the world while not a word of Soviet Jewry crossed the temple pulpit, the very natural question of any Bernie listening and watching all this is: If Ronald and James are brothers, why bother to erect barriers between themselves? If the most important things are love of G-d and of neighbor, let us all love G-d and neighbor together in a common church and—better still—without a church, so as to allow our neighbors, the Buddhists and Shintoists and African pagans, to be loved also. If Jesus and Moses both say the same thing, let us stop this nonsense of Catholicism and Judaism which only divides without unifying. If, as Mr. Epstein says, our children should have a future free of "bigotry," let us junk both the Old and New Testaments, which insist that theirs is the true way and that lead to "bigotry."

Interfaith. The ADL *Bulletin* (March 1975), describing the event, told of a Catholic woman who had walked into the cathedral when Rabbi Sobel was speaking and asked in bewilderment: "What is going on?" The answer is: Interfaith, the great waste of Jewish funds and energy; the great illusion and delusion; the frantic effort on the part of Jews (because it is Jews and not Christians who are the prime promoters of this) to have Christians love them. And *the greatest spur to intermarriage and assimilation* that there could possibly be, as Bernie, noting all "similarities" between the faiths, reasons that there is indeed not the slightest reason not to marry pretty Bridget and thus create interfaith with a vengeance.

The Jewish Establishment is obsessed with the fear of anti-Semitism. It and all its parts spend millions of dollars each year on books, booklets, movies, lectures, banquets, and seminars, all aimed at teaching the Christian that the Jew is really very much like him. The lesson may be lost on the Gentile, but Bernie, in his sublime Jewish wisdom, reasons: If Jews are very much like Gentiles, then it follows that Gentiles are very much like Jews and that Bridget is not very different from Shirley—except that she does not nag as much, and that is good.

Nothing deters the Jewish Establishment. The ADL has a full-time staff for interfaith; the American Jewish Committee has one, headed by the Rabbi Marc Tennenbaum, famed as American Jewry's ambassador to the Vatican (one wonders if he enters, saying to the Roman spiritual Caesar, "Paul, I am Marc your brother"). The Union of American Hebrew Congregations has one, headed by Balfour Brickner. The amount of money wasted could go to build more than a few Jewish schools, so that instead of Christians learning about Judaism, Jewish children might do so.

At a time when Jewish youth is dying of the cancer of assimilation, intermarriage, and alienation brought about in such great measure by the opposition of the Reform movement and the AJC to funds for Jewish parochial schools, they see only vital importance in an Interfaith which will only make the cancer spread more rapidly.

It is interesting to note that the Establishment is beginning to feel the heat of some angry Jews. Their response has *not* been to change their activities but, in typical Madison Avenue religious Watergatism, to change the *title* of their activities. Thus, the Reform movement, led by Balfour Brickner (his response at one symposium on abortion was to defend it with a non sequitur: "It is not abortion that is the problem but the murder of people in Vietnam"), changed the name of its witness to the Christians from the Commission on Interfaith Activities to the Department of Interreligious Affairs. Among the Dialogue Discussion Programs they offer are such things calculated to make us better Jews as:

An Interfaith Weekend Conclave for Jews—"An imaginative, simple, inexpensive, successfully tried program, giving youth an opportunity to explore one another's faith with professional guidance, taking into account young people's need to have fun together." (Bernie, this is Bridget. Have fun together . . .)

An Adult Interfaith Weekend—From drawing board to discussion floor—a handbook detailing procedures for such an adult weekend. "Good for congregational affiliate groups."

Conducting an Interfaith Open House—Two brochures describing how members of any community can better get to know each other.

How many Jews know how much money and effort are expended by the Jewish Establishment on the above? If it were only nonsense, it would be a minor tragedy. But the reality is that not only do millions—that might go for Jewish education to save Bernie from the ignorance and Melting Pot philosophy of the Establishment—not go there, but they go to convince Bernie that all people are alike and share common goals. It is not the Christian missionaries who are the greatest threat to cause Jews to discard their faith. It is the Jewish Establishment with their interfaith Passover Seder at Reform Temple Rodeph Shalom at Philadelphia's wealthy Jewish suburb of Elkins Park (the Jewish Seder led by Rev. Robert Hoag, Abington Presbyterian Church; Rev. John Magill, Gloria Dei Lutheran Church; Rev. Stacy Myers, Jenkintown Methodist Church —and a few rabbis, too). It is the Interfaith Conference on Religion and Human Relations sponsored by the Houston American Jewish Committee, one of a mind-boggling number of such travesties that the Jewish Establishment frenetically holds each year. It is the annual Thanksgiving Service at the Flatbush (Brooklyn) Dutch Reform Church where ten churches and synagogues gather to pray together. This teaches Bernie that all people can thank G-d and that he need feel no special loyalty to his synagogue.

And it is Rabbi Tennenbaum writing in the New York *News* (December 19, 1976):

> Christmas to me means smiles and children and helping the poor and families being together again—values in which Jews have as much stake as Christians. Indeed, that Christmas spirit finds a stalwart companion in our celebration of Hanukkah and together they help light up our lives with the shared spirit of brotherhood and love.

All the "shared and common" goals. All the things that point out the togetherness and sameness of Judaism and Christianity. The lesson is clearer than the Establishment knows . . .

It is surely such things as Interfaith, born of the insecurities of little men who lead the Jewish community, that led young students to ask Rabbi Martin Siegel of Lawrence, Long Island, "to what extent they could be universal through Judaism." Answered Siegel: "I told them that as Jews they were not expected to believe in anything in particular precisely because the emphasis was on a universal community."

There is a basic and irrevocable contradiction between authentic Judaism and Liberalism as a social philosophy. Liberalism preaches the knocking down of barriers and the integration, amalgamation, and leveling of society. Liberalism is rationalism and reason and that is the antithesis of revelation, tradition, and custom. In the words of Ernst Cassirer: "It [reason] dissolves everything merely factual, all simple data of experience, and everything believed on the evidence of revelation, tradition, and authority." The Melting Pot is a basic foundation of Liberalism. Intermarriage and the doing away with differences—certainly the artificial ones that are products of religious and national institutions—are necessary postulates of Liberalism. When Murray Gordon, a liberal, a sociologist, and, very incidentally, a Jew, wrote his book *Assimilation in American Life*, he stated:

> The individual, as he matures and reaches the age where rational decision is feasible, should be allowed to choose freely whether to remain within the boundaries of community created by his birthright ethnic group, to branch out into multiple interethnic contacts, or even to change affiliation to that of another ethnic group should he wish to do so as a result of religious conversion, intermarriage or simple private wish.

Gordon, a Jew, was expressing Liberalism *honestly and openly*. He was saying that Jewishness was not very relevant and certainly should not stand in the way of free choice to do that which a person wishes to do. It certainly should not be allowed to block love and affection and new relations. Liberalism *dictates* intermarriage; it dictates joining clubs that allow Jews and non-Jews to mingle freely; it opposes clubs that insist upon being Jewish lest their children intermarry; it opposes Jewish Community Centers that are only Jewish; it opposes Judaism as a separate, parochial faith, *the only kind of Judaism that can save Bernie from Bridget*.

The American Jewish Establishment *is* liberal. It believes in Liberalism more than it believes in Judaism. In any conflict between the two it *always* chooses Liberalism. The Judaism that it adheres to is a Judaism that is *incidental* to the American liberal life that is the basis of its existence. Albert Arent may say that he is an American Jew, but if pressed he would admit that he is an American and *also* a Jew. And the American comes first. As long as the comfortable, innocuous thing he calls "Judaism" is not in conflict with Liberalism, he can be "comfortable" with them both. But that situation cannot long exist. The club he *must* integrate will be non-kosher and intermarriage will emerge from it. This is the price that the Jewish Establishment is willing to pay for its own peace of body and mind. What Gordon, the totally assimilated Jew, says honestly (he is, after all, a middle-aged Bernie), the American Jewish Establishment believes but cannot screw up the courage to say. Thus, it creates a "cultural pluralism" that is a pack of cards, collapsing in shambles every time Liberalism collides with Judaism.

Intermarriage and Bernie are a direct and necessary product of the "Judaism" of the American Jewish Establishment and no one is more a victim of it than they. Jacob Schiff, one of the lions of the American Jewish Establishment in the later nineteenth and early twentieth century, was a man who practiced a ritual Judaism but who poured the mold for the Melting Pot. It is clear that he never wanted Jews to disappear, to intermarry, to assimilate. He wanted them to be Jewish—in an American, refined, not "too" Jewish way. It was an impossible dream and he paid the price with his own descendents. John Schiff of Kuhn and Loeb, the prestigious brokerage firm, joined the Piping Rock Club (among many others), got into the *Social Register*—and married George F. Baker, Jr.'s daughter Edith. His sister Dorothy, of *New York Post* fame, was married four times—to non-Jews.

What is the result? The ultimate fraud of them all. Faced with the decimation of their own families and members of their Establishment, with the conflict between Judaism's time-honored view of intermarriage and Liberalism's embracing of it, the American Jewish Establishment has embarked on the great feat of proving that intermarriage is really not bad for Judaism, but may indeed be good for it! For years, this Establishment supported fraudulent conversions of Gentiles in order to try to escape the growing intermarriage trend. Today, when the trickle that became a stream is now a flood, they take it one giant step further: They are converting *intermarriage* and proclaiming it Jewish. Thus, we are suddenly inundated with items like the following from a press release of the American Jewish Congress:

> "Philadelphia, March 4 [1975]—The National Women's Division convention of the American Jewish Congress was told today that the high rate of intermarriage in the Jewish community—estimated at one in every three marriages—did not necessarily produce a diminution in Jewishness or Jewish observance.

Or "Jews Said to Ease View on Marriage," the headline of a *New York Times* story (May 15, 1975). In it an American Jewish Committee researcher, Inge Gibel, tells us that Jews involved in intermarriages "are more likely to affirm their religious heritage than in the past" because the Jewish Establishment is welcoming them. And Reform Rabbi Rudin says that "there is as much pull the other way toward Judaism" in an intermarriage as toward Christianity.

A whole host of "studies" of intermarriage are announced, such as one by the American Jewish Committee (February 13, 1976). Why the study? Obviously the groundwork is being prepared to legitimize intermarriage and thus soothe both Establishment and worried Jewish parents who will then be moved to ease their own opposition to it and help in the creation of even more Bernies.

The Jewish Telegraphic Agency in May 1975 reported on the 69th Annual Meeting of the American Jewish Committee in New York. The story began: "Although one of every three Jews now marries outside the Jewish religion, the survival of the Jewish community is not necessarily threatened, according to two noted Jewish scholars."

Leaving aside the question of the depth of these two "scholars," we learn that they are a leading Conservative rabbi, Max Routtenberg, and one Dr. Saul Hofstein, consultant in social planning at the Federation of Jewish Philanthropies and president of the National Association of Jewish Family, Children's, and Health Professionals.

Routtenberg, breaking with the path of traditional Judaism, rejects what he calls "a self-imposed ghetto." (Of course, the use of the pejorative term "ghetto" is calculated to immediately arouse hostility to the idea. What the traditional Jew is saying is that he is prepared to work, live, and come into limited economic and political contact with non-Jews, but sends his children to Jewish day school and limits their friends to Jews). Instead, says Routtenberg, most Jews "have opted to live in the open society and take their chances." He therefore calls for a change in attitude toward intermarriage and calls for efforts to "persuade the non-Jewish mate to convert." (One can imagine the moral or intellectual value of such a conversion.)

Hofstein, however, more accurately reflects the views of the American Jewish Establishment as he suggests that "it might be unwise to seek such conversion actively."

"If a couple has been able to work out its problems and live in

132   THE TRAGEDY: WHAT MAKES BERNIE RUN?

relative harmony," he asks, "do we have a right to disturb that harmony by intruding this question on them if they are not concerned?" Such is the Jewish Establishment type that heads a national Jewish organization. His position is classic Liberalism because he is a classic liberal. Personal "happiness and harmony" transcend Judaism. This is the point of an Establishment rabbi, Everett Gendler, who sees in the increase of intermarriage, perhaps "a new religion in the making," a "new cosmic humanism," and asks: "How then can we do other than relate supportively to such a development?" (*Response*, Winter 1969/70)

Liberalism and Judaism. Two opposing and contradictory creeds, and the Jewish Establishment is committed in the marrow of its intellectual and emotional bones to the former. Their policy is shaped by Liberalism; that is why they kill Judaism and why Bernie runs from the stench of the corpse.

Not only do Jewish ritual and law and exclusiveness fall prey to Liberalism, but Jews themselves are victims of a code that naturally sees people as "humans" rather than as Jews or non-Jews and which frowns upon barriers between races and creeds. For the American Jewish leadership has been in the forefront of every non-Jewish struggle, not only spending huge sums of Jewish funds that might otherwise have gone to Jewish causes and needs, but at the same time turning a deaf ear to Jewish cries and aiding many who were enemies of Jews.

Thus, as we have seen, when Black demands for preferential treatment grew, the B'nai B'rith (which previously had published the results of a ridiculous poll that "proved" that Black anti-Semitism was non-existent) passed a resolution at its Concord Hotel convention (1968) advocating such treatment for Blacks. At a meeting between ADL New York Regional Director, Morris S. Sass, and the angry Jewish Teachers Association president, Dr. Herman Mantell (June 24, 1968), the teacher's organ *Morim* (September, 1969) reported: "Mr. Sass stated that if a Jewish and Black applicant of equal preparation seek the same civil service job, then the preference should be given to the Black applicant."

The chairman of the ADL, Dore Schary, told the B'nai B'rith triennial convention in Washington's posh Shoreham Hotel "not to exaggerate fears of Negro anti-Semitism" (*New York Times*, September 10, 1968). This at a time when Black militants had threatened the lives of Jewish teachers and a number of them had been summarily shipped out of a Black-controlled school district, leading to a teacher's strike.

Albert Vorspan, head of the Commission on Social Action of the Reform Union of American Hebrew Congregations, was the subject of a *New York Times* story (February 5, 1969) that began:

> "Inflammatory" reactions by Jewish spokesmen to anti-Semitic statements among Negroes are stirring the Jewish community to the very brink of hysteria, an official of the Union of American Hebrew Congregations said yesterday.

This was as Black teachers were spreading anti-Jewish hate in the schools, a Black radio program had allowed a viciously anti-Semitic poem to be read, and drives for quotas and reverse discrimination that would destroy Jewish rights were being demanded and implemented.

In 1964, Rabbi Gerald Zelermyer, of the Mattapan area of Boston, was attacked in his home by three Black youths who handed him an obscene anti-Semitic note and then threw acid in his face. The neighborhood, once almost totally Jewish, had become a jungle of crime and fear as Jews who could, fled in panic, leaving behind the poor and the elderly, a pattern that was seen in every major city in America. Said Rabbi Zelermyer: "The sad fact is that the community beyond has sounded a requiem for our area through almost wholesale indifference to our plight." It was more than true. Not only had there been indifference, there had been support for all kinds of liberal and radical programs and individuals that had been enemies of Jewish interests. In a letter to the *Boston Jewish Advocate* (June 11, 1970), Charles Zibbell of Dorchester wrote:

> Jewish liberal lawyers and social workers in the poverty programs organized Blacks to harass and obstruct public agencies and did everything possible to prevent police prosecution of ghetto criminals. . . . Too bad for you old Jews, who now live a life of fear. . . . What you are seeing, by the light of the burning synagogues, is the "chickens coming home to roost."

As Jewish Establishment leaders marched for Civil Rights in the South, supported preferential treatment and averse discrimination for "minorities" (and thus destroyed Jewish rights), backed Chicanos and lettuce and grapes—Jewish problems were either abandoned or trampled upon.

"Leaders Abandon Jews Is Charge" read the headline of the lead story in the *Jewish Post and Opinion* of November 24, 1972. A speaker at the National Jewish Civil Rights Council had attacked the Jewish Establishment leaders for "betraying Jewish needs," saying that they "were insulated from the consequences of their policies, removed by life-styles and locality from problems confronting local communities."

The removal from Judaism of its Divine Revelation and Chosenness removes, too, any uniqueness and special reason for allegiance to it. Liberalism, which is the true faith of the American Jewish Establishment, naturally weakens any special reason to help Jews rather than other peoples who may be "more" oppressed. Liberalism weakens any reason to be Jewish.

At the 1975 American Jewish Committee meeting, Saul Hofstein said: "Somehow, parents need to be helped to affirm that one can be liberal, democratic, against discrimination, yet have a deep conviction about Jewish identity and Jewish continuity."

Somehow. Hofstein does not know how and the AJC does not and no one does, because the two eventually are mutually antagonistic. Why in the world Bernie should not marry a Bridget who is pretty, intelligent, liberal, democratic, and against discrimination can be answered by Jews but not by liberals. The American Jewish leaders have chosen to be liberals and, thus, have no answer.

The Jewish Establishment in America. They make Bernie run. And in no way do they do this more successfully than in their holy war against the one weapon that might give Bernie Jewish pride, identity, and knowledge—*Jewish education.* Maximum Jewish education—the yeshiva, the Jewish day school.

6
The Melting Pot: How It Cooked Jewish Education

> If you would know the well from which your martyred brothers drew their strength to happily go out and greet death, to incline the neck to every polished knife, to every axe poised; to climb the pyre, to leap into the flames, and to die a hallowed death with the words "the L-rd is One"—if you do not know all this, go thee to the House of Study, the old and ancient one.

Thus Haim Nachman Bialik wrote in *If You Would Know ...*

The House of Study! Where on the bitterest of wintry nights and in the insufferable heat of summer, the lights were never dimmed and the voice of the yeshiva student never silenced. The House of Study where the Jew, deprived of state, government, army, and freedom, kept Judaism alive through the study of Torah. Torah! Who among the Bernies, and those who created them, can begin to comprehend what Torah meant to the Jew of old and what it means to the survival of the Jewish people?

There are many religions in our world, many faiths devoted to the worship of the Deity. From primitive man to the sophisticated one who thinks for himself, some intense need has caused him to embrace a philosophy of belief in a Higher Being.

What makes Judaism different from the rest? What aspect of it marks it as unique, as rare, as set apart? It certainly is not prayer. There is hardly a religious sect that does not have its prayers. It is not dietary ritual, for many religions regulate the eating habits of their adherents. Nor is it the setting aside of certain days as holidays and sacred times. None of these makes Judaism the unique, the superb, the amazing faith that it is.

If you would know the well from which our fathers drew their strength, their faith, their holiness—find it in the study of the Torah.

How very true are the words of our rabbis: *"Talmud Torah kneged koulam,"* and the study of Torah is equal to all of other Laws. One says a blessing over a piece of food. It takes, perhaps, five seconds, and the moment of holiness is over. One prays the afternoon service. In ten, fifteen minutes, communion with the Almighty has passed. Even the wearing of the *arba' kanfot,* the fringes; though they cling to the individual throughout the day, he is rarely conscious of them.

But let him open his Book of Books. Let him throw himself into the cool water of the Talmud. It engulfs him, it envelops him, it captures his heart, his mind, his consciousness, his being. The outside world fades and is forgotten. The petty, foolish, mundane world of transitory materialism sinks from beneath his vision. Deeper and deeper he plunges.

The world of the sages Rava and Abaye stretches before him. The world of Talmudic concepts, of *rov* and *karov*, of the 39 *milachot* of the Shabbat, of the eternal ox goring the ever-present cow, of the fantastic realm of the Midrashic Aggadata whirling about him. The present becomes meaningless. Once more he lives in the days of *tumah* and *taharah*, of the Temple sacrifices. Once again he suffers with the Ten Martyred Rabbis, struggles with Bar Kochba at Bethar, mourns with Jerusalem at the Temple site.

Deliciously, he grapples with a *tosafot* commentary, wrestles with a *mahrshaw* commentary, grows frustrated with an incomprehensible Maimonides. The day fades into dusk and the dusk into night and outside the world raves on in its madness, and the Jew learns on.

There is no end to it. Deeper and deeper he plunges, and higher and higher he soars. What are the angels compared to him now! What are kings and rulers and men of wealth! Do not disturb him. He is communing with his Maker. He is ascending the heights of purity, of holiness, of *kedusha*. He is studying Torah.

Verily, it is his life and the length of his days. Truly, it is the secret of the Jew. Consider the difference between the one who does a *mitzvah* mechanically, blindly, unknowingly, and the one who has pored over its origins, its ramifications, its reasons, its secrets, its greatness, its depth, its power. The difference between a religion whose adherents blindly believe and those whose eyes are open to the truth of its teachings.

The Jew cannot be complete without the plunge into the Sea of Torah. Errors, misconceptions, folly, fall away as the Torah waters of study wash across his soul. Boorishness and immaturity, grossness and lowness are cleansed from his being. He is raised to greater heights and his view of the world and those that inhabit it becomes different. He begins to scale the peaks of truth and greatness.

The Torah is his compass, his sextant. It guides him in each and every act of his life. In order to navigate one's way, one must first learn the instruments of direction. In order to act according to Torah, one must learn what these acts are.

The Jewish child reaches the age of study. His parents take him tenderly, proudly, not without a tear of joy, into the *cheder*, the yeshiva. The little ears hear the first letters of the language. The little mouth utters his first Torah sounds:

Kometz—aleph—aw.

You smile, you consider it a little thing. I tell you that before this "*Aw,*" empires fade into insignificance, kings into oblivion. From this sound came forth letters, and from these letters, words, and from these words, sentences. From these came essays and dissertations, explanations and Torah rulings, and from these come life.

And the child, now become a man, continues his studies. He must continue his studies or risk being left on the beach of darkness, of groping, of mundane pettiness. The sea is the wonderful ocean of depths and heights, of closeness to G-d, of analytical vision. Judaism, *true* Judaism, looks at the child and says: "Torah is a sea. Plunge into it. Torah is a garment. Wrap it about you. Torah is a new world. Discover it. Torah is a book. Study it."

If there was one weapon that might have given Bernie pride and identity and a reason for being a Jew, it was Jewish education. Not the pap and nonsense, the insipid irrelevance that he was given. Not the disgrace and abomination known as the religious school, the Hebrew school, the Sunday school, all the creations of the massive, gaudy mausoleums that dot the Jewish landscape and that are commonly known as temples, community centers, and other such places whose senior rabbi is the caterer.

The Hebrew schools, the religious schools that were set up—not to make Bernie a good Jew, but to give him just enough Jewish "culture" so he would marry a Shirley instead of a Bridget, and most especially to prepare him for the great Jewish wrongs of passage, the Bar Mitzvah. The Bar Mitzvah, the human sacrifice that is performed each Sabbath morning in the temples, with the precious little Bernie lamb sheared of the little Jewish wool that he has acquired. The Bar Mitzvah that is not the beginning of a Jew but his end, his spiritual death.

The Bar Mitzvah—the culmination of an empty, vapid, childish, shallow Jewish "education," taught by men and women whose ignorance and lack of Jewish content make them superb vehicles for the "learning" they pass on. The Bar Mitzvah, that obscene cult of ostentatiousness, the ultimate in Jewish status seeking, the competitive drive to bankrupt the pathetic, hapless "father of the Bar Mitzvah." The Bar Mitzvah where the young lamb babbles the words he neither understands nor cares to, to the accompanying *naches*, pride, of beaming women and men who would not know a correct word from a mistake, whose ignorance is sublime and whose disgusting display of conspicuous vulgarity sends G-d fleeing from the mausoleum in wrath. The Bar Mitzvah, whose necessary "religious" interlude was long ago subordinated to the pièce de résistance of the entire immorality play—the reception that follows the ceremony.

And the reception—that sickening waste of money and degradation of Judaism, where materialism runs amok in the guise of religion, where drunks and half-dressed women dance and give praise to the L-rd with African dances, American tunes, and universal abomination. Where the assimilationists, ignoramuses, and despoilers of Judaism beam with patronizing pleasure as the decrepit grandmother, Bubbe, is resurrected from her nursing home or Miami Beach condominium and trotted out to light a candle to the applause of the go-go girls and dirty comedians waiting to do their act.

The Hebrew schools that are supposed to give Bernie the weapons of Judaism to use in a hostile Gentile world. The religious synagogue schools that are created to give Bernie identity and pride— at least enough not to "shame" his parents by marrying Bridget.

The Hebrew school where Bernie sits, shifting restlessly after his five or six hours in public school, and picks at the hieroglyphics they call Hebrew, bored, disinterested, wishing he were a million miles away—all because he must, in two or three years, give Bubbe *naches* so that she will give him a check; all so that he will give Mother an opportunity to outdo the neighbors in a disgusting orgy of social waste; all so that he can do what he must and then, *escape!*

The Hebrew school where he is told that he must be a "good Jew" and then wonders why his parents eat the bacon his rabbi said was forbidden. The Hebrew school where the *rabbi* may eat the bacon the Bible said was forbidden. The Hebrew school in the Hebrew temple where everything reeks of contradiction and hypocrisy. The Hebrew school and its Bar Mitzvahs of which Ned Polsky wrote:

> My parents imposed Jewish tradition on me to the extent of making me take Hebrew lessons and go through a Bar Mitzvah ceremony. . . . To me the Bar Mitzvah ritual was utter nonsense; my chief emotion at the time was shame at not having the courage to rebel against what I knew to be false.

Bernie goes to this Hebrew school and then escapes with joy to his new freedom from religion. He takes with him memories of boredom and a 13-year-old's primitive and infantile view of religion. This is what Jewish "education" he has. These are the weapons he has been given as he enters college.

The Hebrew school of the suburbs, the product of parents who desired to do all that was necessary to be socially acceptable in their new-found areas. They buried the yeshiva and the day school, from which had come forth life and spirit for Judaism; they even weakened the original five-day-a-week Hebrew school by making it three days or less—and they sought to have their cake and eat it, too. Their little Bernie would be a *real* American (read: socially acceptable), while at the same time retaining enough Jewishness to fend off Bridget.

Of course, it was not to be. One could not give bright Jewish youngsters a Jewish education that was farcical to begin with and ending at the 13-year-old level, mix this with a public-school, Gentile-oriented education that did *not* end at Bar Mitzvah but continued on through college with all the questioning of traditional values, and expect anything different to occur than what did.

In his schools and universities Bernie hears the lectures of respected professors, philosophers, scientists. In his philosophy class he learns that religion is an evolutionary process whose beginnings are traced to the need of primitive man to explain the natural phenomena that struck terror into his heart. In sociology he learns of the relativity of cultures, each with different if not opposing morals, ethical and theological concepts. In biology and geology he learns of the evolution of earth and man through hundreds of millions of years. He learns that economics is, according to at least one dominant theory, the determiner of history and the manipulator of religion. In history he learns of the acts of despotism and cruelty of many organized religions.

On the other hand, his religious background consists of attending a Hebrew school for a few hours a week, if that much, in which he crawls through the tortuous effort of learning Hebrew, in which history and laws are presented to a 10- or 11-year-old, and at the age of 13 it ends. His Judaism, that of a youngster, is called upon to match the secularism and agnosticism of universities and intellectuals.

The result is the creation in his mind of an image, the image of Judaism.

Religion, to him, is a man-made thing, which even in its refined stages was the work of wise but ancient men. G-d, to him, may exist (and usually does), but not in the context of an established religion. On the contrary, established religion is something that leads to bigotry and clannishness, and it suffices him that all men believe in the "essentials" of all religions, ethics, and morality. Religion, to him, is outdated and no match for the truths unearthed by science.

When this attitude is applied specifically to Judaism, there is little reason to attend services because one can, if he wishes, pray anywhere without a set form. *Kashrut* becomes an ancient device for health and sanitation which is unnecessary in the era of the Pure Food and Drug Act. Shabbat is a prohibition of work which cannot apply to such laborless acts as driving a car or turning on an electric light. *Mikva* is, once again, a sanitary device associated with unsanitary conditions. Judaism is a form of life that is dying in modern America, and he has no special reason to grieve.

This then, is the image of Judaism. Old, outdated, of a past era: it holds nothing for him. He is absorbed with problems of peace, of racial equality, of economic-social spheres. Judaism, with its outdated rituals, is consigned to the junk heap of medieval nonsense, as Bernie carries through his "integration," "ethics," and "melting pot" to their logical conclusion. He throws parochialism away and integrates, assimilates, melts, dissolves. The Jewish "education" was a paper Torah . . .

No. This is not the Jewish "education" one means when he refers to the weapon that might have saved Bernie as a proud and knowledgeable Jew. Jewish education can only mean the kind that has the soul and the substance of the House of Study described by Bialik. An education that is, first of all, maximum. That is to say, one that takes up as much of the life of the young Jew as possible, not a thing that is an afterthought. In Bernie's case, the Hebrew school is a *supplement* to the "important" part of his education, his secular public school. The very place of the religious school—three days a week, two hours a day, *after* school is over—symbolizes for Bernie its second-class status and relative nonimportance. The minimal number of hours, as compared with his secular school, puts the religious education into a certain perspective.

The pitifully limited time is simply not enough even to begin to give Bernie the knowledge and depth needed to identify with and cling to Judaism. In the hurried few hours, what can he learn more than a stumbling kind of reading, a smattering of Hebrew, a little knowledge-that-is-a-dangerous-thing concerning rituals and history, and, of course, the Bar Mitzvah lessons? What eight-year-old in the *cheder* school of Europe did not know more than Bernie?

And, finally, religious education by its very nature is different from secular training, in that it implies belief in and devotion to G-d. If it is to have any meaning at all to the child, it must be based on awe and prostration before G-d. "The beginning of wisdom is the fear of the L-rd," said Solomon, the wisest of men. Can anyone honestly say that this is the kind of education that little Bernie receives in the religious schools, so many of which are housed within temples dedicated to the belief that the Torah they ostensibly teach Bernie to know and respect is *not* Divine? One may delude himself into thinking that children can be deceived, but children are not so stupid. They are incredibly perceptive and they sense from the totality of the Temple and its school a lack of belief in the things that they are taught as Jewish "culture" and "tradition." When the family, the rabbi, and the synagogue leaders violate fundamental laws to varying degrees, the lesson is not lost on Bernie. For children can forgive adults many things, and their loved ones almost anything. But there is one thing they will not allow to pass in charity, and that is fraud and hypocrisy. And religious synagogue school, thy name is hyprocrisy . . .

If there was anything that might have given Bernie Jewish knowledge and pride and identity, it was the Jewish day school, the yeshiva. Yet here, once again, the upholders of the Melting Pot emerged.

Thou shalt melt, thou shalt integrate, thou shalt Americanize thyself. The Jewish Establishment raised high the banner of the public school and fought, with a zeal no one knew they possessed, the one weapon that might have given Bernie knowledge and a sense of pride and roots. In fear and with hostility, they declared a holy war against the Jewish day school, the parochial school, the yeshiva. They piously rationalized their struggle on the sacred grounds of separation of church and state, but the real reason for their war—

and they took the lead among all Americans in fighting the slightest aid to parochial schools—was their fear and consequent hatred of the parochialism and separatism of the yeshiva. The yeshiva threatened them with too much Jewishness! What would the Gentile say if Jews were too Jewish, if they looked and behaved too differently, if their profile was not properly low? How could one mix easily with Gentiles in the nonkosher country clubs they were so eager to join, how did one assimilate if Jews did not learn to drop the embarrassing customs, habits, and old ritual baggage?

It is the Jewish leaders who have bitterly fought the major Jewish weapon against Bernieism. It is the Jewish leaders who have blocked efforts to get both governmental *and Jewish* funds for the starving yeshivas. It is they who fought the yeshivas and promoted, instead, the public school where Bernies can melt so easily. Let the truth be known:

The American Jewish Congress, The American Jewish Committee, The B'nai B'rith, The Jewish Federations—all the "patricians" who presume to speak for us—are opposed in principle to maximum Jewish education in the form of day schools *because these schools threaten the "integration" of Jews into the mainstream of American society.*

Forget all the nonsense about separation of church and state. When Jewish groups really want something, they are capable of interpreting laws to suit themselves. It is not fealty to the Constitution that prompts Jewish leaders to fight state aid to Jewish schools, because these same groups also oppose large grants from Jewish federations to Jewish education. The real opposition stems from fear and hatred of Jewish day schools, per se. The patricians want to assimilate comfortably, and blatant Jewishness threatens their efforts.

On November 9, 1970, the Board of Trustees of the New York Federation of Jewish Philanthropies met and, among other things, discussed the report of the Functional Committee of Jewish Education, which dealt with the problem of needed funds for Jewish schools. Bear in mind that the report came into being only because of growing, militant protests against the refusal of Federation patricians to give more than a pittance to meaningful Jewish education. The reason for the stubborn refusal of these men, when they find no problems in giving away Jewish money to hospitals and camps that are overwhelmingly non-Jewish, was clearly stated by a member of the board named Benjamin J. Buttenwieser. In discussing and opposing the report, which called for substantial aid to Jewish education, Buttenweiser said:

> There is endless dictum in this report which I think is alien to everything 99 44/100% of the people in this room and affiliated with the Federation organizations negate and vitiate by their own life.

What Mr. Buttenweiser meant was that the report called for maximizing Jewish life and practice and that this went against his beliefs and practices as well as those of almost all Federation leaders. He is right. What the report and many Jews demanded is that the kind of non-Jewish values that motivate the Buttenweisers of this country not be allowed to destroy the Jewish future in America. More and more activists were saying that if Buttenweiser wishes to pursue the valueless "Jewishness" of his generation, that is his privilege. But he should not be allowed to sit on the board of a Federation that has power of the purse over the Jewish future.

Buttenweiser goes on and speaks of the kind of Jewish education found in Israel. That is all right for Israel, he states, "but to try and have that kind of philosophy imported into our American way of life, I think, is a fatal move for this Board to initiate or to champion."

Let us leave Mr. Buttenweiser to his "American way of life" (that has seen Bernie driven to rejection of every Jewish value) and his concluding remarks: ". . . under no circumstances could I, with my views on the separation of Church and State, and the divisiveness of parochial schools, vote for this report."

Aha! There is the crux of the matter: "divisiveness of parochial schools." It is this that disturbs the Buttenweisers of the world and the Jewish groups they dominate. Yeshivas mean that Jews remain separate. Yeshivas are a throwback to the time when Jews demanded that they retain their distinctiveness, despite what the world said. Yeshivas threaten the efforts of Jewish patricians to be accepted in country clubs and non-Jewish Establishment circles. Yeshivas are an embarrassment; yeshivas threaten the liberal values that decree that we all happily melt; yeshivas create "anti-Semitism" because they retain Jewish differences and the Buttenweisers of the world fear that hatred of the Jews will begin to end only if we drop our stubborn insistence upon being so very "different."

Church and state? Constitutional issues? Nonsense! It is not these

things that bother Jewish patricians. What disturbs them is that
their efforts to make Jews assimilate, thus strengthening their own
drive to retain status and prestige with the non-Jew, will be
threatened by the Jewish yeshiva.

The above words are not those of B. J. Buttenweiser alone. They
are the words of all the Buttenweisers who make up the leadership
of the American Jewish Establishment. From the outset, this
Establishment has determinedly fought government aid to parochial
schools, and has joined with a number of secular and civic associa-
tions—most of which are also predominantly Jewish—in a group
known as PEARL (Committee for Public Education and Religious
Liberty). The Jewish Establishment is represented by the following
groups: American Jewish Congress, American Jewish Committee,
Association of Reform Rabbis of New York and Vicinity, B'nai
B'rith, Jewish Reconstructionist Foundation, Jewish War Veterans,
National Council of Jewish Women, New York Federation of
Reform Synagogues, Union of American Hebrew Congregations,
Workmens Circle, and others. The amount of power and money
that is at their command is enormous and their target is—Bernie. It
is PEARL and the Jewish Establishment that have successfully shot
down every move on the part of the *government*, which recognizes
the desperate plight of parochial schools and which attempts to aid
them *indirectly* for those services and education that are purely
secular.

Thus, two Pennsylvania statutes attempted to furnish "auxiliary
services" to children in nonpublic schools up to a cost of $30 per
child. The program included guidance, testing, remedial and "other
such secular, neutral, and nonideological services as are of benefit
to nonpublic school children and are presently or hereafter provided
for public school children of the Commonwealth." It also called for
the state to lend to nonpublic schools "textbooks which are acceptable for use in any public, elementary or secondary school." In short,
efforts were being made by decent, fair-minded legislators to find
some way to help religious schools *in their secular and totally nonreligious* programs so as to keep the wall that separates church and
state and, at the same time, aid schools and children.

Rather than attempting to find in this—as did so many legislators,
Democrats and Republicans, liberals and conservatives—a constitutional and fair way to help their own Jewish yeshivas, the major
Jewish groups leaped to the attack. The Pennsylvania Jewish Community Relations Council (an arm of the Jewish Federations there)
was joined by every major Jewish group, this time including Con-

servative Judaism's United Synagogue of America, in an appearance that went to the Supreme Court. "Not one inch of compromise," was the Jewish cry. No funds of any kind, directly or indirectly, even for totally secular subjects. Thanks to their efforts, the legislation was killed by the High Court, as has been every attempt to find a decent compromise, including giving aid—through tax credits—to the *parents* of the child and not to the school itself.

In an appearance before the Committee on Resolutions (Platform) of the Republican National Convention, Moses I. Feuerstein of Torah Umersorah, National Society for Hebrew Day Schools, presented an effort at fair compromise. He proposed to the delegates, in part:

1. An increase of all services, facilities, materials, that are secular and nonideological.
2. Grants for facilities for physical instructions, science, language, and related fields (which are purely secular).
3. Ways and means for scholarships or vouchers to students, or for grants, tax credits, and the like to parents.
4. State support for those services (clerical, custodial, administrative) which are used exclusively for secular, neutral purposes.

Had the Jewish Establishment been sincerely concerned with the plight of Bernie, had it really been troubled by the awesome alienation of young Jews, it would have made a fair effort at accepting all or some of these points. But the yeshiva is the enemy and there is to be no compromise.

The National Jewish Community Relations Advisory Council, which includes every major Jewish community council, and the Synagogue Council of America, the umbrella group for Reform, Conservative, and the largest Orthodox rabbinical and synagogue bodies, issued this decision, with only the Orthodox dissenting:

We are opposed to government aid to schools under the supervision or control of any denomination or sect, whether Jewish, Protestant, or Catholic, including outright subsidies, transportation, textbooks, and other supplies.

In February 1976, PEARL, not missing an opportunity to strike at any budding aid to yeshivas, filed suit to prevent public school teachers who specialized in therapeutic aid to the handicapped from being assigned to such functions in private schools. Dr. Bernard Fryshman of the Orthodox Agudath Israel termed the PEARL action "a deplorable attempt to deprive poor handicapped children of corrective and remedial services so that they should not go through their lives handicapped." It should be noted that the Jewish Establishment groups which fought against the aid to the religious lower-class handicapped, are among those who cry the loudest against "injustice" and "insensitivity."

The plight of the yeshiva is an increasingly desperate one. The high costs of education—from construction of schools and their upkeep to salaries and other expenses—are staggering. Inflation has made deficits grow to the point where schools are in danger of closing and, most important, have forced tuition to shoot up to the point where lower middle-class and, of course, lower-class parents cannot afford to send their children.

Nor does the tuition, even when paid fully (and, by far, most parents are not able to do that) begin to cover the cost of each child. In a ghastly kind of joke in this richest Jewish community in the world, yeshivas must find extra income by such things as bazaars, rummage sales, and Bingo. Naturally, the moralists who are in the forefront of the opposition to yeshivas are the first to condemn the Bingo methods used by the struggling schools just as they point their hypocritical fingers at yeshivas whose growth has come about because of parental fears of integration in the public schools.

The fact is, were there sufficient funds for yeshivas and day schools, tens of thousands of Jewish children who now receive no such education would be going to the all-day Jewish schools and enjoying the benefits of maximum Jewish education. The vast majority of the potential students who do not go are children from poor and lower-middle-class families who simply cannot afford the tuition payments. It is these deprived Jews who are the major victims of the Jewish Establishment which is so concerned over injustice in Asia and Latin America. Indeed, many of these children are not only deprived of the Jewish education that more affluent children receive, but they invariably come from neighborhoods in the inner city (their wealthier brethren have fled to the suburbs where they moralize to others about integration) where the public school is a jungle and menace to life and limb. If their motives in seeking a yeshiva education are not primarily for the sake of Torah, let it be seen within the context of the truly physical dangers of the public schools and the words of the Talmud: "Let a man ever concern himself with

Torah and commandments even for an improper motive because from the improper motive he will come unto the proper one." The hypocrisy of wealthy, liberal Jews who have escaped forced integration by fleeing to the suburbs and then level charges of "bigotry" against the yeshiva is mind-boggling.

The needless turning away of tens of thousands of Jewish children, the overcrowded schools, the inadequate facilities, the underpaid teachers, the yawning deficits, the perpetual teetering on the verge of bankruptcy—all these have no effect on the Jewish Establishment. For it is committed to throttling the spread of the Jewish day school, which threatens to create a generation of young Jews that will understand the bankruptcy and ignorance of the present Jewish leaders and organizations.

The Union of American Hebrew Congregations (Reform), in 1972, made its position clear:

> The Union of American Hebrew Congregations has historically opposed using public funds for nonpublic elementary and secondary schools, believing that such aid would infringe the separation of church and state and have a damaging impact on public schools.
>
> Therefore, consistent with the traditional opposition of American Reform Judaism, we oppose recent proposals to allow income tax credits for tuition paid to such nonpublic schools.

Note that the operating factor in the statement is the "damaging impact on public schools." More concerning that later.

The B'nai B'rith has traditionally been opposed to aid to yeshivas. At its 1976 convention in Washington, D.C., this largest of the Jewish "service" organizations, affirmed "its opposition to public aid to sectarian schools" even though that aid might be indirect (busing, hot lunches, secular textbooks). Despite a question by a minority proponent of indirect aid, Steven J. Riekes of Omaha ("What is the danger of providing math books to parochial schools? Those who oppose it sound as if the Inquisition is around the corner"), the Establishment again voted against Bernie.

The opposition is clearly one based on fear of and hostility to the yeshiva per se. What the yeshiva with its thoroughgoing Judaism represents is anathema to the assimilated of the Jewish Establishment who would rather see Bernie go by the wayside than become a religious, observant Jew.

There is no doubt that among all the destroyers of the Jewish day school and of the Bernies it alone can save, the name of the American Jewish Congress leads all the rest. Dominated by liberal Jews who in any clash between Jewish and liberal values will opt for Liberalism, it has been the leading force in the struggle to strangle the yeshivas. Its own general counsel, Leo Pfeffer, a man who has already gone down in Jewish infamy as the lawyer who leaps into every fray against aid to Jewish schools, has been "loaned" to PEARL to serve as their general counsel.

Following a 1973 "victory" in the Supreme Court against government aid to parochial schools, the Associate Executive Director of the Congress, Richard Cohen, taunted a columnist in one of the Anglo-Jewish papers for attacking the organization's role. In the *Jewish Press*, July 27, 1973, he wrote:

> The sound of Marvin Schick gnashing his teeth in frustration over the Supreme Court decisions invalidating public aid to parochial schools was music to the ears of many of us.

Cohen's and the Congress's opposition is a direct continuum of the bitter hostility to the yeshiva that has existed for decades and for the same basic reason—the yeshiva is the antithesis of the Melting Pot. In it, Jewish children do not melt; they remain Jewish, very Jewish—*too* Jewish.

For the Establishment opposition to the yeshiva is rooted in the time-dishonored fear of "What will the Gentile say?"—in this case, the fear of what the Gentile will think of a people that separates itself from the majority American culture. It is an opposition that extends back many decades. One of the most important Establishment figures of the early twentieth century, Louis Marshall, condemned the yeshiva in the *Jewish Forum*, June 1925, as creating a "wall of difference" between its people and the outside world. In a letter to Rabbi Solomon Gandz on December 3, 1928, Marshall stated his firm opposition to the establishment of Yeshiva College. "It is," he said, "destined to failure and is sure to do much harm to the best interests of Jews in America. . . . *It converts the Jew into a self-created alien.* In my opinion such an institution is not only unfortunate but it is absolutely unnecessary" (my italics). And, of course, by fighting the yeshiva on those grounds, Marshall and the Establishment gave birth to the millions of Bernies they now wonder and puzzle over.

The *American Israelite*, organ of the Jewish "grandees," angrily wrote (As reported in the *American Jewish Chronicle*, February 10, 1908—my italics):

> The New York Yeshiva is an anachronism for which the United States has neither the time nor the place and every dollar spent for its maintenance is that much wasted and worse. A legitimate use can be found for every dollar that the Jews of the United States can spare and there is none to waste *for transplanting into American soil an institution of the medieval ghetto.*

The Reform Rabbinate has been vigorous in its opposition for the same reasons: "The Jewish all-day school, like Jonah's gourd, has come up in the night of despair. It will wither in the broad daylight of renewed faith in freedom and the democratic process," said Victor E. Reichert, in a paper read at the Reform rabbinical body's Central Conference of American Rabbis in Cincinnati in 1950.

And Sam Rosenkranz, speaking at the 1962 convention of Reform's National Association of Temple Educators, stated that the Jewish day school presents "a threat to general public education in the United States and to our liberties."

Over and over again the *true* reason for Jewish Establishment opposition to the yeshiva emerges. It is too parochial; it separates Jew from Gentile; it segregates Jews; it is a threat to us because it makes us self-created aliens—and what will the Gentiles say? Anti-Semitism will grow unless Jews mingle and show that they have no horns or tails and it will wither away "in the broad daylight" of Jewish melting and dissolving in the public school. And so it was the public school that became the Jewish Establishment's Holy Grail.

The public school! This was the way to equality, to uniformity, to mixing, to the death of anti-Semitism. The Jewish shepherds urged their flock to send Bernie to public school, and the flock, as eager to mix as the shepherds, needed little urging. Bernie went to public school.

In its efforts to convince the public to support its holy war against the yeshiva movement, the American Jewish Congress enlisted the aid of a leading Conservative rabbi, Robert Gordis, one of the deans of Conservative movement and editor of the Congress sponsored magazine, *Judaism*. (Gordis's most notable achievement was his attempt at defining Revelation as a thing that happened but necessarily so). In their January 1976 issue of *Congress bi-Weekly*, the AJC reprinted, with approval, an address given by Gordis before the Synagogue Council of America (italics added):

> The day school, laudable as its objectives are, represents an act of separation from the general community. *We need to recognize that this aspect is a drawback, not a virtue.* This removal of children from the society of their peers is a price we have to be prepared to pay in order to give an intensive Jewish education *to a minority*—even a substantial minority— of Jewish children. For their ranks will provide desperately needed leadership for the Jewish community of tomorrow.
>
> But if we stratify American life completely and permanently through government support of parochial and private schools— and this is the ultimate end of the process—the results are bound to be deleterious. . . .
>
> We Jews have a civic duty not merely not to undermine the public school but to aid positively in its reconstruction and improvement. The fact remains, however, that any large-scale financial contribution to parochial schools from the government will reduce the funds available for the public schools.

And Joseph Robinson of the Congress, in an article in *Sh'ma* on December 25, 1970, called it a Jewish moral obligation to save the public schools so as to aid the black underprivileged children:

> Should we recognize the obligation of American society to undo the damage of past oppression? Should we accept the obligation to educate black underprivileged children? Or should we abandon the poor and simply rescue our own children from the educational hazards they are increasingly encountering in the cities—by removing them to suburban public schools or to urban nonpublic schools?

As always, Jews must save the world—in this case, the minorities of the urban areas—and no sacrifice is too much for that. In order that Blacks and Puerto Ricans receive their just due, *our* children must give up the opportunity for maximum Jewish education, *our* children must risk losing their *identity*. Jewish children must become Bernies so that Blacks and Puerto Ricans will gain what the white Christians took from them.

The truth is that Gordis is a deeply confused clergyman whose thought processes in this regard appear schizophrenic, a problem shared by many of his colleagues. He is not prepared to accept the separation and parochialism of Judaism, the injunction that the Jew indeed be different and separate lest he fall into the trap of assimilation. And so, he walks the tightrope, part of him crying out for the need to mix with others. This will let Jew and Christian see that "we all possess basic goals and aspirations in common," that there are "shared personal experiences," that there is "human solidarity." There is little question that this is what the public school can do. In fact, it usually succeeds so well that Bernie is overwhelmed by the truth of Gordis's "truth" and asks the eminently simple and logical question: "So why be a Jew?" "Why have *any* Jewishness?" "Why have *any* Jewish schools?"

Naturally, as a Conservative rabbi, Gordis finds this thought troublesome and he cannot muster the courage to follow through to the logical conclusion of doing away with the divisive yeshiva. And so he piously proclaims the need for *some* yeshivas. Some?

Yes, since there is a need for a certain amount of new Gordises to shepherd tomorrow's flocks, Jews must be prepared to make the sacrifice of removing a few—a select minority, an elite—"from the society of their peers" to give *them* an intensive Jewish education. Who will be the elite? Not for nothing did Gordis create a day school of a sort in his own temple . . .

Of course, Jewish youth in general should make the sacrifice of maximum Jewish identity and risk physical attacks in public schools as well as the loss of their Jewish soul. The Jew must sacrifice. But rest assured that the Jew who must sacrifice will not be the children of the Gordises or of the elite.

And what of Mr. Robinson's concern for the poor and the underprivileged? *Black* underprivileged, of course. Is there a thought for the *Jewish* underprivileged, the *Jewish* poor? Does he care about the right of the poor religious Jew to whom a religious education is more important than anything else; is the American Jewish Congress pontificating to its Jews to help *them*? And is there a concern for the poor and middle-class Jews whose children face terror and beatings in public schools; is *this* not a form of "underprivilege" and "deprivation" that the Robinsons do not suffer, since they do not live in Brooklyn or the Bronx? What of the underprivileged Jews who wish to give their children the Jewishness that Robinson does not possess and who wish to know that their children will go to and come home safely from a school which is not a jungle?

That the allegiance of the Jewish Establishment to public school is not so much love of the democratic public school as much as

hatred and fear of the religious implications of the yeshiva, is clear
from a special task force report issued by the American Jewish
Committee in October 1972. Faced with the rising demand for better
and maximum Jewish education, the task force admitted that it was
increasingly difficult to stem the tide away from the public school
and suggested another way to "save" Bernie from the only kind of
meaningful Jewish education that could possibly make Jewishness
relevant to him. Said these opponents of the day school system
(italics added):

> One significant area for educational innovation is the devel-
> opment of private Jewish schools along the lines of institutions
> like St. Paul's, Groton, and Portsmouth Priority. . . .
> There have been the beginnings of one or two Jewish-
> sponsored secondary schools. These schools, *unlike the tradi-
> tional Jewish day school, could accept non-Jews as students.* . . .
> They can gain the loyalties of a constituency which sends its
> children to the "top" schools but will not send them to
> yeshivas. . . . *The Task Force endorses* the embryonic efforts to
> develop such schools and recommends further explorations of
> the viability of one such school in a number of metropolitan
> centers.

The outrageous fraud of the Jewish Establishment was never
more nakedly manifested. Gone, suddenly, is the struggle for the
democratic public school as we hear support for not only private
schools, but the snob, upper-class, wealthy, elitist kind of school, à
la St. Paul's. Not only is this a clear turning of the back on all the
lower- and middle-class Bernies who could never afford such a
school, not only is it a cynical acceptance of parents who wish *only*
to escape public school integration and have their children go to a
status school, but it is an effort to escape the yeshiva and wreck it.
If, somehow, the Establishment can persuade parents that they
can have a private education (free of Blacks) that is "Jewish" (but
not traditional or even religious), that is sufficiently liberal so that
it will also accept non-Jews (and one can imagine how Jewish the
curriculum will be), then the Establishment can pour funds into
these schools, boast of its support of "Jewish education," and be free
of the need to explain why it is not helping the Jewish day school.
No, it is not democracy that troubles the Establishment. It is fear
of the parochial Jew, the separatist Jew, the meaningful Jew, the

Jewish Jew. The yeshiva threatens the Establishment because it produces honest youngsters who look at the emperor even as he is haughtily marching to the cheers of his followers, and who point at him, saying: "But he *is naked;* the Jewish Emperor Establishment is naked of Jewishness!"

And today, as the shepherds run frenziedly about surveying Bernie and asking him, "Where did you meet Bridget?" he calmly answers: "Why, in the public school; in the public school to which you sent me." Who made Bernie what he is? The Establishment groups and leaders who took a Judaism of particularism, of separatism, of uniqueness, of *difference,* and—in their fears, insecurities, and ignorance—created an American brand that leveled all uniqueness, "proved" that Jews and Christians were not different, and eliminated every logical and moral reason to be different. *They* created Bernie.

And having fought to make sure that Jewish schools do not get *Gentile* money, the Jewish Establishment tries as much as possible to limit its *Jewish* funds.

In an impassioned appeal in October 1975, the then head of the Orthodox Rabbinical Council of America, Rabbi Fabian Schonfeld, described the Jewish day schools of New York City as facing "economic chaos and collapse" and said that they are "in danger of financial bankruptcy." He called upon the Federation of Jewish Philanthropies to establish a minimum of 5,000 scholarships of $1,000 apiece for these schools, saying:

> The day school and Jewish education in general are being starved to death while beautiful statements in praise of education are being made. They are threatened with economic chaos and collapse because of inadequate support from American Jewish and philanthropic groups. . . . If we are to prevent further alienation and a loss of Jewish values, we must change our policies and place Jewish education, and particularly the Jewish day school, at the top of the list.

Rabbi Schonfeld was not talking about government aid that the Jewish Establishment was able to fight by raising the red herring of separation of church and state. He was calling for *Jewish* groups to give *Jewish* funds to *Jewish* education. He was asking Jewish groups to save the Bernies that they, in such great measure, had created. The rabbi is not naive. He knows that the Jewish Establishment is opposed to maximum Jewish education per se; he knows that they prefer Bernies to Baruchs. He knows that miserly allocations for Jewish education are no accident, but a deliberate policy based on the non-Jewish values that possess the Jewish Establishment leaders.

According to a fact sheet issued by the Council of Jewish Federations and Welfare Funds on August 2, 1965, of the 30 to 35 percent of funds raised by communities that were spent within the United States (rather than raised for Israel), only 3 percent went for what was called "religious and Jewish education." And understand what is meant by "Jewish education": it is a catchall phrase, deliberately misleading the Jew who seeks to learn how much Jewish money is being allocated for real, hard-core Jewish education, i.e., day schools. Under "Jewish education" the federations include, first of all, the expenses and salaries of the unnecessary Boards of Jewish Education that they have set up. The major part of the funds that the New York Federation, for example, allocates to its Board of Jewish Education goes for upkeep and salaries and administrative expenses. The money that could so easily go directly for scholarships goes instead to officials, secretaries, office expenses, and the like.

The *Jewish Week* is a New York weekly dominated by the Federation, which devotes pages each issue to photos, blurbs, and flattering comments about the group. On October 26, 1975, it reported, "The Federation of Jewish Philanthropies last year provided $2,750,000 for Jewish education through the Board of Jewish Education." At first glance, it is an impressive statement; it was so designed. But a closer reading reveals that this money is consumed in great part by the Board's administrative expenses and the rest is used for "all types of Jewish schools, ranging from the Orthodox to the secular" as well as for "educational programs conducted by Federation-affiliated camps, community centers, and child care agencies."

Understand what is being said here. The proposed budget for 1976/77 was $26,345,171. Of this, the *total* amount for education of *all kinds* was less than $3,000,000, or about 10 percent. Of that money, not only was a good quarter to a third spent on administrative expenses, but the rest went mainly to the spiritually bankrupt temple religious schools (one-day, three-day-a-week institutions that mass-produce Bernies) or to such varied nonsense as Jewish art, Jewish dances, Jewish poetry, and all the rest that is so irrelevant to anything meaningfully Jewish for Bernie.

When the real, the bottom-line question is asked: how much did the New York Federation of Jewish Philanthropies, the wealthiest of them all, give to the 50,000 Jewish students in the strangled day schools? The answer is a ludicrous $500,000, about $10 per child . . .

Jewish education is the most important item on our agenda. It is a question of Jewish spiritual survival. But it is a stepchild in the mind of the Jewish Establishment, and even in the best of communities it is merely one of many other beneficiaries. The order of priorities is tragically perverted and there must be a drastic reordering of them. There are two evils that cry out for removal. The first is the nonsectarian nature of the present Jewish federation.

When a Jew gives to his Jewish federation, it is not the same as giving to the Community Chest or the United Fund. The citizen who gives to one of the latter, consciously and willingly is giving to a nonsectarian fund that supports all causes regardless of creed. Not so a Jewish federation or welfare fund. The Jew who gives to one of these is a person who wants Jewish funds to go through a Jewish group to a Jewish cause. He expects NAACP funds to go to Blacks and Biafran relief to Biafra and nothing else. He asks and expects the same for Jewish funds given to a supposedly Jewish federation. But it is not so; Jewish funds are allocated by federations to non-Jews and to institutions that often are *detrimental* to the Jewish cause.

Huge amounts of federation funds go to Jewish Community Centers. Generally, in middle-sized Jewish communities, they are by far the largest recipients of Jewish federation monies; even in a city like New York, where the center plays a major role in Jewish life, nearly $7 million—almost 3 times the total funds spent on Jewish "education" and about 14 times the amount given to all the yeshivas—was allocated to these centers.

In September 1976, Rabbi Isaac Nadoff of Beth Israel Synagogue in Omaha, Nebraska, bitterly attacked the federation there for refusing to hold a hearing on charges he had made concerning the Jewish Community Center. "At present," said Nadoff, "more than 50 percent of JCC youth are non-Jewish." Seeking to challenge the open membership policy of the JCC, Nadoff was told by the federation that he must take up the question with the center committee. "I asked for an audience with the center committee but it was never granted to me," says Nadoff, adding the interesting fact that the unrestricted policy was "unanimously endorsed by the Omaha Board of Rabbis."

The vast majority of JCCs have non-Jewish members and in many of them the percentage of Gentiles is extremely large. The least of the problems is that this affects the activities and programing by reducing their Jewish quality and quantity. Obviously, when a large part of your center's membership is not Jewish, these members will not be interested in Talmud classes, in Jewish Holocaust programs, and in studies of Judaism. Basketball games, dances, and *fun* is what will characterize the JCC because that is what its membership clientele will demand. Jews have no need to spend their funds so that Gentiles can play basketball and go swimming.

But there is, of course, a far more serious implication. Not only do the JCCs provide a content that is increasingly non-Jewish and irrelevant, but they have become breeding grounds for interdating and intermarriage. The Jewish community, through its funding of the federations' order of priorities, subsidizes its own spiritual death and pays for the creation of Bernies by the thousands. Whereas only 3 percent of federation funds are spent on education, more than twice that, 7 percent, is spent on the irrelevant and dangerous JCCs.

The use of Jewish funds for non-Jewish causes and non-Jewish beneficiaries is endemic to all the federations by virtue of the fact that the vast majority of their allocations are to institutions that are not Jewish and that cater to anyone. "Jewish" hospitals are figments of the imagination. There are no "Jewish" hospitals, for all people get sick and all people should pay for hospitals. Jew, Christian, Muslim, and atheist need hospitals; there is no need for "Jewish" hospitals that are funded in *any* measure by Jewish federations. These hospitals are often not even kosher; Jews who have been placed in "non-Jewish" hospitals have found that frozen kosher dinners are available to them as readily there as in any "Jewish" institution. Indeed, the non-Jewishness (and at times anti-Jewishness) of these hospitals may be seen in the years-long stubborn opposition of Long Island Jewish Hospital to installing a kosher kitchen, despite an offer by a wealthy Orthodox Jew, A. B. Joffe, to contribute $100,000 for it. Beth Israel Hospital in Boston was accused in federal court in July 1975 of refusing to hire an Orthodox Jewess, Judith Rafalowicz, because she informed the hospital that she "would not work on Jewish holy days." It should also be noted that numerous religious Jews working at the Federation office in New York City have had difficulties because they insist on leaving early enough on Fridays to avoid violating the Sabbath.

The hospitals get no less than *$5 million* from the New York Federation while the 200 day schools starve for money. Let all men pay for and build hospitals, nonsectarian ones, the United Way.

There are camps, settlement houses, employment and guidance bureaus, social welfare institutions of all kinds, the majority of whose clients are not Jews but which are subsidized and supported by the Jewish federations. Consider the following examples of institutions and groups funded by the New York Federation of Jewish Philanthropies:

Jewish Board of Guardians, Court Clinic and Court Liaison and Referral Services—This agency provides social services through the court system for juvenile delinquents and potential delinquents coming before the courts. A great percentage of the youths serviced are non-Jewish and in many cases have committed criminal acts against Jewish victims.

Federation Employment and Guidance Service—More than $700,000 was appropriated by Federation for this agency. A look at its Manhattan office will find the vast number of clients to be non-Jewish. In addition, antipoverty agencies give this organization summer youth jobs called "slots." A great percentage of these slots have gone to non-Jews who are then placed in Federation camps.

Federation Camps:—$1.25 million was allocated to Federation camps. While a number are totally Jewish, there are others that have a high percentage of non-Jews. Not only are Jewish funds not used to send needy Jewish children to camp, but the mixing of Jews and non-Jews is a direct cause of interdating and intermarriage. In one case, that of Camp Usdan in Wyandanch, Long Island, a Jewish camper, refused a scholarship, complained that 800 Harlem children were bused into the camp daily. They had full scholarships and the busing costs were, of course, also absorbed.

The Educational Alliance on the Lower East Side—This institution, the recipient of a Federation grant of more than $500,000, has a long and proud history of aiding Jews. But that is past and at present well over half of the clients serviced are non-Jewish. The irony is that many anti-Semitic Puerto Rican extremists enjoy the benefits of the Jewish Educational Alliance; a few years ago an exhibit there of "community poetry" included an anti-Semitic poem.

The use of Jewish communal funds for non-Jewish services and nonsectarian agencies is only part of the problem. The other half is the fact that the priorities of the federations are disordered. Many decades ago, when Jews poured into the United States and immigrant and governmental services were few or nonexistent, it made sense for the Jewish community to set up hospitals, old-age homes, and social services that were otherwise not available. Today, these are not the burning needs of American Jewry. It is Jewish education that now cries out for massive funding. It is Jewish education—the real kind, the yeshivas—that clearly must be the major recipient of Jewish monies.

There is no need for the Los Angeles Jewish Federation to give $143,000 to the wealthy, patrician, do-little America.i Jewish Committee. There is not an ounce of justification for its grant of $73,000 to the American Jewish Congress with its dangerously anti-Jewish battle against aid to yeshivas. The Jewish War Veterans, a main activity of whose aging members is playing cards at their meeting halls, does not deserve $9,000.

In Miami, the Hillel Community Day School received $8,500 from the local federation in 1973 while the American Jewish Congress got $12,500. The South Dade Hebrew Academy received $5,000 while the National Jewish Welfare Board received $19,000. The Hebrew Academy, the largest day school, received $50,000 for all of its many students; the American Jewish Committee and the Anti-Defamation League received the same amount for doing little or nothing. Out of a total budget of $3 million raised for local and national needs, the Miami day schools received less than $65,000! Is it any wonder that Bernie prefers the Miami beach to the Miami day school?

And the very same Jewish groups, B'nai B'rith, American Jewish Committee, Synagogue Council of America, which fight government aid to yeshivas, do not lift a finger to assure them Jewish funding. When the NAACP needed money to overcome an adverse court judgment, the AJC in September 1976 rushed to raise $20,000 for the organization while the Synagogue Council of America pledged to call its member agencies to support the drive for money for the group. But the Jewish organizations have no fund-raising drives for the yeshivas they choke by cutting off government aid. Indeed, when the American Jewish Congress was attacked for not giving funds to Jewish schools, Richard Cohen replied, in the *Jewish Press*, July 27, 1973: "So what? Congress spends hundreds of thousands of dollars annually for adult Jewish education programs including Yiddish and Hebrew language albums; publications on Jewish art, music, and literature; the distinguished quarterly magazine *Judaism*, and the popular review of Jewish interests, *Congress bi-Weekly*."

The fraud is so established that one wonders whether it can ever be dislodged. All of the Congress "educational and cultural" achievements mentioned by Cohen are so meaningless, so irrelevant to Jewish survival, that if they were eliminated in toto tomorrow, no one would know they were gone. Bernie will not be saved by

Cohen's Congress culture. Every penny spent on it might have been used for real religious training. The Congress works on the well-known law: spend money on something, *anything*, to show that you have done something, and you can get an allocation next year to do the same.

Consider the irrelevancy of the Congress's Martin Steinberg Center. A letter sent out over the signature of Program Director Jeff Oboler on November 26, 1976, was "happy to announce the two main public events" for December. Jewish funds went for the following vital contributions to Jewish identity:

> We will feature Rafi Guber, a talented composer and folk singer who composes his own songs using both Hebrew and English lyrics. His music reflects the American folk rhythms of the 60s and some of his later compositions have the melody and sound of Yemenite Jewish music. . . . On Sunday, December 12, we will have our second monthly poetry reading featuring the works of three distinguished American Jewish poets. . . . Raphael Rudnick is the author of two poetry books published by Random House. . . . He has lived in Holland for the last few years. . . . Layle Silbert is a member of the New York Poet's Cooperative. . . . Maxine Silverman describes herself as a Polish Jew from Sedalia, Missouri . . .

The poets will, of course, fill Bernie with massive Jewish pride and identity; if these are the two main events of Congress culture, one has some good idea why Bernie dies a little more each day. The Congress will not give money to yeshivas because it hates and fears them. It will pay lip service only to the kind of vapid and fraudulent "Jewish" culture that signifies nothing.

In 1975 in Philadelphia the National Women's Division of the Congress voted to file a friend-of-the-court brief in behalf of a Boston physician, Kenneth Edlin, convicted of manslaughter for performing an abortion. These progressive women pledged to promote "free access to abortion" for all women. The AJC was nothing if not consistent. Having done its best to destroy Jewish souls, it was now committed to do the same for their bodies.

The Congress is typical of the Jewish Establishment that has destroyed Bernie. It is a dangerous group because it purports to speak for Jews. It is dangerous because it is *not* a do-nothing group. If it were to fade away, all Jews would be better off.

As for the federations, Rabbi Irving Rosenbaum of the Loop Synagogue in Chicago said it best in an article in the *Chicago Jewish Sentinel* on April 22, 1976:

> Unless there is a speedy, dramatic, radical, and revolutionary change in the thinking of our [Chicago] Federation and in that of the other Jewish Federations in the United States, they will almost certainly have caused the death of the American Jewish community. . . .
> Our own local statistics indicate that enrollment in Jewish schools of all kinds has dropped almost 50 percent in the last 25 years [there are almost 90,000 *fewer* children in Jewish schools today than there were 10 years ago]. . . . The rate of intermarriage is without question somewhere between 30 and 40 percent. Where in the name of Heaven does the Federation think its contributors are going to come from 10, 15, and 25 years from now? From the children of intermarriage? From Jews who by happenstance married other Jews but who have no intellectual or emotional basis for commitment to a Jewish community? Of course not. . . .
> We need a speedy, radical, and revolutionary change in our thinking. *That means there can be no budgetary limits on the amount spent for Jewish education as long as the money spent produces educated Jewish children.* If current income is not enough, let us borrow from banks, issue bonds, or mortgage our endowment funds. Surely, Jewish survival in the United States is as important as it is in Israel—and we have done all of those things for Israel (italics added).

But of course, there is a difference. The yeshiva, the Jewish day school, meaningful Jewish education, is a *danger* to the Jewish assimilationists who run the community. The functionaries, the professionals, the men in the Jewish grey flannel suits with ever-present pipes in their mouths cannot abide the maximum Jewishness that labels them for the ignorant and un-Jewish people they are. The yeshiva is *too Jewish*; better a Bernie than a Baruch.

Yet these people—who are responsible in the first place for the growth of the ailienated young Jew—continue to guarantee the destruction of the Jewish future. Funds for community centers that cater to a majority of non-Jews are always available; this, after all, is a "Jewish" cause. Money for hospitals whose clientele is predominantly not Jewish can always be found; somehow, this falls under the federation charter. Money for unwed mothers, 90 percent of whom are not Jewish; money to keep up community centers which are breeding grounds for intermarriage; money for every conceivable institution that bears little or no resemblance to any Jewish cause or need—this money is always available.

But funds for Jewish education, the heart of Jewish survival, are verboten.

Who created Bernie? Clearly, the Jewish Establishment. And clearly we must never forget it; we must always remember. And seriously consider the suggestions that have been raised about withholding our funds from the Establishment groups and, instead, establishing democratic federations committed to supporting truly Jewish causes—primarily Jewish education. It is money that has given the secularized Jewish Establishment barons control of the Jewish community. Let it be money—denied them—that brings back control of the community to people who wish, also, to bring back Bernie.

7
Bankruptcy

Why be a Jew?

It is an agonizing cry from the souls of tens of thousands of young Jews who assimilate, integrate, and disappear into the outer space beyond Judaism. It is *the* cry, *the* question. It is asked by young men and women who have seen the emptiness and the vapidness of the Judaism they grew up with. It is asked by young Jews who have seen the ugliness and the vulgarity of their empty temples and the fraud and bankruptcy of their temple rabbis. It is asked by young people whose "Judaism" gives nothing, absolutely nothing, in terms of ideals, self-sacrifice, and meaning. It comes from those who equate the "Judaism" they know with ostentatious wealth, fat and contented leaders paying lip service to G-d and "religion," and the reality of that religion in the form of rabbis who do not believe in the Divinity of Torah or (increasingly) in G-d and in lay people whose ignorance of anything Jewish is compensated for by Hadassah and UJA checks.

The seeds of Bernieism in the United States were sown when modern Jewish leaders—secular and religious—began to destroy any logical reason for being Jewish, any rational cause for pride in "Jewishness." When enlightened and emancipated Jews did away with the uniqueness and specialness of Judaism, they created Bernie.

When they denied Revelation and said that the Judasim that was handed down over the centuries and that had kept Jews alive and separate, was not Divine but created by men; that it was a composition of myths and superstitions shared by many ancient peoples and that the Torah is the product of many different men over many centuries—there remained nothing to distinguish Juda-

ism from any other modern religion. If the Sabbath was not
ordained by G-d, why bother to observe it, and how did the parents
who violated all except perhaps candle lighting grow angry at those
who ignored that, too? Either Judaism was from G-d or it was not.
If yes, it had to be observed, in toto. If not, the one who tore out 103
pages was not one whit different from the one who threw away the
entire book.

When they denied the concept of a Chosen People, they made the
Jew no better, if no worse, than a Ghanaian or Zimbabwean or a
Swede. If most nationalism was increasingly perceived by the Jewish
intellectual to be at best ludicrous and at worst madness, and if
Jewish nationalism was essentially like all the others, then why in
the world raise up barriers between peoples and creeds because of
some antiquated concepts?

Those who murdered Bernie took a Judaism of their ancestors that
was strong and powerful enough to withstand Inquisitions and
Crusades and pogroms and Kishinevs and Auschwitzes, big and
small. It was a Judaism that lived because its adherents were ready
to die for it. It was a Judaism of the *zayde* who believed in G-d and
proved it by observing His commandments. It was a Judaism that
came from G-d and not from man. It was a Judaism whose rabbis
and leaders knew Torah, not the latest best-selling book list, and
who did as they said, setting a supreme example for the Bernies of
old who knew why Judaism was different; who never for a moment
thought of Bridget.

The murderers took all this and threw it away, exchanging it for
"American Judaism," a grotesque mixture of Myron Cohen jokes,
Miami Beach, UJA checks, Hadassah membership, Jewish food,
and Moshe Dayan eye patches. It was a "Judaism" that was stripped
of all nonessentials so as to lighten the burden on the long-distance
Jewish swimmer through the American waters of assimilation,
equality, and brotherhood. It was a "Judaism" whose adherents
beamed as their leaders got it down to "ethics."

This school of Jewish confusion and desperation was symbolized
by a letter from one Carolyn A. Lisberger that appeared in the April
1951 issue of *Commentary* magazine. She described as her reasons
for identifying as a Jew:

> An identification with a group that has a common heritage,
> a historical culture, an ethics that are rooted in a Jewish hu-
> manistic concern down the ages. . . . And it is this emphasis on
> humanism that keeps me a Jew.

Ethics! As if that was the beginning and end of Judaism. As if Christians and Shintoists could not be ethical too. As if Bridget was necessarily less ethical than Shirley. Ethics, intoned the well-paid rabbi from his magnificently furnished pulpit, ethics—that is Judaism. If that's all there is, then Bernie knows that Judaism has lost any exclusive hold on him. Everyone today is ethical. George Meany is ethical and Nelson Rockefeller is ethical and Rev. Moon is ethical and Prince Sihanouk is ethical and the late King Faisal was ethical, as are his uncountable sons. Is that all there is to Judaism? If that is all there is, then stop lecturing Bernie as he marches into the sunset with his ethical *shiksa*.

In the 1961 summer issue of *Midstream* magazine, Nat Hentoff, one of the Jewish intellectuals who had participated in the *Commentary* symposium on what Jewishness meant to them, replied to an attack on him and others by Shlomo Katz. In his answer he describes his debate with his critics and says:

> I have asked this question of others who claim that I am somehow abandoning Jewishness. I have asked them to tell me *what* this Jewishness is and I have yet to hear anything but diffuse sentimentality and references to the fact that there is a Jewish history.

Hentoff then moves on to the question of "Jewish" ethics and values:

> Is there indeed? In what way does this Jewish morality differ from the secular egalitarianism to which Jews and non-Jews have contributed throughout the history of Western Europe? *I want to know what there is in Judaism for a non-believer....* If there is a specific Jewish humanism, how does it differ from atheistic humanism (italics added)?

Emil Fackenheim, one of the thinkers of the Reform movement, has the uncanny ability to cut through a problem, analyze it exceedingly well, draw the proper conclusions, and then lose the strength to follow through personally. In his December 1951 *Commentary* article, "Can There Be Judaism Without Revelation?" he boldly stated (italics mine): "If revelation must go, with it must go any possible *religious* justification for the existence of the Jewish people." And then he says:

To be sure, it is always possible to seek refuge from this dilemma in evasive rhetoric. So. . . . much is heard about "Jewish values" created by the "religious genius" of our forefathers; to these it is asserted, modern Jews have a unique obligation. . . .

There are no more "Jewish" than German or Russian values, or for that matter, Communist or capitalist. . . . If we Jews have indeed produced religious genius we have given it, long ago, to the world; we cannot and dare not keep its insights to ourselves. We try in vain to save Jewish religious particularism on nonsupernatural grounds. . . . If, then, revelation is impossible, only one religion remains tenable in the end: the religion of humanity, expressed in what one might call a "bible of mankind," a compendium of what is best in world literature and art.

Of course, this is what Bernie has been saying all along. He is honest. He is not afraid or a fraud.

In a pathetic attempt to answer Bernie (and, one suspects, himself), Dr. Joseph Landis of Queens College in 1963 presented a paper to the National Conference of Jewish Communal service in Atlantic City, in which he admitted the problem of Bernieism and concluded: "Since we cannot convince him of the Judaism of G-d and Torah, let us make him a loyal *secular* Jew, "committed only to Jewish nationalism."

How sad, and how futile. Bernie knows that Jewish secular nationalism is as empty and vapid as all the rest. If he is an *American* by birth and citizenship, what is this "Jewish" *nationalism?* Is it mere Jewish descent? He will, then, impute to it as much importance as does the Polish or German or Norwegian or Italian American. Surely, none of those Americans spends too much time agonizing over marrying an American descended from some other "national" background. Hentoff said it directly: "A secular Judaism is impossible to maintain for much longer," and clearly an irreligious Israeli of Jewish national descent would not think very long about marrying a *shiksa*. To the secular nationalist, Bernie would say:

"You see, my secular nationalist friend, unlike you, I see nothing at all very special or logical about nationalism, per se. I see nothing very rational about setting up boundaries and barriers, separate governments, armies, parliaments, economies, exchange rates, and languages. If anything, nationalism is a barrier to world brother-

hood and one of the major fomenters of conflict and war. If I were
a secular nationalist, I would be hard put to explain why Jews
should remain separate and not assimilate and I would struggle for
a rational explanation of Jewish behavior—stubborn and ob-
stinate—over two millennia of Exile, as they suffered every conceivable manner of persecution and yet refused to disappear.

"There is nothing special about a Jewish tank or jet plane,
nothing special about an independent state of your own with a
Parliament, prime minister, national airline, and social-economic
political problems; all nations have them. There is nothing special
about a scientific institute, universities, and lawyers, physicians, and
sanitationmen; all nations have them.

"Without belief in the Jews as a Chosen People of G-d, there is
not the slightest interest for me in them more than in any other
people.

"And if you wonder why secular Jewish nationalism, Zionism, has
proven to be such a disastrous failure among youth in Israel; and if
it bothers you that the youth questions the basic axioms that, to you,
are truth incarnate, going so far as to dispute the right of the Jews
to Israel and even joining an Arab spy ring; and if you are disturbed at the fact that so many Israelis have little ties to world
Jewry and so many would like very much to leave the country and
make a great deal of money elsewhere, and if the Jew in Israel looks
more and more like any other people and feels nothing special about
himself and his state—learn an important lesson.

"Secular Jewish nationalism—no more than any other kind—can
give no rational reason to a sensitive and intelligent young person,
to see anything special about his people or his state. The beginning
of the moral and spiritual crumbling of secular nationalism is all
around us to see. *Your* love of Jews stems from *nostalgia*. Because
of this, you either avoid the contradictions or are incapable of
seeing them. The young Israeli or the young assimilated Jew in
the Exile, however, is not a Jew by habit or by nostalgia. He asks
the logical questions and gets no logical answers—because you are
not capable of giving it to him and *no secular nationalist is*."

What in the world do all those who make Bernie run, think he
is? A fool, a backward imbecile? What do they expect him to do
when the B'nai B'rith publishes a "Jewish Heritage (!) Book" titled
Face to Face that explains the Torah and revelation in these terms:

To the modernist [Jew], the first criterion of the truth of a
proposition or of the validity of a principle is not its con-

formity with tradition but its consonance with reason and experience. Far from judging all things by the standard of Torah, he tests Torah against the standards by which he judges everything else. *And only in so far as Torah passes muster does he accept it as authoritative* (italics added).

Let the Torah "pass muster." And by what standards do *we* judge the Torah? By reason and ethics? Then by all means let us begin to worship *them*. What a nonsensical and fraudulent thing is this "Judaism" of the B'nai B'rith and its fellow-perverters of Judaism, and how well Bernie knows it. He accepts the concept of the B'nai B'rith and decides not to be a Jew but a man of reason, ethics, and rationality. He judges everything by those standards; he chooses all that is rational and "true" (by his standards) from every religion and every secular creed and every philosophy. Following the advice of the B'nai B'rith, *he* creates G-d in his own rational Bernie image.

Is there any wonder that David Daiches writes (in *Commentary*, italics added):

> I want American Jews to face the issues honestly and stop pussyfooting. If they believe, as by much of their conduct they seem to suggest, that in a modern democratic state it is possible to develop an ecletic humanism which draws some nourishment from a variety of religious traditions but which is not committed to any specific religious position, then let them boldly say so and face the logical consequences—acceptance of assimilation as an ideal. . . .
>
> But to remain Jews out of mere pride, or fear, or jingoism, or habit, to cultivate a Jewish consciousness while ignoring or disbelieving or glossing over the ideas and doctrines which constitute the Jewish heritage—this appears to me both illogical and unintelligent. If you believe that the Jewish religion can be prettied up into a modern mixture of Freud and Jefferson and kid yourself into calling your fancy synthesis Judaism [as was done in that absurd book, *Peace of Mind*], then I suppose no one can prevent you: but don't then sneer at assimilationists—*they are at least honest about what they are doing.*

It is a brutal, savage, and true indictment. It is Bernie speaking. Bernie wants to know what is exclusive about Judaism, what is unique, what is special, what it has that other religions do not.

And those who murdered Bernie have no answers for him. The head of the B'nai B'rith has no answer for him. The temple caterer has no answer, nor the Board chairman, nor the Sisterhood president. The temple rabbi has no answer for him. Mother and Father surely have none. All of these have no answers for him *because all of them have no answers for themselves.*

"And Reuben answered them, saying: 'Spoke I not unto you, saying: Do not sin against the child; and ye would not hear? Therefore also, behold, his blood is required.' "—Genesis 42.

All of them—Jewish organizations, temples, rabbis, parents—have sinned against our children; now their blood is required. All that could possibly be done has been done to alienate those children from Judaism and to make them fail to see anything particularly different about it or any reason to identify with it. They gave them dross and told them it was gold; they gave them mediocrity and said that it was greatness; they gave them a ritual that catered to status and obscene ostentatiousness and called it the Judaism of our fathers; they told them to be liberals and revolutionary fighters for all other people without ever teaching them the history and glory of their own, and expected them to grow up to be proud Jews. Little wonder that our children—understanding the fraud and meaningless sham—forsook their faith and people. For they could not help believe that everything their rabbis and parents and Jewish leaders told them was Judaism was that—and if that was a sham, they wanted no part of any of it.

And so they turned off on drugs and turned on with Ho Chi Minh and Trotsky. And all our added budgets for AZA basketball leagues and all our lavish, catered, Roman Bar Mitzvah feasts and all our multimillion-dollar temple-mausoleums could not turn the tide. We sinned against our children and now their blood was required. They brought home their Gentile wives and left behind their Jewish heritage.

Judaism lives or dies on the unique fact that G-d revealed Himself at Mount Sinai and gave the Jew a truth that no one else has. Judaism lives or dies on the fact that the Bible and the Talmud with their laws, commandments, statutes, and ordinances were divinely revealed and that the only way to holiness and true goodness comes from the observance of Torah laws. This is what kept Bernie's *zayde* and *bubbe* Jewish; nothing else. This is a reason for being Jewish. This is a reason for not marrying Bridget. All the rest is fraud and bluff. Poor Bernie, victim of the worst kind of robbery, the taking of his heritage and reason for being. If only he realized that the "Judaism" that he saw his entire life was any-thing but that. If only he realized that he was the victim of the worst kind of spiritual swindle. How fortunate he would be. How joyous and happy and meaningful would his life become if he could rediscover the Judaism of his ancestors that was sold on the American continent for 30 pieces of dross. Jewish is beautiful if you do not play games with it—or with yourself. If only Bernie understood, how fortunate he would be. He could then turn in his Bridget for a reason for being. A reason for being Jewish. And there is a reason.

Two
THE GLORY: WHAT MAKES BARUCH PROUD?

8
The Answer

JERUSALEM, 1977—
Now, Bernie, you know the tragedy, the bankruptcy of the false
"Judaism" you were fed. Indeed, you knew it without having to
open this book and read these pages. *You lived it*, and, I say with a
sad heart, you have been twisted and crippled by it. You were
robbed by all the good people who gave you everything in life
except the most important things—truth, meaning, identity.

But never think that what you have seen is the real Judaism.
Far from it. The Judaism that you never saw, and never were
given to properly understand, exists and awaits you. Stop for a
moment and consider it. Forget about trying to escape from your
people, your heritage, and your destiny. Forget all the nonsense
that poses as "Judaism"—the mausoleums that pass for temples;
the rabbis who preach salvation for all causes except the Jewish one;
the people who created G-d in their own image, making Him
emerge in the form of a UJA Israel Bond, Bar Mitzvah caterer,
Catskill Mountain resort, bagels and lox, graven image. Stop for a
moment and find yourself again. Let me help you understand who
you are, who your people are, what the times we live in mean for
you for them, what the future holds for you, your people, and
Israel. Forget the tragedy and consider the glory:

"Surely this great nation is a wise and understanding people"
(Deuteronomy 4). "Do ye thus requite the L-rd, O foolish people
and unwise" (Deuteronomy 32). Ah, what a great people this could
be. What a magnificent state it could create, what a future it would
have, what a redemption there would be. If only it were a wise and
understanding people . . .

What a glorious and happy world there would be for this people and what blessings would be showered upon it and what majesty and kingship would be its own to have. What ascendancy and holiness, what truth and freedom, what redemption and liberation, what an end to its sorrows and pain—if only it were a wise and understanding people. But it does not understand, and refuses to be great, and flees from the glory of its role, and seeks to escape the blessings of that wisdom that could be its own. And so it becomes what it has become today.

Two verses, two paths, two choices, and we have chosen the madness: "O foolish people and unwise." The nation that was wise and understanding has become void of counsel and confused in judgment. The people that was clever and perceptive stumbles blindly and unseeing. It calls darkness light, and vows that falsehood is truth. It embraces absurdity and prostrates itself before empty delusions. It rejects greatness and insists upon pettiness, spurns majesty and prefers mediocrity. It is a confused and perplexed people whose senses and feelings fail it.

It fails to see the awesome tragedy that approaches; or sees it and fails to understand what it sees; or understands it and fails to comprehend how to save itself. It beholds reality and rejects it; trembles in fear and seeks refuge under the shelter of falling trees; stumbles and seeks support from broken reeds. It hopes for redemption in foolish irrelevancies, petty politics, vain nonsense. It seeks miracles and refuses to acknowledge them, is offered salvation and ignores its outstretched hand. It teeters on the brink, stares at the horror that lies after the fall, and seeks to escape to safety even as it stumbles toward the precipice.

It is a confused and frightened people, a foolish and blundering nation, a multitude that forgets whence it came, hence has no idea where it is going; that has forgotten the source of its existence and pays the price in agony, indecision, and foreboding. The Children of Israel, who cast away a treasure, wander like spiritual beggars and intellectual paupers, pleading for alms and beseeching aid, all the while falling into a depression that is a growing nightmare.

It is the worst of times when it is in our hands to make it the best of them. We live in a moment in history such as this people has never seen, a moment of Divine decree, that holds within it the promise either of glorious final Redemption or of horrors such as we have never experienced, but a foretaste of which was given us three decades ago.

O foolish people! Would that we had the wisdom and understanding to seize the moment and save ourselves! Would that we had the counsel and knowledge to bring eternal liberation and Redemption upon ourselves, our children, and their children after them! But instead we sit paralyzed in a stupor and a stupidity, an ignorance and a blindness, as the epic tragedy draws closer and closer.

We do not understand. Though we all consider ourselves wise and perceptive, learned and clever, we do not understand. There are those in the Exile who understand nothing, absolutely nothing. Having cut themselves off from faith, people, spirit, body, Jewish ties of any kind, having been born "free," declaring their independence of their heritage—in their own eyes they are no longer Jews. They are Americans or Frenchmen or Europeans or "human beings." They came to the crossroads of life and turned in the other direction.

There are others who, having reached a comfortable and reasonable accommodation with Judaism, giving little and asking little in return, happily drink in the sweet nectar of a sweet Exile. Their horizons are clear, their brows unfurrowed, their hopes high, their future calm. Both are blissfully ignorant of what this moment means, of what Destiny is decreeing for them, what awaits them—as Jews.

Both kinds propose while Heaven grimly waits to dispose. The night is inky and they do not even know there is no light. They stroll blithely through their world, not knowing they are trespassing, not feeling the awesome moment that is upon them and that will shatter them like a broken potsherd. The book is open and the hand writes and the judgment is sealed, yet the clever people, "wise and understanding," luxuriate in their ignorance and do not begin to know that they are calmly snoring on the edge of the precipice. They live their days of quiet unreality, walking calmly through the suburbs of the shadow of death until they fall, unexpectedly, into its pits.

But there are others who *do* sense a foreboding of doom, who feel its fingers on our souls. There are those who look out the window at the world and know a chilling fear. In the Exile, their children drop from the Jewish march of history, falling away to lie on the road of life, victims of strange waters and ideologies, assimilation, intermarriage, and the prevailing curse of our days—sheer indifference to being Jewish. These people are ravaged by the cancer of the spirit while at the same time they sense the growing tide of an unprecendented Jew-hatred from which they instinctively recoil, as it carries in it the promise of a cruelty that will not be satiated until the fires have consumed every Jew. A world is going mad. The ground trembles beneath their feet in the Exile as the Gentile grows insecure and violent and the perpetual scapegoat waits, trembling, to be noticed. They sit nervously in their fleshpots and insecurity girds their loins. They sense something in the air, something impending, something foreboding, something terrible. The world prepares to destroy itself and the Jew will be a victim twice over.

And in the Land of Israel, 29 years young and 4,000 years old, the Jew stands and watches the icons breaking, the illusions pricked, the sureness and certainty battered, the idols shattered, the ideals tattered. Israel stands at the center of vicious circles, surrounded by rings of enemies who seek its destruction, enemies whose power grows daily as unlimited manpower and inexhaustible wealth create huge armies that improve steadily, equipped with the latest in technology that an entire world falls over itself offering to them; enemies whose confidence grows, convinced that time is on their side and that Israel is doomed. Their missiles threaten our cities and their terrorists haunt the lives of women and children. Their vow is never to cease fighting, though it be for a hundred years or more; they present us with a future of never-ending conflict. Their threats burden our economy with unbearable loads, as we require billions for defense and the citizen groans under his taxes, even as the cost of living zooms upward under the lash of inflation. And the enemy's political wiles have isolated us from former allies, so that we stand alone, a growing pariah under intolerable pressure from the world to make fatal concessions. Meanwhile our only ally grows closer and closer to our enemies, and we watch fatalistically as its interests and ours drift apart even while it begins to apply more and more pressure—political, economic, military—to force us to concede that which we know we should not.

The hostility and hatred we have faced for so long have made us weary and depressed, so that we see, side by side, a startling drop in Aliyah to the country and an alarming rise in those who leave to seek their fortune elsewhere. The relentless hatred causes our youth, already paying the price for the bankruptcy of an educational system and now faced with the seemingly never-ending war, to begin to question its own right to the land. There are those in Israel who see this and are terrified, sensing a crumbling and a disintegration.

What will happen? The question is put by those who *do* see and fear, and who, in the recesses of their minds and hearts, ask the unthinkable, the ultimate question: Can Israel be destroyed, G-d forbid! And the tragedy is that those who *do* feel the foreboding, who do sense this terrible moment, also fail to understand. They do not begin to understand what the moment is, why it is, and whence it came. They fail utterly to grasp its cause, and so cannot possibly arrive at the solution.

Thus they stumble about wildly and desperately, learnedly, and expensively. In the Exile they create commissions and study groups, committees and congresses, recreations and anti-defamation leagues. They create idols named liberalism and education, democracy and secularism, party ties and courts, public relations and respectability, humanism and brotherhood, sisterhoods and temples, Reform and reform, melting pots and low profiles. And they believe that these will save their bodies from the Gentile haters and their children's bodies from their Gentile lovers.

And in the Land of Israel, in the face of the creeping exterminators, they create new governments, new personalities, musical chairs, minority-majority governments, new protest groups, "peace," "flexibility," "allies," appeals to world conscience, treaties, realpolitik.

All of the Jewish wiles—and above, Heaven smiles grimly. For in all their pathetic and desperate programs, plans, schemes, solutions—in all their irrelevant foolishness—the one thing that makes sense is absent. The one little word that means everything is missing from all their plans: G-d.

There is a Jewish Destiny and we do not begin to know or to care. But ignorance or indifference are irrelevant, for that Destiny is a decree that will not be altered and we foolishly ignore it at our own peril and that of our loved ones. The Jewish Destiny is in motion and we live in a moment that is crucial to it, for it is in our hands to bring it to a glorious conclusion or attempt to ignore it. Depending on our choice will come majestic and swift Redemption or, first, agony and tragedy, both unprecedented and unnecessary.

There is so little precious time left! So little time for us to comprehend this destiny and do what we must in order that we be spared agony and unspeakable tragedy. Enough of the foolishness and the meaningless irrelevancies, the pettiness and nonsense. It is time to recall what the Jewish People is, what its destiny is ordained to be, how to think and act in order to bring upon our heads the blessings of the final glorious Redemption and how to give meaning to our lives. It is time to remember who we are to stand in awe before the Omnipotent Jewish G-d, the Jewish G-d of History. If we do not understand that Jewish history, that what *will* be is a directed thing that *must* be, we will be completely incapable of understanding what is happening today and what will happen tomorrow.

The G-d of the Jews *is*. He exists. He is the G-d of creation and the G-d of History. If He is not this, He is nothing. Only a G-d who creates, directs, decrees, shapes, and ordains the present and future is worthy of being worshiped, deserving of being a G-d. Only a people that believes that its G-d called the world and its inhabitants into being and controls and decrees their destiny has any logical and intellectual reason to worship Him. A world that is haphazard and a destiny that is at the beck and call of finite man is a world that has no G-d. A G-d that has no control and decisive decree over the fate of man is a myth, a plaything conceived by man, a thing deservedly consigned to the dustbin of antiquity.

"In the beginning G-d created the heaven and the earth." Thus the Torah begins its message to the Jew to let him know that the Jewish G-d exists as a real entity and not as some intellectual plaything. And the Psalms tell us:

> The heavens declare the glory of G-d, And firmament showeth His handiwork. . . . Before the mountains were brought forth, Or ever Thou hadst formed the earth and world, Even from everlasting to everlasting, Thou art G-d. . . . For a thousand years in Thy sight are but as yesterday when it is past. . . . Thou carriest them away as with a flood; they are as a sleep. . . . How manifold are thy works, O L-rd! In wisdom hast Thou made them all; the earth is full of Thy creatures. . . . Thou hidest Thy face, they vanish; Thou withdrawest their breath, they perish, and return to their dust. Thou sendest forth Thy spirit, they are created; And Thou renewest the face of the earth.

And the G-d of the Jews is the G-d of Truth. At the side of His Omnipotence stands His Omniscience. He who created Man knows what is the truth and the proper path for His creation. He knows the reason for the creation of man, and He knows the true path— the only path—that can lead to the fulfillment of that purpose, the only way that can bring man both happiness and goodness. How absurd for the creation to quarrel with its Creator, how laughable that it presumes to tell Him what is best! "Woe unto him that striveth with his Maker," cries Isaiah. "Shall the clay say to him that fashioneth it: 'What makest thou . . .?' " The G-d of History and the G-d of Truth—this is the G-d of Israel.

The existence of this G-d and the belief in Him is the foundation of foundations for the Jew, for from this comes necessarily the path that the Jew must follow. The commandment of commandments is *to know G-d*. And so in his great work, the Mishne Torah, Maimonides opens with the following: "The foundation of foundations and the pillar of wisdom is to *know* that there is a First Cause and He brings forth all that exists . . ."

"And I shall betroth thee unto Me with faith, and thou shalt know the L-rd." To *know* that there is a G-d and that He is the G-d of History and Truth is to believe in Him with perfect faith. To know Him is to stand with that awe that we call *yirat shamayim* —fear of heaven—as a supplicant before his master. It is to stand with the love of a son for a father. To believe totally and *to know the L-rd* is to know that He is Omnipotent and Omniscient, that He, the L-rd, is G-d over all Creation. That is true faith and true awe. That is reality; that is Judaism.

We should recall the words of the simple Jew whose prayerbook is open and directed to a real and living G-d. This is how a Jew who knows G-d prays:

> Thou art the Flame and I the straw—and who should have mercy upon the straw if not the Flame?
> Thou art pure, and I am sinful—and who should have mercy upon the sinful if not the Pure?
> Thou art the Supporter and I the falling one—and who should have mercy upon the falling one if not the Supporter?
> Thou art the Shepherd and I the flock . . .

The words of the Jew who looks to the real G-d and who daily whispers: I believe, I believe, I believe . . . *I know!*

Before such a G-d there is fear and awe and in the face of such a G-d other kinds of fear disappear. Awesome fear emerges as the Jew stands before Omnipotence and knows that nothing in this world matters in the face of the unlimited strength of the Divinity. And earthly fear disappears in the knowledge that the Chosen People of this Omnipotence need fear no nation or might or force in this world and that the Jewish Destiny is guaranteed by the G-d of History. It is time that we considered this G-d of History carefully and what He implies for us, the Jewish people individually and collectively, and for the State of Israel.

What a pity that the vast majority of Jews do not understand who they are and *why* they are! What a pity that they have fallen victim to ignorance and to ignorant shepherds. What a pity that they understand neither the Chosenness of the Jew nor the sublime magnificence of the total Torah way of life. In their abysmal lack of knowledge and superficial gleanings they see and hear of commandments and rituals and find them inexplicable or ludicrous. Being told that the Sabbath forbids "work," they cannot grasp why switching on a light is forbidden. Having heard that *kashrut* is a hygienic thing, they cannot see why government-controlled and well-cooked pork is forbidden. They suffer from the problem of the three blind men who wished to know what an elephant was, with each one touching a different part. The one who touched the tail "understood" that an elephant is a rope; the one who touched the tusk "learned" that an elephant is a spear; and the one who touched the leg "realized" that the elephant was a pillar.

One cannot understand Torah and the true path of Judaism without seeing the entire purpose and architectural blueprint, without knowing what the structure is supposed to look like. For the commandments are but bricks in a structure and only when seeing the planned totality can one understand why each brick serves a logical purpose. There are some Jews who never learned anything of their faith and others who learned a dangerous little. Both can never say: I do not believe in Judaism, for one who has never learned it deeply does not know what *not to believe*. One must study Judaism at the feet of those who believe and know it. Not for nothing did the rabbis say: "Great is study because [only] it leads to doing." Only the one who has studied Torah can understand it fully, and the ignorant one can never become G-d-fearing. So let us learn together.

"The world and all within it were created only for the sake of Torah." Torah, the Jewish code of law, the life-style and life of the Jew. His map, his guide, his existence. The Jewish G-d of Creation created the world for the sake of Torah, in order that its principles and truths might be translated into practice and life. And the Jewish people was chosen by G-d as the vehicle for living and teaching His Torah. *That and that alone is the Jewish raison d'être; that and that alone is the reason for creation.*

All that ultimately occurs, eruptions of wars and catastrophes, the rise and fall of empires, in the end have no meaning except that they affect the fortunes—or misfortunes—of the Jewish people, the messenger of G-d. The Jewish nation is, indeed, the heart of the world and there is no reason for the existence of empires, kings, rulers, masses, or systems except for their influence on the Jewish people and their fate.

And so it was that on a day unlike any other in the annals of this world an entire people stood at the foot of a burning mountain, upon whose peak the L-rd had descended in a fire "and the smoke thereof ascended as the smoke of a furnace, and the whole mount quaked greatly. And when the voice of the [shofar] horn waxed louder and louder, Moses spoke, and G-d answered" in a voice that shattered the atmosphere and thrust itself into the souls of the people who stood by, as it called out: "I am the L-rd thy G-d, who brought thee out of the land of Egypt, out of the house of bondage. Thou shalt have no other gods before me" (Exodus 20).

Unlike anything that ever happened before in history, the G-d of Israel appeared before *all the people*. Not only Moses, not only the elders, not only a few "chosen" ones saw and heard the manifestation of G-d. Each and every Jew, every man and woman and child, saw and heard for themselves so that no Jew would ever be able again to question, doubt, or cynically mock. Here was the uniqueness of future faith and belief based solidly on *observation*. And that is why the First Commandment does not begin with "I am the L-rd who created the heaven and the earth," for that is a thing that the people did not see for themselves. Rather, "I am the L-rd who brought you out of Egypt," where you, yourselves, with your own eyes, saw the incredible miracles of the plagues and the splitting of the Red Sea, all the miracles of observation that culminated in this standing at Sinai and hearing G-d. This was the Revelation that was the ultimate proof of G-d, that caused the Jew to shout: I *know* G-d! Upon the Revelation at Sinai, Judaism stands or falls.

Sinai! It was the moment of annointment. The Chosen Moment for a people chosen for greatness, for difference, for uniqueness, for the carrying out of the role of the Chosen. And the Jewish people became the People of G-d.

Not another Sweden or another Poland; not another pale replica of West or East; not one more part of the capitalist or socialist camps; not one more but the only one. The *only one* chosen by the G-d of History as His own, as His unique people:

> For thou are a holy people unto the L-rd thy G-d; the L-rd thy G-d, hath chosen thee to be His own treasure, out of all peoples that are upon the face of the earth (Deuteronomy 7).

The Jew became a nation, but more—much more. He became a religio-nation. At the moment of Revelation he was also commanded a Torah—the Divinely created and revealed laws that were to be his "life and length of his days." That he was to study when he sat in his house and when he walked on the way, and in the evening and in the morning. It was to be the blueprint of his life because it contained the truth and the way to the purpose of man—holiness. A Written Law and an Oral one, both revealed by the Almighty, this was what the Jew was commanded to observe, and this was the reason—the only logical reason—that he cried out: "All that the L-rd hath spoken we will do."

It was a treaty, a covenant between Israel and its Maker.

The Jew was, from that moment the Chosen one. He was sanctified, hallowed, *and set apart from all the nations.*

"I am the L-rd thy G-d *who hath set you apart from the peoples.*" Separation and difference. And each week, as the Sabbath day draws to a close, the Jew raises his cup of wine and performs the *mitzvah* of *havdalah*—separation. And he says: "He who separates the holy from the ordinary, light and darkness, *Israel and the nations* . . ." Israel and the nations. The one stands alone to one side, and all the others, together, on the other.

But this chosenness is not a contemptuous concept of racial superiority or a master-nation concept for the sake of enslaving and trodding upon peoples. This separation is not division and isolation for its own sake. "And the L-rd did not set His love upon you, nor choose you because you were more in number than any people —for ye are the least of all people."

Nevertheless, "Ye are the children of the L-rd your G-d . . . for thou art a holy people unto the L-rd thy G-d; the L-rd thy G-d hath chosen thee to be His own treasure, out of all peoples that are upon the face of the earth."

The separation is but preparation for the true unity and oneness of man; the chosenness is not a cheap and undemanding thing but an obligation, a mission, a difficult one. It is a yoke, magnificent and glorious, but a yoke, nevertheless, that weighs the Jew down even as he happily groans beneath it. Why chosenness? Why separation from the other nations? Why be a Jew and not a "human being"?

"For thou art a *holy* people." Holiness. To live the kind of life that sees one sanctify himself and rise to holiness, to rise above the mundane, the profane, the animal. "Ye shall be holy for I the L-rd thy G-d am holy!" Be holy! This is the commandment, this is the obligation, this is the mission that is meant by being Chosen: "Ye shall therefore be holy because I am holy!" Over and over again the Jew is given his orders and instructions, his directional signals and map of life. "And ye shall be holy unto me for I the L-rd am holy and have set you apart from the peoples that ye should be Mine."

Only by being set apart, only by being separated and different can the Jew learn how to be His, can the Jew avoid being dragged down by the environment and influences of a culture that degrades and desecrates, that profanes man even as it turns him into the animal. Holiness can only be achieved by living a certain kind of life, and when that life is attacked and challenged and threatened by alien and contradictory forces every day and in every way— there can be no holiness, there can be no purpose to Chosenness.

What is this holiness? What is it and how does one achieve it? Man is a creature unique among all the myriad creations of the L-rd. On the one hand there is that tiny, dwarflike, finite creature of whom David the Psalmist said: "What is man, that Thou art mindful of him?" This is the man of brutal and cruel selfishness, of sordid and animal-like yearnings. Indeed, at times he is far worse and far more brutal than any animal that roams the earth, for man alone kills for pleasure, he alone can be a sadist, reveling in the pain and suffering of others.

And even when man lives a life that is free of such blatant evil, what is he? In the ultimate plan of the universe, the individual who passes through life fleetingly—like some innocuous atom whose presence or absence impresses no one and, apparently, makes not the slightest difference in the wider scheme of things—is not logically important enough to merit consideration. When one contemplates puny man against the background of the universe, he truly does appear to be of no importance or relevance. If we can belittle the significance of an entire generation and gloomily declare: "One generation passeth away, and another generation cometh; And the earth abideth forever," then it would appear to the rational thinker that one minute element of the generation— one person plucked from the billions—is unworthy of great attention, let alone deep despair.

But the insignificance of man in terms of his Maker is only one side of the coin of life. In relation to his G-d, we can speak of man as "are not all the mighty as nothing in your presence and the men of fame as if not existing and the wise as if without knowledge and the perceptive as if without understanding—because the majority of their deeds are empty and that part of man that is greater than the animal is really nothing, for all of life is vanity?" But this is only in relation to man and his Father in Heaven.

For the same David who gloomily looked at finite man in terms of the Infinite Divinity and wondered aloud why G-d should remember this puny creature, also answered his own question by looking at the Divine spark that was, despite all, placed within the soul and sang forth: "Yet Thou hast made him but little lower than the angels . . ."

Little lower than the angels! Can we grasp such a thing? Is this creature, who eats and sleeps and sometimes hates and does shameful things and descends to such pettiness and depths of evil unimaginable, is he truly to be considered as being possessed of such greatness of soul that he is but little lower than the angels who serve the L-rd in total purity?

Yes, and perhaps higher. For the celestial creature who cannot help but always refrain from sin, because he was created without temptation or capability of evil, never comes face to face with the daily struggle of soul that is the lot of that unique creature called Man. The heavenly being that must always be good never knows the inner struggles of Man, who is capable of doing good or evil and has the awesome responsibility to choose good. And if such a man can consciously reject evil and ugliness and mediocrity; if he can purposely choose good and beauty and greatness—what a magnificent and awesome thing he is! "See, I have set before thee this day life and good and death and evil . . . therefore choose life!" The man who can overcome his inner selfishness, his ego and natural self-interest, is the man who achieves holiness. The man who achieves holiness rises to that beautiful magnificence that Creation was meant to produce.

For holiness—the purpose of man—is aimed at taking the ego and self-centeredness that is at the root of all ugliness and evil and harnessing it, submitting it to the discipline of man. All that is evil in the world occurs because of the selfishness of man and his refusal to sublimate his own desires and interests to goodness and morality. One steals because he places his own desire for money over the moral imperative; one murders for the same reason. The "I" that is within man, grown wild and unharnessed, can destroy a world. It is only when that "I," that ego, is disciplined and subordinated to goodness that the selfishness and self-centerdness that leads to all that is ugly and evil can be eliminated.

We live in a world that revels in "freedom," in the right to do what we wish. Rights and freedom have become the watchword of our times, and they grow like some cancerous disease into license and moral anarchy. For the Jew there can be no such thing. For the Jew there can only be the yoke of the heavenly kingdom.

The yoke of the heavenly kingdom! The heavy and beautiful yoke, the difficult but magnificent burden that makes the Jew strong through obedience and free through submission. "There is no freedom except though the engraved tablets of the Law," say the Rabbis. The Jew who thinks that he has freedom because he can do whatever he will, with license and no bounds to his desires, is not free but rather a slave to his passions. He *cannot* stop, he *cannot* overcome his ego and wants, he cannot bring his will to bear. He is a slave of materialism.

Such a person, though he begins by declaring his right to do all things only if he harms no one else, *must* in the end reach the point where he has become an addict of his own desires, incapable of struggling against them. Then, when it comes to a choice between his own needs and the moral rights of others, he will turn on the others with savagery and determination, all the while rationalizing away his actions.

Judaism demands limitation, discipline, subordination of the ego, self-centeredness, and freedom of man because it declares clearly that "unto the L-rd is the earth and all that it contains." There is no such thing as man's ownership of anything on this earth. He is a tenant, allowed to use the property of the Almighty on definite conditions, all of which underline the concept of admitting that G-d is the creator and owner of all that exists. The Jew may eat bread, but the precondition is the blessing. He may earn money, but he must give a tithe, 10 percent, to the poor. His property is limited because it is *not* his property. And the concept extends to his wealth and *his body*. One cannot do with his wealth as he sees fit, nor use or abuse his body as he chooses. An abortion is murder; the body does not belong to the woman. Suicide is a sin because man has a role to play that he cannot escape and his life is not his own to do with as he sees fit.

To feel the pain of the oppressed and the hunger of the needy, to give of one's property and one's time to soothe and ease their wants, is not so much to have the needy *take*. More important, it is for the Jew to learn to *give*. The Jew who gives admits that his wealth is not his; he cries out his faith that the L-rd will fill and replenish his own wants and he smashes his selfish nature that cries out: It is mine! Torah social justice is not a plan to have the needy take, but to demand that the fortunate give.

Holiness, the smashing of the will, spiritual elevation, and uprooting the animalism that is within us—this is the Jewish G-d and this is His Chosen People. The one cries out the uniqueness of his G-d with the words: "Shma Yisrael, hear O Israel, the L-rd our G-d, the L-rd is One." The other smiles at His children, wrapping his arm in *teffilin* that reads: "Who is like your people Israel, the one nation on earth."

Nothing less than making *man* good will make the *world* good; nothing less than a holy human race will make a world holy. It is illusion to believe that one can make a people better by changing the form of government. No change in the system of society will make that society better, for there is no such thing as "government" or "society." There are only the individuals who comprise the government or the society and the whole is nothing more than the sum of its parts. If the parts are rotten and corrupt, the whole must emerge the same. If the people are selfish and egotistical, society will emerge the same, regardless of the form of government that it uses. An ugly world will never be made beautiful by attacking the symptoms. It is man himself who must be changed and made better. Then and only then can the world which he makes up become better, too. The holiness of the human being guarantees the holiness and beauty of his world. Even if this is a long and difficult process, it is the *only* way. Of such things did the rabbis say: "There is a long way that is short and a seemingly short way that is in reality long."

And how does one change man's natural inclination to be selfish? "For the inclination of man's heart is wicked from his youth." How do we harness this and raise man to holiness? One cannot simply *teach* man to be good any more than one can teach a painter to paint by lecturing to him. One must himself paint in order to become a great artist, and one must practice the habit of discipline and harnessing of the ego if one desires to smash selfishness and achieve holiness.

"The commandments were given to Israel to purify people." Here is the way the Almighty, creator of man who knows all of his workings and ways, knew that man could be brought to holiness and purity. The *mitzvot*, the commandments—they are the way, the only way. "And you shall fulfill all my commandments, and then shall you be holy unto your G-d."

A child awakens in the morning. How natural for him to arise and, feeling hungry, rush downstairs to immediately eat. Nothing stops him from fulfilling his desire and, in general, except for obvious instances, he lives a life in which he is free to do that which pleases him. The concept of freedom has become one in which the individual sees it as his right to do what he wishes, all the while pushing further out the boundaries of that permissiveness. It is *my* property and I have the right to do with it what I wish if I do not harm anyone else. It is *my* life; it is *my* body, it is *my* . . .

The Jewish child of Torah awakens in the morning. He is just as hungry as any other one. But he knows that before he can go downstairs and eat he must wash his hands a certain way, with a blessing; put on his skullcap and four-fringed garment, with a blessing; say the morning prayers; and then go down to the breakfast table—but not yet to eat. Again, he washes his hands with a blessing and says the blessing over the bread. *All this before the first bite of food enters his mouth.* All this so that he will know that there are things more important than his immediate desire to eat.

And so goes his day, and so goes his life. Not a life of self-torture and asceticism, for Judaism is as opposed to the extreme of total self-denial as it is to that of hedonism. Rather, a life in which he does not so much attempt to abolish his ego as to hallow it. Of course the Jew can eat—but his diet is limited and disciplined. Certain creatures are totally forbidden him; certain foods cannot be mixed; all meals are sanctified by blessings before and after. Food—the very essence of the animal—becomes a thing that is hallowed and disciplined. It is not "reasons of sanitation" that are at the heart of kosher food laws, but reasons of sanctity and morality. The Jew who daily builds up the habit of doing without and sacrificing in relatively small things, grows into the Jew who finds sacrifice in urgent matters infinitely easier. The Jew who conquers his animal lust for food learns to make himself the master and not the slave to lust. He has already climbed far up the mountain to holiness.

And so with all the commandments that the Torah has woven as a thread through every hour and phase of the life of a Jew. Each one comes to discipline him and to purify him, to remind him who he is and where he is meant to go. The Sabbath teaches him that the desire to earn money and to live a material life must be harnessed so that for one complete day out of every seven there is a literal separation of man and Materialism. The foolish, myopic Jew who looks upon the Sabbath as a burdensome thing cannot comprehend the greatness that lies in a complete day of holiness, in which man is totally divorced from wealth and its pursuit. The ignorant Jew who cannot understand why the light switched on constitutes "work" does not understand that it is not so much "work" that is forbidden on the Sabbath as *production and creation, so as to acknowledge G-d's creation of the universe*. The unlearned Jew who scoffs at the laws of ritual purity and the ritualarium, which require sexual abstinence between husband and wife for nearly one half of every month, one half of their lifetime together, has not the slightest grasp of the magnificence of a concept that hallows marriage, recognizing the beauty of sex when it is a part of love and family rather than an expression of lust. If for half of a lifetime the husband and wife must set physical togetherness aside, then they must forge another bond, one of mental togetherness, in which both realize that their spouses are not commodities, but people with talents and capacities. The lust and ego and animal desire that are so much a part of sex at its ugliest become modified and purified and sanctified when Torah raises sex to its most beautiful.

The commandments were given to us so that we might purify and discipline ourselves and reach that holiness that is the purpose of man. But the commandments that were given to rid us of our ego and selfishness can only achieve this purpose if we do them out of selflessness and not *out of ego*. The Jew who practices ritual and laws because they appeal to him, who does not recognize them as being Divine but merely "ethical" and "good" in his own view, destroys the very purpose and the effect of the commandments and turns a religion of awe and obedience into a personal whim. Only the Jew who obeys the laws *despite* his feelings and, indeed, despite the fact that some may be against his personal preference or moral code, is truly smashing his ego and reaching holiness. This is the essential difference between what is wrongly termed "Orthodoxy" (Torah-true Judaism would be a more definitive term) and the counterfeits of Judaism—Conservative, Reform, and all the rest.

A Reform temple may have an organ and a Conservative one mixed pews. That is not what sets them apart from true Judaism. That is merely a manifestation, a *symptom* of the difference. The real difference lies in the Jew who suits Torah to his own code versus the Jew who knows G-d and accepts upon himself the yoke of the heavenly kingdom, the heavy and magnificent yoke that makes man free through submission to the Almighty. Thus spoke the rabbis:

> Why does the paragraph of *Shma* (Hear O Israel . . .) precede the paragraph of "If thou shalt hearken . . ." (that speaks of the observance of the commandments)? In order that he should first accept upon himself the yoke of heaven and only afterwards the yoke of the commandments.

Again:

> How do we know that a man should *not* say I cannot abide pork . . . but should rather say: I can eat the pork but what can I do if my father in Heaven has decreed otherwise? It is said: "And I have separated you from the nations that you should be Mine," that you should be separated from them for My name's sake *and accept the yoke of heaven.*

No Jew who does not accept the Revelation at Sinai and the Divine origin of the commandments ever fulfills even one commandment! The Jew who logically or emotionally finds a commandment to his liking, and observes it for that reason, turns the commandment of G-d into a desire of man. And he derives no benefit; nothing within him changes; his ego and self-centeredness are not one bit modified. Only the Jew who knows G-d, believes fully in Him, stands in total awe of Him, and fulfills the commandments *because He so ordered and for no other reason*, reaches the understanding and true purpose of the commandments.

When Moses first entered the palace of Pharaoh and said to him: "Thus saith the L-rd, the G-d of Israel: Let My people go . . ." the Egyptian monarch, supreme ruler of his land and of the greatest empire of its time, replied: "Who is the L-rd, that I should hearken unto His voice to let Israel go? I know not the L-rd . . ."

The course of human history has been that of G-d's effort to make man "know the L-rd." The purpose of man is to rise to holiness through the bending and subjugation of his will to the L-rd. Man, the animal, becomes man the creature "little lower than the angels" only through humbly making his will subordinate to his Maker. The knowing of G-d, the recognition that there is a G-d and that he is the L-rd, is the first step to the smashing of one's ego with all its ugly selfishness and its obsession with self-gratification. To be free, to do "one's thing," to cast off restraint, is not to know G-d but to place one's own self on a divine pedestal.

To know G-d, and to know specifically the G-d of Israel, is the only way to create a human race which is humble and small, holy and good. It is the only way to understand the concepts that comprise holiness, the ultimate goal of man. It is the only way to understand the methods that lead to the attainment of that holiness which will put an end to the self-centeredness from which stem all the evils of the world.

The Jewish people is the instrument of G-d, chosen by Him to teach the world to "know the L-rd." It is the Jews who were directed to practice the theory of holiness, to bring into reality the Man that is just a little lower than the angels. Jewish history is the story of the successes and failures of the Jew in his mission and the rewards and punishments of G-d. It is a history filled with the tragedy of both Gentiles and Jews seeking to escape from the yoke of heaven, denying the existence or the authority of the L-rd, stating: "I know not the L-rd . . ." and choosing self-gratification over humble holiness, with all the selfish and sordid evils that stem from this.

The end of the historical trek is told over and over in the Bible and in the Talmud. The end of days will see the earth "filled with the knowledge of the L-rd," the ultimate future will be one of "On that day, the L-rd will be One and His name One." The destiny of man is to ultimately know the L-rd G-d of Israel, as the Omniscient and Omnipotent, and conversely to know himself, at long last, as the created, the finite, the humble being who stands eternally at the mercy of his Maker. How it will come about is dependent on the Jew understanding his historical and immovable destiny.

And as the Jewish people was chosen to be a special people, so was a land selected to be a special land. The Chosen People were given a Chosen Land, and as the one was holy and raised above all peoples, so was the other hallowed and lifted above all lands. The Land of Israel was given by the Almighty, Creator and owner of all lands, unto His Chosen People for the purpose of living there, possessing the Land, and creating within it a Chosen society.

"Get thee out of thy country, and from thy kindred, and from thy father's house, unto the land that I will show thee"—G-d's commandment to the first Jew, Abraham. That land was the Land of Israel, given by the King of the Universe to the people that He had chosen. Over and over again was this land promised to Abraham, to Isaac, to Jacob. To Moses as the Jews were in exile, in the slavery of Egypt: "And I will bring you in unto the land, concerning which I lifted up My hand to give it to Abraham, to Isaac, and to Jacob."

The Jewish people were to be a light unto the nations, but it is impossible to be so in an exile, where a minority not only cannot influence the majority but becomes twisted and corrupted by it. The only place where the holy Jewish society can be created is in a separate, sovereign Jewish homeland. That land is not meant to create one more little national entity; it is a holy land that cannot abide desecration and that spits out those who defile it. "Lest the land spit you out should you defile it, as it spat out the nations that were before you." The Land of Israel; eternally Jewish, eternally holy, its boundaries promised by the Almighty to His people:

> Everywhere whereon the soles of your feet shall tread shall be yours. From the wilderness even unto Lebanon, from the river, the Euphrates, even unto the uttermost sea shall your coast be. There shall be no man able to stand before you, for the L-rd your G-d shall lay the fear of you upon all the land.

There can be no escape from our special relationship with our G-d, and those who embrace the strange gods of our times merely follow in the follies of similar foolish Jews who attempted to flee their destiny in times past. In the end, every fleeing Jonah meets his whale, his Gentile who spits him out. He remains sadder but wiser, knowing that one can never flee the Jewish G-d and that the worlds of the Gentile and Jew are irrevocably separate.

From the moment that the Jew was chosen for his special role he was chosen for special obligation. If one is selected for magnificent portion and lot, then it is accompanied by special responsibilities.

> If ye walk in My statutes, and keep My commandments, and do them. . . . I will give peace in the land . . . and none shall make you afraid. . . . And I will have respect unto you, and make you fruitful, and multiply you; and will establish My covenant with you. . . . And I will walk among you, and will be your G-d, and you shall be my people"

That is the honor and the prestige, and side by side, the Torah (Leviticus 26) continues:

But if ye will not hearken unto Me, and will not do all these commandments . . . I will set My face against you, and ye shall be smitten before your enemies; they that hate you shall rule over you; and ye shall flee when none pursueth you. . . . And I will bring the land into desolation . . . and you I will scatter among the nations . . . and your land shall be a desolation, and your cities shall be a waste. . . . And as for them that are left of you, I will send a faintness into their hearts in the lands of their enemies; and the sound of a driven leaf shall chase them. . . . And ye shall perish among the nations, and the land of your enemies shall eat you up.

Here is the promise and the warning, the blueprint for the destiny of the Jewish people. And what was promised was fulfilled. The Jew did not hearken, refused to be wise and understanding, and rejected the Torah that is his life and air that he breathes. And he was driven from his land and thrust into an Exile in which "driven leaves" cast terror into him and Gentiles cursed him, humiliated him, trampled upon him, beat him, spat upon him, stole his money, drove him from land to land, burned him alive, stole his children, drowned him, and gassed him—and roared with laughter as they did it. The Chosen who refused to carry out their mission and who sought to be like the other nations received the full measure of punishment, drank deeply of the bitter cup of hemlock.

But this is hardly the final act on the stage of Jewish Destiny. For there is an end to the punishment, to the chastisement, to the Exile. There is a final, beautiful, and glorious majesty that marks the last, the final step:

Thus saith the L-rd: Refrain thy voice from weeping, And thine eyes from tears; For thy work shall be rewarded, saith the L-rd; And they shall come back from the land of the enemy. And there is hope for thy future, saith the L-rd; And thy children shall return to their own border (Jeremiah 31).

The smallest shall become a thousand, and the least a mighty nation. I the L-rd will hurry it in its time (Isaiah 60).

There is a "time" of Redemption for the Jewish people. There is a final Redemption, a final day when the majesty and kingdom of the L-rd shows itself before the eyes of the nations and the Law and Kingdom of Heaven reign forever and forever. On that day will the glory of G-d and His people Israel be enshrined and the final Redemption attained.

We live today in the final era, in the footsteps of the Messiah. It is incumbent upon us to understand this and to clearly know its consequences.

We are deep into the period of *atchalta d'geulah*—the beginning of the Redemption. One who gazes upon the incredible millennia of wandering, suffering, and miraculous survival of the Jewish lamb among the 70 wolves; who has seen the terrible Holocaust; the phenomenal return of a people exiled for more than 18 centuries as it resurrects its state, brings to life a language, and gathers in the exiles from a hundred lands of dispersion; the miraculous victories against overwhelming odds of 1948, 1956, 1967, and 1973, the most miraculous of them all; the astonishing liberation of historic Eretz Yisrael with our return to the Wall, to Hebron, to Judea and Samaria—one who has seen all these miracles and signs of G-d and does not believe that we are a divine people and this is the era of the Redemption and the beginning of the Jewish State that can never be destroyed—is blind.

Yet such there are. There are the vast numbers of nonobservant who do not believe in G-d or who pay a lip service to Him that renders Him irrelevant. They see in the State of Israel a state like all other states, the product of a nationalism like all other nationalisms, a natural and rational phenomenon. For them there is no hand of G-d, no beginning of a divine Redemption, no miracle. Since it is a state like any other, there are no guarantees; such a state has no Divine insurance policy. Such a state can be destroyed and it is thus only natural to look at the black clouds of destruction and consider dangerous concessions or emigration to Canada.

But even in religious circles there has long been a debate over the religious legitimacy and place in history of the State of Israel, centering about the very honest question: How can the religious Jew see the Hand of G-d in a state which was created and is run by Jews who are not only nonobservant but who quite clearly either deny G-d or are at best indifferent to His meaningful existence. How can one compare this state with the first two which were created by believing Jewish leaders and which were both destroyed precisely because Jews behaved in the manner of the Jewish rulers of Israel today? Indeed, many religious Jews refuse to give religious recognition to the state, or at best accept it on a de facto basis, while a large number of others disregard the seeming contradiction and declare that the state *is* the expression of Divine Will, though they are hard-pressed to explain themselves logically.

The key to understanding our era and our future lies in comprehending the true meaning of the creation of the State of Israel, why in a generation such as ours the Redemption has begun. The Prophet Ezekiel, in one of the most dramatic and profound visions of the Bible (Ezekiel 36), spoke to the Jews of his time, and beyond, of the day when the Exile would end and the Jew would return home:

> And I scattered them among the nations, and they were dispersed through the countries; according to their way and according to their doings I judged them. And when they came unto the nations, whither they came, they profaned My holy name; in that men said of them: These are the people of the L-rd, and are gone forth out of His land. But I had pity for My holy name which the house of Israel had profaned among the nations, into which they came. Therefore say unto the house of Israel: Thus saith the L-rd G-d. I do not this for your sake, O house of Israel, but for my Holy Name which ye have profaned among the nations, whither ye came. And I will sanctify My great name . . . and the nations shall know that I am the L-rd . . . when I shall be sanctified in you before their eyes. For I will take you from among the nations, and gather you out of all the countries, and will bring you into your own land.

Here is the essence of our times. Here is the reason for the rise of the State of Israel and the impossibility of its destruction. It arose and was created to wipe away the humiliation of *hillul hashem*, the profaning of the name of G-d!

"And when they came unto the nations, whither they came, they profaned My holy name." *The very presence of the Jewish people in Exile*, scattered among the nations, a minority without a home, a group defenseless and exposed to the whims and power of the majority, a people persecuted because it is weak and has lost its land, government, army, and pride—that in itself is *hillul hashem*.

And it is obvious why it must be so! When "men said of them: These are the people of the L-rd, and are gone out of His land." The nations look at this weak and defenseless people upon whom they trod, whom they persecute, rob, despoil, and shame, saying: "If these are the people of the L-rd and we can do this to them, *He is*

weak, powerless, or nonexistent!" It is the scorn and disdain of the
Gentile for the Jew and his G-d of which the Psalmist cried: "Wherefore shall the nations say: Where then is their G-d!"

To the Gentile who can, with impunity, trample upon and
murder the Jew *there is no Jewish G-d*, for if there were He would
not allow such a thing to be. And so the Gentile mocks this Jewish
G-d and declares Him to be nonexistent. And this is *hillul hashem*,
from the Hebrew word, *hallal*, meaning vacuum, empty, void.

In the awesome description of the final days when the nations will
gather for battle with Israel, the Prophet Ezekiel describes their
utter defeat by G-d and says: "And My holy name will I make
known in the midst of My people Israel; neither will I desecrate My
holy name to be profaned any more . . ." And the Biblical commentator Rashi says, simply: "The degradation of Israel is the desecration of G-d's name."

It is through the Jew that the Jewish G-d is either profaned or
sanctified. When the Jew rises to the heights and emerges victorious,
it is not only he but his G-d who is vindicated and exalted. And
when the Jew is beaten and disgraced, it is the name of his G-d that
is profaned for seeming inability to save him. The essence of
Auschwitz lies not in the murder of Jews but in what that murder
implied for the existence, power, and truth of their G-d. If we could
degrade, humiliate, gas, and burn all those helpless Jews, sneered
the Nazis, "where then is their G-d!" There was never a greater
Hillul Hashem than this.

And so we understand, finally, the true meaning of *hillul hashem*,
and through it the reason for the rise of the Jewish State in our
times and the irrelevancy of the religiosity or nonreligiosity of its
leaders. "I do not this for your sake, O House of Israel, but for My
holy name which ye have profaned among the nations." It is *not*
because the Jew was worthy of it that the State of Israel came into
being. Whether the Jew remained the same or became worse was not
relevant, because it was not as a reward for his piety and deeds that
G-d created the State. Indeed, as the age of science, rationalism,
materialism, and internationalism raced ahead with giant strides, it
became clear that the Jew would never become better, only worse.
For the Jew was eagerly backsliding. So the Jewish G-d decided that
He would no longer tolerate the profaning of His name, the disdain
and mockery of the nations, and He decreed that there should rise
a Jewish State *which is the very antithesis of the Exile*.

If the Exile, with its humiliations, defeats, persecutions, minority
status, and supping as a beggar at the tables of others, is *hillul*

hashem, then an independent Jewish State which gives the Jew a home, a majority, his own land, his own army, and his own trampling of the enemy on the field of battle *is the very opposite*. It is *kiddush hashem*, the sanctification of the name of G-d! It is the reaffirmation, the proof, the witness to His presence and dominion, His control of the earth and all therein.

"For I will take you from among the nations and gather you out of all the countries and bring you into your own land." Where then is "their" G-d? Here He is, with all His power and omnipotence! Here, in the fact that a people that wandered to the four corners of the earth could return; here, in the sudden, stunning resurrection of Jewish armed might; here, in the incredibly swift military victories that gave rise to awesome legends of Jewish might and prowess; here, in the rise from the ashes of an independent Jewish State where the Jew is not beaten but *who beats, if need be*. Here is "their G-d," here is *kiddush hashem*.

When the L-rd brought the Jews out of Egypt, he culminated the victory with a total destruction of the Pharaonic Egypt that had said: "I know not the L-rd." And G-d tells Moses: "And I will beget Me honor upon Pharaoh, and upon all his host. . . . And the Egyptian shall know that I am the L-rd." And again Rashi says: "When the Almighty takes vengeance against the wicked, His name is raised and glorified."

"When I shall be sanctified in you . . ." It is through the Jew that G-d is sanctified; the elevation of the Jewish people is the elevation of the Jewish G-d. *This* is the meaning of the creation of the Jewish State—sanctification of G-d, the beginning of the final Redemption. Here is the key to comprehending exactly how the final Redemption will come, the key to saving the Jewish people untold tragedies, to escaping from the clutching fear and depression, the confusion and nagging doubts, that grip the Jew today in Israel and the Exile.

"I am the L-rd, in *its time* will I *hurry* it" (the Redemption). The rabbis comment on the apparent contradiction in these words of the Prophet Isaiah (Sanhedrin 98): "If the Redemption has 'its time,' a fixed and set time, then how will G-d 'hurry' it? Either there is a set time or it is flexible." And they answer: "If they [the Jews], merit it, I will hurry it; if they do not merit it, it will come in its fixed time."

The Redemption is assured, but it can come in one of two ways. Either by merit, and thus gloriously and swiftly, or despite our sins, and thus painfully and not until its fixed time. The creation of the State of Israel and the initial return of the people was the miraculous first step in the beginning of the Redemption. It is also G-d's final offer to us to reach that redemption "hurriedly."

A redemption that is not "hurried" but comes in its fixed time is, to be sure, a guarantee that the Jewish people and its state that came into being by Divine decree will never be destroyed. But it means something else, too. It means that we have not merited *swift* Redemption and that terrible and tragic punishments and sufferings will be visited upon the Jewish people before the Redemption comes. Suffering such as we have never endured but which we tasted a few decades ago and which we sense beginning to envelope us today.

The choice before us is a stark and simple one. If we fail to understand and believe, thus choosing not to "merit it," we opt for the Redemption to come "in its time." In the Exile, the Jew will be decimated as G-d brings down destruction on the lands. A universal economic, social, and political crisis will bring wars and destruction upon the nations. At the same time, the crisis will unleash a specific Jew-hatred that will see the Holocaust and genocide repeated against the Jews of the most comfortable of Western lands.

In Israel, the growing strength of the enemy and his success in isolating Israel politically and economically will cause a disastrous drop in the morale and fighting spirit. Israel will see a drying up of immigration and a rise in emigration, further bolstering Arab confidence, and an unabating armed struggle by the Arabs, who will not be satisfied until the entire state is eliminated. We will see terrorism escalated, wars of attrition elevated, and bloody concessions forced out of frightened Israeli governments as the threat of missiles aimed at our cities, the impossible cost of sophisticated weapons, and the loss of irreplaceable soldiers turns our horizons bleak and our future black.

> And if there be yet a tenth in it, it shall again be eaten up (Isaiah 6).
>
> For I will gather all nations against Jerusalem to battle; And the city shall be taken, and the houses rifled (Zechariah 14).

The Jew in the Exile will be utterly destroyed and despoiled while the State—though there is a Divine surety that it cannot be destroyed—will suffer overwhelming losses, tragedies, and disasters. Yet the key to preventing this unnecessary impossibility lies in our hands. It lies in our meriting redemption, in our truly believing that we are in the final era. It lies in our knowledge that how the Jewish Destiny emerges depends on whether we are faithful to the Jewish Idea. How sad that in the Exile and in the Land, among both nonobservant and observant, there is a tragic lack of understanding of the Jewish Idea and Destiny that breeds failure to do what must be done to hurry the Redemption.

We must have faith in our G-d and our destiny and return to Him and the mission He has given us. *Tshuva*—repentance and return! "Return unto Me, saith the L-rd of hosts, and I will return unto you." (Zechariah 1). A return to Torah and Judaism, a return to the special holiness and special greatness of the people of G-d. This is imperative lest we suffer the consequences of a redemption that tarries until "its time." Return to G-d and commandments, the sweet portion that is ours, the inheritance that raised us up from all the nations and that enables us to say, each morning: "Happy are we, how good is our portion and how sweet is our lot." The return to Torah and the sweet freedom of obligation and meaning of life. *Tshuva*—return. Return to a real and total Sabbath; to a real and total *kashrut*; to a real and total submission of our lives to the daily commandments. But there is more.

For how many are there who observe the commandments daily but who are men of little faith—irreligious observers of ritual, practitioners of folklore. The essence of religion is faith, and commitment to Him and this the Almighty seeks. Through faith will come swift Redemption; without it, there will first come agony. It is commitment to the *mitzvot*, the commandments—the difficult ones that call for the most deep-seated belief, that seem so dangerous to cling to, that G-d demands. The Jews who do not believe in G-d and do not observe His commandments are joined by those Jews who practice commandments and profess to believe in Him but who do not really; their bankruptcy emerges when they are called upon to make the genuine sacrifices that can only be understood if one truly believes.

"Great is the Faith that Israel manifested in Him who spoke and created the world, for Israel's reward for their faith in the L-rd was the resting upon them of the Holy Spirit." And we find, similarly, that Abraham inherited this world and the world to come only through the merit of his faith in the L-rd, and Israel was redeemed from Egypt only through the reward for faith, and the Exiles will not be ingathered except through the reward for faith.

It is faith, belief, and trust in G-d which make up the key to the Redemption.

Faith in the Jewish Destiny, in the belief that if the Jew remains true to his G-d and his heritage, he can never be destroyed. Belief in the power and the will of his G-d to destroy the enemy. Faith and belief that all the horses, chariots, jets, and nuclear weapons in the world are as nothing before the G-d of History; that the rational and "logical" and "obvious" and pragmatic wither away before the power of the Creator and Destroyer, the G-d who shapes and forms.

And if this faith and belief are to have any real meaning, they demand that the Jew live both his personal and his national life according to them; that the individual and the nation must make their decisions in the light of their faith in G-d. They mean gazing upon a "real" world that appears to be fraught with danger and that calls for a "rational" retreat from duty and obligation, and to deliberately choose the opposite path of seeming madness, because it alone is the path of fidelity and faithfulness to Jewish values and because G-d will protect those who have faith in Him. This is the path of Yisrael Saba, of ancient Israel, the "madness" that sustained them and kept them alive. The path of logic would have called for an understanding that it is impossible to wander in Exile for 2,000 years; that it is not logical to stand alone and persecuted against an entire world; that if one is faced with death or conversion, one chooses conversion. That would have been the path of rationality— and the end of the Jew. Our fathers were "madmen," and because of them, we survive. That is the *truth* of the Jewish belief.

If we really believe that Abraham followed the path of the fiery furnace; that Nahshon leaped into the Red Sea; that Gideon led 300 soldiers into battle against the mighty enemy; that David walked into combat with the giant Goliath; and that Isaiah spat in the face of the all-powerful Assyrians—then we have cited cases of Jews who truly believed in the only way belief has any meaning, who *at the moment of truth* risked their lives on the assumption that the G-d of History did indeed exist.

It is not enough to be a comfortably practicing Jew. Too many "atheists" practice a superficial religious observance, yet join the irreligious in crumbling before the fear of man. We know the Jew who believes in G-d until the war sends him flying back to the Exile. The Jew who believes in G-d until his son is asked to become a freedomfighter. The Jew who prays for Zion from a safe distance of 5,000 miles. Under all their prayer shawls is a body that denies the Jewish G-d of History.

The true believer is the Jew whose values are clear and unpretentious, who knows what is finite and what is infinite, what is

permanent and what is transitory, what important and what meaningless. He knows what is expected of a Jew and leaps into the
battle to perform as expected, regardless of the odds of man and the
chances of success predicted by "experts." He walks hand in hand
with a real G-d and knows that ultimate success *must* be his because
of the Companion beside him. And he knows that it is not the
breath of life of the Gentile or the finite human that gives and
assures us existence, and that the criteria of one's actions must be:
Is this the way of Judaism or not? Is this my obligation or not? If
it is, plunge into it and fling yourself into duty. Success will be
yours because the G-d of the Jews is the G-d of History. If not, flee
from it despite its alluring promises and temptations because you
will surely fail, because G-d so decrees.

Faith, trust, and total belief in G-d is the foundation of foundations, the key to the Redemption and the meaning of the rabbis
(Makkot 24) when they declare that the Prophet took the 613
commandments of Judaism and set them all upon one foundation:
"But the righteous shall live by His faith" (Habakuk 2).

The coming of the final Redemption with "hurried" glory and
majesty that will spare us death and agony is dependent upon the
sincere faith and total belief of the Jew in his G-d, the G-d of
Omnipotence. And to know whether we are a generation that truly
possesses this faith, trust, and belief there are clear and demanding
yardsticks—for the Jew in the Exile and for the Jew in the Land of
Israel.

The first of these demanding and difficult yardsticks of faith is
Ahavat Yisroel, love of each and every fellow Jew. The Torah
commandment is clear: "And thou shalt love thy fellow Jew as
thyself." And the commentators explicitly state: "We must have
mercy on a Jew and on his property as we would ourselves and on
our property." This love is not a simple thing. It calls for sacrifice
on behalf of the Jew in need. "Thou shalt not stand by thy
brother's blood." And the words of the rabbis are clear: "How do
we know that if he sees a fellow Jew drowning or a wild beast
dragging him or bandits coming upon him that he is obligated to
save him? It says: Thou shalt not stand by thy brother's blood."
And if the Jew is threatened and all else fails, know that Judaism
demands *and obligates* even violence, as it says: "If one comes to
slay you, slay him first." No, not Quakerism—but good Judaism.

The history of our era is filled with instances when the Jew did
not hear the cry of his fellow Jew. The Holocaust took the lives of
6 million Jews and Free World Jewry knew as early as 1942 of the

genocide—and they stood by their brother's blood. Despite the knowledge that Allied bombing of the death camps and the railroad lines and bridges leading to them, over which rode the cattle cars with their countless new victims daily, would save hundreds of thousands of lives—they stood by their brother's blood. The reason? Fear that demonstrations and protests and sitdowns at the White House might lead to anti-Semitism. Fear of what the Gentile might think overcomes awe of the commandment of the Almighty. Because of this lack of faith in G-d in all its nakedness, we carry the blood of countless Jews on our souls.

The refusal for nearly half a century to take up the plight of Soviet Jewry in an activist, angry powerful fashion again stemmed from fear of what the Gentiles would say—and do. Every Soviet Jew who today has been lost to us through assimilation is the direct result of this failure to leap to his aid. That which Jews have done for so many other peoples they refused to do for their own. Again, we stood by our brother's blood . . .

The commandment to come to the aid of the oppressed Jew holds within it two components. As a Chosen People with a common destiny, the Jew has a special relationship to each and every other Jew. "And thou shalt love thy fellow Jew as thyself" is derived from the special ties that bind all Jews into a special nation of G-d.

The failure to care about the Jewish poor and the Jewish residents of threatened neighborhoods and the Jews who were victims of reverse discrimination—all are failures of Jewish love for Jews. But added to this is the fact that the oppression of a Jew is a desecration of G-d's name which makes imperative the Jewish bending of all efforts to put an end to it. Failure to do this because of fear of what the Gentile will say is a failure of faith and trust in G-d, a failure to pass the test of the first yardstick.

For both the Jew in the Exile and the one in the State of Israel, there is the test of standing firm against the betrayal of Jews though that means going against what the Gentile might say, though it means threatening one's own interests. In the Land of Israel there has been created not a Jewish State, with a foreign and domestic policy firmly rooted in Judaism, but a state of Jews, Hebrew-speaking Gentiles, who ape the Gentile world, who create their Western culture in Hebrew, who Gentilize a Jewish-dream. Fear of what the Gentile will say and of his attitude toward the state—the same fear of the Ghetto Jew—creates a state that betrays Jews and Jewish values.

Are there Christian missionaries in Israel who steal Jewish souls, and should they be banned? Yes, but they are not—because to do so would be to risk angering the Gentile and endangering political ties with the Christian world.

Do there exist Jewish communities in the world with no one to help them and does the State of Israel possess the military skill and power, to do so? Did Israeli troops stand for years near Damascus and hear the cries of oppressed Jews and do nothing until they assented to an agreement that freed *Israelis* and ignored "foreign" Jewish brothers? Do Arab diplomats stroll the boulevards of the world freely without fear, knowing that what Israel did for its own citizens—when it killed terrorists all over the world—it will not do for "foreign" Jews because this flies in the face of accepted world international norms and will bring down the wrath of needed allies upon Israel?

Did not Israel, all the while it had diplomatic ties with Moscow, deliberately suppress the Jewish activists there and refuse to aid or to publicize their struggle? Did not Israel lie and slander Soviet Jewish activists because they wanted to anger neither the Soviets nor the U.S. ally which sought détente with Moscow? How many Soviet Jews were sacrificed in this way?

Does not Israel deliberately refrain from speaking openly about the threat of physical anti-Semitism in the Western world and especially the United States, for fear of what both Gentile and Jew will say, and thus contribute nothing to peace of mind to the Jew who faces destruction?

Does not Israel know that it is a Jewish crime to deport and extradite Jews from Israel, to bar them from entering the Jewish State, and still do this because not to do so might anger the Gentile?

And does not such fear inevitably come home to roost when the government knows war is coming and still refuses to call up reserves or strike the first blow, because it is important that the Gentile not think that we began the war, so that we pay for his love in Jewish lives?

The Jewish State has an obligation to be the guardian of Jews both in Israel and throughout the world. This is the *Jewish* policy, yet the state betrays it. It follows the fearful path of Jewish leadership and communities in the Exile who sit timidly when called upon to risk their own interests on behalf of Jews, weighing every act on the scales of Gentile reaction. They are small men, within and without the Land, men of little or no faith, for they refuse to endanger themselves or to sanctify G-d's name.

For the Jew, Jewish interests take precedence over others. The yardstick is never "What will the Gentile say?" but rather, "What shall the Jew do?" Faith in G-d and an unflinching determination to stand by fellow Jews is the clear test of Jewish faith that will hasten the final Redemption.

The second yardstick is for the Jew of the Exile. For him, the answer is to return to G-d and to the unique Jewish way of life, the commandments of the Torah. Failure to do so will make a mockery of all the efforts of foolish people to solve Jewish problems in the Exile. Those who leave the path of Judaism must ultimately pay the price; only by a return to Torah can the Jew save himself.

But there is more involved here than a mere return to observance within the fleshpots of the foreign Exile. There is an integral part of return to G-d that is not understood even by countless ostensibly religious Jews and without which there is no Redemption for them. *There must be an immediate return of the Jew of the Exile home, to the Land of Israel.* The importance of this obligation lies in the fact that the return to the Land of Israel is:

1. A major commandment of the Torah.
2. A commandment which is particularly important due to the sacrifice and commitment that it demands.
3. A commitment that manifests understanding of and faith and belief in the Jewish Destiny and the Jewish G-d and that sanctifies His name.

It is impossible to speak of a sincere and genuine Jewish return to G-d without the fulfillment of this major commandment, which is equal to all the commandments of the Torah. Failure to obey this major commandment is, in itself, a failure to merit Redemption.

Millions of Jews remain in the Exile because they simply do not consider themselves Jews in any meaningful sense. Millions of others have made a convenient accommodation with their schizophrenia and see their future in what they now call the Diaspora (a much more comfortable and less insecure word than "Exile"), visualizing themselves as "Americans (or what-have-you) of the Jewish faith," and enabling themselves in this manner to dutifully support Israel as nonresident enthusiasts and charity-givers.

The tragedy of the vast numbers of Jews who are so far from any meaningful Judaism or so ignorant of its fundamentals lies in the fact there is almost nothing one can do to persuade them to leave the Exile and live. They simply do not comprehend when we speak of the *mitzvah* to live in the Land of Israel, or say that Jewish

Destiny—for them—is tied to the Land. But far more culpable are
those others who know that to live in Israel, aside from any question
of Jewish destiny, is a commandment of Judaism and still deliberately and tortuously explain it away.

"And thou dispossessest them, and dwellest in their land"
(Deuteronomy 12). Considering this verse, the rabbis of the Sifrei
state: "The dwelling in the Land of Israel is equal to all the *mitzvot*
in the Torah." Similarly, the Tosefta (Avoda Zara 5) states: "A man
should dwell in the Land of Israel even in a city with a majority of
heathens rather than outside the Land even in a city with a majority
of Jews. This teaches us that the dwelling in Israel is equal to all the
mitzvot." The Talmud (Ketubot 110b) states: "He who dwells outside of the land is likened to one who has no G-d."

The great Talmudic scholar, commentator, and authority, the
Ramban (Nachmanides), states that this *mitzvah* of dwelling in the
Land is a positive commandment in the Torah which is *"for generations, obligating everyone."* He brings proof for his contention from
the Sifrei which tells of Reb Elazar ben Shamua and Reb Yochanan
Hasandlar, who planned to leave Israel to study Torah in Netzivin
(outside of Israel). When they reached the border "they remembered
the Land," wept, tore their garments, quoting the verse "And thou
dispossessest them," and returned to Israel. Since they lived after
the destruction of the Temple, it is obvious that this commandment
is binding on our generations, too, and their equating it with all
the *mitzvot* of the Torah shows that it is not only a rabbinic injunction. The authority, Hidushei Mahrit (Ketubot 110) brings down
the opinion of the Ramban and approves. From the words of the
Tur, Even Haezer 75, it also appears clear that this is a *mitzvah*
binding upon all Jews in our time.

Yet the "Zionist" leaders do their Zionizing from America, except
for paid junkets to Israel where they spend the public's money on
unnecessary conventions. And the religious Jew, who doesn't even
have their excuse, remains with all the other Jews in Exile. They,
at least, do not *know* that rabbinic authority ever existed. But the
religious Jew, who is so cautious about his observance of every
major and minor commandment, tradition, and custom; who, if
there is a harsh and more lenient opinion, will always choose the
harsher one, to be more pious; who prefers to be sure and eat *glatt*
kosher meat rather than simply kosher—suddenly becomes most
liberal, tolerant, and lenient; suddenly finds an individual minority
opinion and stakes his future on it. The religious Jew builds his
New Jerusalem in Brooklyn or Golders Green or Toronto and his

rebbes hold court while his rabbis sermonize there, and the *yeshivot* and *mikvas* go up and down there, and the Golden Galut, the beautiful golden exile, becomes home.

"Next year in Jerusalem!" This is the bold lie uttered every Yom Kippur and Passover by a Jew who sits, wrapped in *tallit* and religion and piously observes the great *mitzvot* and the *minutiae*, while fuming at the "irreligious." Each year he raises his pious eyes to heaven and with total nonchalance lies as he shouts to his G-d: "Next year in Jerusalem!" For next year, he fully intends to remain in Brooklyn or Golders Green or Toronto. What a warping of a magnificent religion; what deceit and hypocrisy. Here is the Jew who takes a dream of 2,000 years, pays lip service to it, then ignores and abandons it. His hot tears on Tisha B'Av for return to Jerusalem, his three-times-a-day plea to have his "eyes behold thy return to Zion" are hollow; in them we see the nakedness of the *irreligious Jew* who observes *mitzvot* . . .

Disregard the rationalizations and the clever explanations of all those Jews, observant and nonobservant, explaining their presence in the Exile. The Jew does not stay there because he "does more for Israel by staying and sending money," or because he "can give Israel political support," and the religious Jew does not sit without a G-d because "Israel is not religious enough." All of these are shameful excuses to soothe guilty consciences. The reason that good Jews, observant and nonobservant, remain in the Exile during the great miracle of Redemption is because it is more comfortable there; because it is "dangerous" in Israel; because it is too hard to begin a new life; because it is too difficult to learn a new language; because it is too painful to lower one's standard of living.

These are the reasons; all else is fraudulent nonsense. The Jew in the Exile is the true descendant of the Children of Israel who, while traveling in the desert after being freed through great miracles from bondage in Egypt, after having been privileged to stand at Mount Sinai and to hear the voice of G-d speak to them, suddenly wanted to go back to Egypt *because they had no meat!* "And the Children of Israel also wept on their part, and said: Would that we were given flesh to eat! We remember the fish, which we were wont to eat in Egypt for nought; the cucumbers, and the melons, and the leeks, and the onions, and the garlic" (Numbers 11). We remain a people that exchanges greatness for meat; destiny for garlic . . .

And if the "religious" Jew rationalizes away a *mitzvah* because his values have become as corrupted and warped as those of the irreligious, so too, on the question of recognition of this moment in

206 THE GLORY: WHAT MAKES BARUCH PROUD?

which we live, the Jewish Destiny and the Era of Redemption in which we find ourselves, he remains as small and as uncomprehending as the Sabbath violator.

The existence of the Exile is intimately connected with the future of the Jewish people who live there, and is determined by the irrestible path of the Jewish Destiny. There is no future for the Jew in the Exile, the Almighty is eliminating it and the Jews who remain there. A great upheaval of crises and wars will sweep the nations of the Exile and a wave of Jew-hatred and holocaust will arise, and in the end the Jew there will be destroyed. The Jewish Destiny in the Exile is either to leave or to be destroyed.

The Exile, despite the refusal of the comfortable Jews to admit it, can never be anything but a punishment and a curse, a sin for those who voluntarily remain in it. Everywhere that the Almighty wishes to warn the Jewish people of the direst of punishments, that punishment is always Exile: "Take heed to yourselves that your heart be not deceived and ye turn away and serve other gods and worship them . . . and ye shall perish quickly from the good land which the L-rd giveth you." And in the terrible chastisement of the Torah that is read in the synagogue in a low, hurried manner, a whole series of calamities and punishments are presented that culminate in: "And the L-rd shall scatter thee among all the peoples from one end of the earth even unto the other. . . . And among these nations shalt thou find no peace; neither shall the sole of thy foot find rest."

Punishment and curse: this is the essence of the Exile, for only because of our sins were we exiled from our Land in the first place. And the Almighty *will not allow us* to remain in the Exile, comfortably preferring that to a return to the Land of Israel. We already can see the signs, if we wish to, in the series of crises that increasingly grip America: The growing psychological crisis of loss of confidence and belief in the basic institution of democracy and in the centuries-old belief that America was always right in its dealings and in its wars. The political crisis that spreads as the military growth of the Soviet Union threatens the Free World and even American security. The racial crisis that has not gotten better but which sees rising expectations sharpening anger, resentment, and separatist tendencies among minorities and fear and hatred among the white majority. Social problems that see long-held beliefs and authorities cast away and a rootless kind of America growing and searching desperately for truth and an anchor. An economic crisis that assures that the quarter century of spectacular American luxury and wealth will never again return. All of these crises are growing into a spectacular explosion, and the scapegoat will again be the Jew. The Exile is ending whether we like it or not, and let no Jewish leader, blind and ignorant, soothe us and lull us to sleep.

The Exile *must* be eliminated because the Redemption of the Jew is totally tied to his leaving the place where he is a stranger, a persecuted and despised minority. The existence of the Exile is a contradiction of G-d's majesty and of the Jewish Destiny. If G-d is bringing Redemption to the Jew and creating His Kingdom through the return to Zion, there cannot coexist an Exile that symbolizes Jewish persecution and dispersion, and Jewish refusal to acknowledge his destiny. As long as the Jew remains in Exile, there remains a desecration of G-d's Name.

For the Almighty knows that, left alone, the Jew will never return from the fleshpots—and so He does not leave him alone. Our rabbis say, concerning the verse "And among these nations shalt thou find no peace," *if they were able to find peace, they would never return to Israel.* The tragic knowledge of the loss of faith among the Jews leads to the only assurance that the Jew will *not* remain, because the Gentile will not *allow him to remain* . . .

By deciding to stay in Exile, the Jew does two things. He both ensures his own destruction, because G-d is determined to eliminate the Exile, and he displays his ignorance of the path of Jewish Destiny, else his refusal to acknowledge it. Ironically, his punishment is the very destruction he is convinced cannot happen to him in the Exile, but only in Israel to which he will not go. The insistence of the Jew on remaining in the Exile, his refusal to go up to the Land of Israel, is a rejection, knowingly or unknowingly, of the Jewish Destiny.

And of such men did rabbinical giants like Rabbi Yehudah Halevi and Rabbi Yaakov Emden speak when they deplored the Jews who create their Jerusalems in the Exile:

> The Rabbi: You have shamed me, King of the Khazars. And this sin [the refusal of the Jew to make an effort to return to the Land of Israel] is that which prevented the fulfillment of G-d's destiny during the time of the Second Temple, as it is said: "Sing and rejoice, O daughter of Zion" [Zechariah 2]. For the Divine form was prepared to descend upon the world, as in the beginning had all the Jews agreed to return to the Land with a willing heart. But only some returned and most, and their

leaders, remained in Babylonia, desiring the Exile and their labor in order not to be separated from their homes and affairs (Sefer HaKuzari, Rabbi Yehudah Halevi).

There is not one in a thousand who is aroused to settle in the Land to dwell there but rather one in a state and two in a generation. No man seeks its love, considers searching or seeking its welfare and good, and does not expect to see it. It appears to us as we sit in comfort outside the Land that we have already found another Land of Israel and Jerusalem, similar to it. Because of this, there came upon us all the evil when the Jews sat in Spain and in other lands in comfort and great honor from the days of the destruction, many years . . . and then were exiled from there until there remained not a trace of the Jews in those lands (Rabbi Yaakov Emden, in the introduction to his prayerbook).

For the Jew of the Exile there is no choice. He will either leave willingly and upright or flee in panic—if fortunate—or be destroyed. The decision to return from the Exile will save his life, and at the same time serves as a major yardstick of his faith and a major step in his return to G-d. If he believes and returns to the Land, he will help bring the Redemption of the Jewish people in the Land of Israel "hurriedly." If he does not believe and if he remains, he and his loved ones will be destroyed and he will contribute to tragic and unnecessary suffering to the Jewish people. The irony is that the safety which the Jew seeks in the Exile is an illusion, for the Exile is doomed while the "dangers" facing Israel can never destroy the State because of G-d's vows and the Jewish Destiny.

But if Jewish Destiny decrees the destruction of the Exile, it does not simply end with that. In the Land of Israel, too, there must be faith and belief and here, too, there is a yardstick. How sad that the Chosen People has created a Hebrew-speaking Portugal. Israel has become a state that produces Gentilized Hebrews, a Levantine creature that stripped from its citizens a Judaism of centuries and substituted for it the culture of Dizengoff Street. The results are everywhere. It is a state where an automobile, an apartment, a washing machine, the latest American fashions, are the topics that obsess people. It is a state that sees people dream of the Golden Land, the land flowing with milk and honey—America—and make daily efforts to emigrate there.

There must be *tshuva*, repentance and a return to G-d and the unique chosen path of the Jew, the cleaving to the commandments of the Torah. Without this, there will be no hope. But it is not enough to merely cleave to those commandments that we automatically think of when we consider "religious observance." To be sure, the observance of the Sabbath, *kashrut*, and the like are essential parts of the Jewish return to G-d, but there is something at least as important that must accompany them, and that the observant face as a challenge no less than the nonobservant. An indispensable, perhaps the most important, test of Jewish return to G-d is the belief in His Omnipotence that manifests itself in the difficult and seemingly impossible task of *staunch and unflinching refusal to betray the Land of Israel by violating the prohibition of giving any part of it to a non-Jew.* "And thou shalt not give them permanent ownership." To give away land to a non-Jew in Israel and thus remove Jewish possession and holiness from it is a violation of Jewish Law. How many times more so to give it away under pressure and Gentile force!

The surrender of any part of the Land of Israel is a violation that is forbidden even at the cost of one's life. In the case of a decree on the part of Gentiles that demands from the Jewish *people* as a class the violation of *any* commandment, the law is that the Jew must die rather than violate that commandment, since the Gentile decree against the people is a desecration of G-d's name. (See Maimonides, *Hilchot Yesodei HaTorah* 5:3.) In the case of the Land of Israel, which *itself* is a national commandment—i.e. it belongs to the Jewish people—the demand that parts be given up is a demand that the Jewish people violate a law and thus an inadmissible desecration of G-d's name. Moreover, it is clear that the whole question of conquering and fighting for the land has nothing to do with the question of "self-preservation taking precedence over commandment." If it did, Jews would have never gone to war whenever they were attacked, but would have submitted quietly to being conquered, paid taxes, *and lived.* Yet they did not. They always fought the enemy who attacked them; such a war was always considered an obligatory war, as is every case in which Gentiles attack Jews.

What is more, to give up any part of the Land of Israel or even to return any part of the lands outside the boundaries that were conquered by us through the miracles of G-d, particularly in this era when each victory is a special proof of His greatness, is to reverse the miracle, to desecrate the Name of G-d just at the time when His final victory is upon us. Retreat is more than retreat from land; it is retreat from sanctification of G-d's name, from the awesome miracle of 1967. In that year, the Messiah knocked on the door and shouted: Open! Open and I bring you the final Redemption! Do we remember the two weeks that *preceded* the Six Day War? The two weeks in which Arabs danced in the streets of their cities in gleeful anticipation of the total destruction of Israel? Do we remember how frightened Jews were and how they thought in their inner recesses: Is it possible that yet another holocaust is coming and that a Jewish state that emerged after 1,900 years of exile will go under after only 19 years of independence?

And then the miracle came. Not only was Israel not destroyed, but the unstoppable Jewish forces poured across the borders that comprised a pittance of their homeland and smashed westward, eastward, north, and south. Jerusalem with its Temple Mount and Western Wall; Hebron, city of the Patriarchs; Judea and Samaria and the Golan and the Gaza and the Sinai. All the places where the Bible was written and lived; all the land that had been enslaved by strangers—all now *returned* to the bosom of the Jewish people.

We stood on the verge of the final Redemption—if only we had had the courage and the faith to grasp it. The Messiah knocked and said: Open! The key to the door was faith. Faith that if we had leaped upon the liberated lands and cried out: These are ours and they have returned to us; if we had joined them officially to the State of Israel and made them part of it; if we had called for free and unrestricted Jewish settlement in every part of the Land of Israel—if we had done this without fear of what the Gentiles would say, the Messiah would have walked through the opened door and brought us the final Redemption.

But we did not. We were people of little faith, and in some cases none. We hastened to bar Jews from settling in the city of Abraham, Isaac, and Jacob. We forbade Jews from exercising their rights, their *obligations* to settle in the Land: "And thou dispossessest them, and dwellest in it their land" Jews were barred and Arabs assured that the land was theirs. Little wonder that the world says the same thing and demands the return of the "Arab" lands. The greatest of the foolish sins of the leaders of Israel is clearly the one of taking a miracle and turning it into an ordinary thing: taking holiness and making it profane; taking Sanctification and retreating back to Desecration. All because of lack of faith.

"The exiles will not be returned except through faith" as it is said: "And I shall betroth thee unto Me with faith and thou shalt know the L-rd." No retreat; the entire purpose of the rise of Israel is to guarantee that the world shall know the L-rd, shall admit and proclaim that the L-rd, G-d of Israel, is the true G-d. The only way that the struggle between Israel and its enemies can end is through that acceptance. Any retreat, anything less than full admission by the Arabs that the L-rd is the true G-d and that the Land of Israel, His land, belongs to His people, falls short of the Divine purpose. Peace is wonderful but the call of Heaven in this moment of Redemption is for the final purpose of the world to be reached: "And the L-rd shall be King over all the earth; on that day shall the L-rd be One and His name One."

That is why there can be no retreat, why a refusal to retreat based on "military strategy," or "political logic," or any other secular reason not based upon faith in G-d, will be of no avail.

There are perfectly logical reasons to reject the madness of retreat before an enemy that is sworn to destroy any Jewish state of any size or shape. Even the "practical" and "logical" person knows in his heart that a "Palestine" on the borders of an Israel is but the first step to the next effort to eliminate what is left of the Jewish State. But that is not the heart of the question. Geographical status will not save Israel. "Israel is delivered by the L-rd," and He can save His people though they live in a state far tinier than the present one. Retreat from the Land is not a military question, it is a Jewish one. Retreat removes from the Holy Land the name and ownership of the L-rd. Retreat under pressure and through fear is an act of faithlessness. Retreat from any part of the Land is prohibited.

"Not one inch of retreat" is not a political slogan but a religious one. It is Jewish policy for a Jewish people that believes. To cleave to such a policy in the face of awesome enemies, international isolation, and pressure from allies calls for immense faith and belief. And that faith and belief will determine how the Redemption comes. Contrary to what the men of little faith believe, it is the lack of faith, the willingness to betray the Land, the Law, to desecrate G-d's name, which will bring wars and agonizing tragedy before the final Redemption. And it is holding fast to the Land, ignoring pressures and fears of friend and foe alike, that will guarantee the hurried final victory.

The Jew always works on two parallel levels. He does not merely pray and trust in miracles; he also prepares for battle by all natural means. Yet he realizes that not with the strength of his arm alone can victory come, and he turns to G-d for help in his time of need. It is when he combines both of these—power of his arm and trust in G-d—that he can overcome the same impossible odds and enemies that would otherwise overwhelm him.

The Jewish Destiny calls for the Jew to refuse to betray the miracle of Redemption by returning any part of the Land of Israel under any circumstances. And it calls for not returning even a non-strategic part *outside* of the Land of Israel's borders unless there is no desecration of G-d's name, no limiting and reducing of the miracle of His victory; in other words, unless the enemy lays down his arms, pledges a total peace, and recognizes the majesty and kingdom of the Jewish G-d through His people, Israel. To stand before this test will require a rejection of the fear of isolation, all-powerful enemies, and the need to submit to the demands of "allies" whom we "need." But this, after all, is the true and only test of real faith.

We must never fear to be alone, for that is the Jewish blessing that has saved the Jew from assimilation and that will make the final miracle and the Jewish victory all the more astounding. The saving of Jewish lives does not allow the return of the Land—what little men and of little faith are those who say so. The threat to life cannot dictate a return of the Land, because if saving lives is the criteria, then it may also dictate the return of *the State*.

What lack of trust and faith lies in the hearts of those, both observant and nonobservant, who would give up parts of the Land of Israel! What a failure to understand the gravity of this act, and what a failure to understand the *mitzvah* of the conquest and settling of the Land!

If we seek an answer to what the Jewish response is to a call to give up parts of the Land, we must as always seek that answer in the Jewish sources. And, as always, there is a precedent. "The deeds of the fathers are a sign unto the sons."

When Jephthah of Gilead ruled (Judges 11), he was confronted by the king of Ammon and his people who moved to the border and prepared for war with Israel. When Jephthah sent messengers to him to ascertain the reason, the Ammonite king replied: "Because Israel took away my land, when he came up out of Egypt, from Arnon even unto the Jabbok, and unto the Jordan. Now therefore, restore those cities peaceably."

The parallel is striking. An enemy who comes and demands the return of the "conquered territories," and who presents an alternative: there need not be war, with loss of Jewish youth. There can be peace, if the Jews will return the territory. And the Ammonite is not even speaking of what we now call "the inheritance of our fathers"; he is referring to the *eastern* part of Eretz Yisrael, the part that is now known as Jordan. And he speaks of an end to belligerency (of a conference, perhaps?) where the "conquered territories" will be returned, thus "giving peace a chance."

In the face of all this, and with knowledge that some people are advising that "the preservation of life decrees the giving up of land," Jephthah, the leader of his people in his generation, replies to the enemy: "Wilt not thou possess that which Chemosh thy god giveth thee to possess? So whomsoever the L-rd our G-d hath dispossessed from before us, them will we possess." And he goes to war. And Jews fall. But he does not give up a part of the Land of Israel.

And when Moses chose twelve spies to spy out the Land of Canaan, he chose twelve leaders and chiefs, scholars versed in the Law. And they returned and cried out (Numbers 13):

> The land through which we have passed to spy it out, is a land that eateth up the inhabitants thereof; and all the people that we saw in it are men of great stature. And there we saw the Nephilim [giants] and the sons of Anak, who come of the Nephilim; and we were in our own sight as grasshoppers, and so were we in their sight. : . . And all the congregation lifted up their voice, and cried . . .

What were the men of wisdom who spoke these words saying? Were they simply traitors or timid creatures? No, they were speaking of "reality" and "logic" and were stating the obvious "facts," that it is not possible for a grasshopper to fight giants. They were making their own *halachic* ruling that the preservation of life overruled the Land of Canaan.

But it is not true. The conquest and the settling of the land does *not* fall before the danger to life; it is the one *mitzvah* concerning in defense of which one is commanded to place oneself in danger. For without war there is no Land of Israel for the Jewish people, no Jewish state safe from enemies. The *mitzvah* of settling the Land is intimately tied to the danger to life. Those spies who sought to return to Egypt and live rather than die in battle; who sought to return to the Exile and perhaps create a Jerusalem there, were wrong. They have come to be known forever as the Generation of the Desert, not worthy of entering the Land, men of little faith who were doomed to die in the wilderness. Whose children entered the Land, fought for it, and inherited it.

As Jephthah summarily rejected any return of Jewish land in return for an Ammonite "peace," and as the Jewish G-d angrily punished the twelve spies who sincerely felt that to go up to the

Land of Canaan in the face of giants was suicidal, so we must learn, that the conquest and holding of the Land of Israel is irrevocably tied to faith and to the potentially tragic sacrifice of Jewish lives. It is fear of man that keeps Jews in the Exile from coming to live in the Land; it is fear of man that drives Jews to give up parts of the Land. It is fear of man that creates a Jewish State that behaves like any other state, sacrificing Jewish interests and Jews out of fear of angering the Gentile and violating his concepts of international norms. It is fear of man that turns the Jew into a worshiper of *avodah zara*, literally "foreign worship." The G-d of the Jews is a jealous G-d who demands *total* worship, total belief and trust in Him as the *only* force on earth. When we fear man and at the same time violate Jewish laws, we commit the most heinous of Jewish crimes, *avodah zara*.

And there is yet another yardstick—the Arabs who live within the State of Israel. Is anyone so foolish as to believe that they love the state in which they have lived for all these years and in which so many were born? Is anyone so naive as to believe that the Arab citizen of Israel loves that country? What is Israel if not a Jewish state, committed a thousand times over to the freedom, sovereignty, culture, language, religion, and national destiny of Jewish people, to the concept of a Jewish homeland with a Jewish majority and Jewish control? It is said so very clearly in the Declaration of Independence of Israel; in the basic law of Israel, the Law of Return (that grants every Jew the automatic right of citizenship); it is the underlying logical principle of Zionism, that is, Jewish nationalism. Why have a country with merely *many* Jews in it? That may already exist in Brooklyn . . .

An Arab may have his own religious and cultural and social and economic rights in a Jewish State, but he will never be equal to a Jew any more than Jews are equal in Moslem Egypt. And since the Arab knows that he was once the majority in a country that was called "Palestine" and is now a minority in one called "Israel," it stands to reason that he will never accept the Jewish State. No country with two separate peoples, each claiming that the land is theirs, can ever know peace. Israeli Arabs are a time bomb who promise us a Northern Ireland or a Cyprus.

The Arab birth rate is enormous, while Jewish women—progressive to the end—fight overpopulation in India by not having babies. And when one adds the tragedy of liberal abortion in Israel that murders tens of thousands a year, and the growing emigration of Jews from Israel because their Jewishness is too weak to compete with their desire to make money or to escape military service, one sees a distinct threat to the survival of a Jewish State *by democratic means*. What will happen when, in a brief 10 years, Arabs comprise a quarter of the population with 25 Kneset members? Think of their political power in a fragmented Kneset and think of the demands for "autonomy" in the Galilee that will have an Arab majority. And in 50 years? Is it inconceivable that they will be a majority with the democratic right to rule the Kneset and Israel, change the name of the state to "Palestine," and abolish a Zionist state in favor of a "democratic, secular Palestine"?

One cannot purchase Israeli Arab friendship and good will with economic and material benefits nor with educational opportunities. Quite the opposite. The Arab outpaces the Jew in quantity and begins to grow in quality as more and more Arabs attend schools and universities. And the intellectual Arab is the most dangerous of all, because he is the most nationalist and frustrated. Moreover, the Arab intellectual will be joined and aided by Jewish intellectuals who have no identity of their own, are even more frustrated, and who see in Zionism and the Law of Return doctrines that make the Arab nonequal to the Jew. They see, too, in our failure to immediately declare the liberated territories Jewish, proof that they are not really ours and that we are, indeed, conquerors by might and not by right. We will see more and more young Jews support the Arabs by demonstrations, riots, and espionage. We will see the Arabs growing cleverer and speaking more and more of a "secular, democratic Palestine" in which Jews and Arabs can live "together." And this at a time of weariness with continuing war, the heartache of more and more Jewish deaths, and pressure from enemy and "friend" alike.

Furthermore, the Arab who lives in the Jewish State, and rejects its concept and its exclusive Jewish ownership, is in effect rejecting the ownership and sovereignty of the Jewish G-d. He is saying: *I do not know the L-rd*. This rejection, the stoning by Israeli Arabs of Israeli soldiers and their rioting against Jewish sovereignty, their call for a description of Israel as a "binational" state—all these are desecrations of G-d's name.

What is the solution to the Arab problem? It is more than clear. While there is yet time we must push for emigration with compensation of the Israeli Arab, who is most dangerous because he is neither equal to the Jew in Israel nor an Arab in the eyes of other Arabs. He will attempt to prove his "Arabism" by fighting the Jewish State. Emigration, within the context of an *exchange of Arab-Jewish populations*, is vital.

Beginning in 1948, more than ¾ million Jews fled Arab lands. The flight of the Arabs in 1948 was but the other side of the coin of what in effect was an exchange of populations. It is time to complete that process by an emigration plan which would offer full compensation for property and the transfer of Arabs either to other Arab lands or to lands in the West. After World War II, the Poles and Czechs—who had learned to their horror what a hostile minority within their borders could mean—*expelled* 8 million ethnic Germans *without* compensation. India and Pakistan exchanged 10 million Hindus and Muslims as each fled to the newly created states in 1947. The result was a homogeneous situation rather than one of perpetual bloodshed and hatred.

What prevents Israel from taking this logical and sane step that is classically expressed by the rabbis in the concept: "He who has mercy on the cruel is destined to have cruel to the merciful"? Only one thing! fear of what the world will say. Again, lack of faith—the yardstick for our times.

To return to G-d and the commandments. To return from the Exile. Not to return any part of Israel. Not to turn Jews and Jewish interests away out of fear of what the Gentile might say. To remove from our midst those who reject a Jewish state and destiny. These are the things that will determine the future of the Jews, the exact path of the Jewish Destiny. The destiny will be whatever we make it, either "in its time" or "hurried," and the demand that is thrust on us is to manifest in *concrete* action, total faith and trust in G-d. By our readiness to do this, to sacrifice, we sanctify G-d's Name and prove ourselves worthy of Redemption.

"But I will be hallowed among the children of Israel" (Leviticus 22). "*Give of yourself* and thus sanctify My name"—*Rashi.* How does one sanctify the name of G-d? How does the Jew rise to what G-d demands of him? Only through his readiness to give of himself, through commitment to *mesirut nefesh,* willingness to give his soul, if necessary. To be ready to give up the comfortable fleshpots and move to a country where internal difficulties are legion and which external enemies threaten to destroy; to refuse demands by bitter enemies and needed allies to give up parts of the Land, thus increasing the threat of bloody war; to fly in the face of world opinion and norms and refuse to violate Jewish laws and obligations—all these are terribly difficult things. But by doing them, by "giving of ourselves and thus sanctifying G-d's name," we *force* G-d to bring the Redemption "hurriedly." We lift our eyes unto G-d and say: "We believe in you; we trust in you and we sacrifice for you. We face a terrible danger and we go out to battle and you *must* help us. You *must* bring us Redemption because you promised it. By our faith we have merited that Redemption and you are obligated to bring it."

There is nothing more fundamental to the Redemption than faith. Indeed, it is possible that if the Jewish people were totally lacking in *mitzvot*, but possessed the one attitude of true and sincere and willing faith in G-d, along with a preparation to translate that faith into concrete sacrifice, they would at least bring the Redemption to the doorstep of reality. This is the meaning of the rabbis who say: "If Israel observes the Sabbath properly even one time, the son of David [the Messiah] comes." (Midrash Rabbah, Shmot 25). For the Sabbath is the cornerstone of belief in G-d and in His omnipotence. It is testimony to His creating the world, possessing it, controlling it, directing it, overpowering it. If we believe in that which the Sabbath represents, we bring the Redemption closer.

And this, it appears to me, is the deeper meaning of the Talmudic statement that Habakuk set the entire 613 commandments upon one, "and the righteous shall live by his faith." That though the Jew, for a myriad of historical and social reasons, no longer observes many of the *mitzvot* but clings with truth and with dedicated sacrifice to the sincere and pure belief that G-d will save His people and *acts* on this, this is so great that it will bring close the Redemption, for upon faith does the entire Torah rest and through faith is the Jew saved.

And is this not what the Rebbe of Gur, author of the Sfat Emet, means (Tehilim 31): "In [the Purim prayer] Shoshanat Yaakov, we declare that all who have faith in G-d will not suffer humiliation. This includes not only righteous people but even individuals who possess only faith and whose actions alone might not render them worthy."

The converse is also true. If the Jew, though he be filled with commandments "as a pomegrante," lacks faith in the Jewish Destiny, in the Jewish G-d, and is that cursed one who "trusts in man and makes flesh his arm"; if he is prepared, as swiftly as any nonbeliever and scoffer, to practice the art of realpolitik and diplomacy, giving up Jews, land, and faith, rather than standing fast and trusting in G-d; he can only delay the Redemption and bring tragedy down upon the heads of the Jewish people. He is as much an atheist as the atheist, as much a disbeliever as the disbeliever he so scorns. He is the man of little faith, and of him do the rabbis speak when they say: "What causes the righteous to fritter away their table in the future to come? It is because of the lack of faith that was within them" (Sotah 48).

I believe that, in a generation so lacking in deeds and so small and orphaned—*true* faith and readiness to sacrifice with trust in G-d is enough to merit a 'hurrying' of the Redemption at least in great measure, and if not bringing it immediately, at least bringing us close to it so that we are saved terrible tragedies and sufferings.

"What does the L-rd thy G-d require of thee, but to fear the L-rd thy G-d, to walk in all His ways?" (Deuteronomy 10). And the rabbis so correctly ask: "Is fear of G-d, then, such a small thing, that Moses poses the question as if it were a simple task?" The question is in order. The fear of G-d, the true fear and awe that makes one realize how Omnipotent and Almighty He is, and how one must therefore not only fear to disobey Him but also be joyous in the knowledge that such an awesome G-d can destroy the mightiest of enemies and turn back to dust the most powerful of empires, that one must stand firm with trust in Him against the most terrible of all dangers—is such fear a simple mater? Is it acquired easily?

Of course it is not! It is a terribly difficult thing, a small matter only to a man like Moses, whose faith and trust enabled him to give up an empire, stand up against a Pharaoh, against a whining, complaining, threatening people for 40 years, and then not enter the Land. But that is what the Jew is called upon to be. Simple or not, that is what is demanded of the Jew.

The very essence of faith is not simple. It is never needed in a condition of relative safety and security. Faith is called upon only when the night is inky black and there appears to be no hope. Faith is meaningful only when the sword is on the neck. Faith is what separates the truly religious from the irreligious, the truly believing from the nonbelievers. At that moment of truth we see who girds his loins and buckles on his sword and who, in the midst of his "piety," prepares to sacrifice people and land "because of danger to life."

When that symbol of faith, the first Jew, Avraham Ha'Ivri, Abraham from the "other side"—the whole world on one and he on the other—heard that his nephew Lot had been taken captive by four kings, "*vayarek et chanichav*," he hurried his servants, only 318 of them, to go to battle against four armies! (Genesis 14). And the rabbis take the word '*vayarek*'—hurried—which also comes from the root meaning 'green', and say (Midrash Rabbah, Genesis 14).

> Rabbi Yehuda said: They [his servants] turned green [frightened] faces to Abraham and said: "Five kings could not stand up to them and we will!" Rabbi Nehemiah said: Abraham turned a green face to them and said: "Nevertheless, I will go out and fall, if need be, for the Sanctification of G-d's name."

We are a generation cursed with little men and little faith, an orphaned generation without leaders and without men of stature, neither statesmen nor teachers. Woe to a generation of little faith!

What will happen?! The best of us cry out in despair and confusion. We stand before a vast array of enemies whose manpower and funds are unlimited. They have powerful weapons that can reach our cities and bloody our soldiers. They have many, many allies who support them, train them, fund them, and may even threaten to intervene on their behalf. They have terrorists who threaten the lives of women and children. The world leaves us in isolation and we have few allies, indeed only one real one upon whom we desperately lean and to whom we frantically look for arms and support as it forces us to make "painful" and dangerous concessions.

We are weary of a seemingly never-ending struggle, and our weakness leads us to postulate all manner of illusions and delusions of hoped-for peace. Perhaps we should compromise, return this or that part of the Land, recognize the "Palestinian" people, support the creation of a "Palestinian" state, "give peace a chance," trust the Arabs to have undergone a change of heart and to accept Israel into the region. And we delude ourselves because we despair.

We are told that the only alternative to our delusions is war—here is a chance for peace. We are told that, in any event, we have little choice because the Soviets can destroy us and only the United States can prevent them from doing so, while at the same time it remains our only supplier of weapons. Therefore we hear that it is justified to accept a cease-fire that stopped us as we were prepared to decimate our enemies and save the lives of thousands of our soldiers; that it is justified not to strike the first blow because we need the understanding of the world; that it is justified to retreat from Sinai and from parts of the Golan and from parts of the West Bank. That it is justified, even, to sacrifice brothers and sisters in Syria for agreements demanded and needed by allies. We are told that this must be because it is a practical, logical, realistic policy.

And so we forget G-d and the Jewish Idea and are gripped with fear of Man. And we remain in the "safety" of the Exile, supping from its fleshpots. We seek the love and peace of man by giving up the land of G-d. And in the best of times, both in the Galut and the State, we set our policy by what the nations will say—and betray the Jewish Destiny.

Men of little faith and little understanding rule us, men who insist upon being grasshoppers rather than giants. Both in the Exile, where never have so many Jews been led by such tiny ones, and in Israel, where those who lead the state took a miracle and turned it into an ordinary thing, the Jew will pay for the lack of faith of his leaders. The same men who angrily fought the "alarmists" who demanded mass evacuation of European Jewry in the years before the World War; who refused, until 1942, to declare that the aim of Zionism was a Jewish State lest this offend both British and Arabs; who created a policy of *havlaga*, self-restraint, refusing to attack Arab terrorists who murdered Jews with impunity from 1936 to 1939; who knew of the Holocaust but buried its news, because they feared to offend the British or to make the war a "Jewish war" and risk anti-Semitism; who created and encouraged a Kastner; who turned Irgun and Sternist soldiers over to the British; who, in America, destroyed a generation of Jewish identity through their efforts to "melt" and bowed and scraped at brotherhood and inter-faith meetings while proving to their youth that there was indeed no difference between Jews and non-Jews—these men and others like them spiritually destroy the Jew of the Exile and lead to his coming physical destruction, urging him to remain in the Galut so that he will not leave except through the boot of the Gentile, his bombs, or his chimneys. And similar men rule in the Land of Israel and continue to commit the most atrocious of Jewish crimes, taking the miracle of return to Zion, the 2,000-year-old-dream, and turning it into mundaneness.

No wonder such people tremble before the dangers they see; no wonder they hasten to betray Jewish values. For they see only what their pragmatic eyes behold; they are incapable of seeing anything beyond. Those who believe that Jews are ordinary people, a nation like any other nation, who do not believe in G-d or who pay lip service to Him, can understand only what their physical senses tell them is "real." Such people naturally look with eyes of "logic" and reject the "mystical" and "irrational." They measure everything in terms of "reality"; if there is a danger of war in Israel, one simply does not go there to live but remains in the "safe" Exile. If Israel has no allies, then it is "logical" not to act boldly lest we lose the support of the one we have. If we need weapons, it is "logical" that we not antagonize the one that gives us those weapons because it is only its weapons that give us victory. And if the price of the weapons is betrayal both of the Land and of other Jews, as well as a mad risk of disaster, we must take that risk and we must do the betraying.

This is how the Jew becomes a Gentile, how a Chosen People turns into an ordinary one. How a people that has no faith collapses in fear before man, betrays Jews, Judaism, and Land and then pays for its fear and lack of faith through the natural consequences of its actions. The explosion of destruction that will come about in the Exile will catch and destroy it. Its retreat will bring the enemy closer to Israel and encourage him to launch bloody wars in the heartland of the Jewish State. The Jews who are oppressed in the Exile, for whom nothing is done, will not add their precious infusions of quantity and quality. *The Almighty repays us measure for measure, and our punishments follow from the consequences of our sins.*

It is incumbent upon us to stop our mad Gentilization of ourselves, our failure to know who we and our G-d are. It is incumbent upon us to understand our greatness and believe in it, so that we do not cheapen ourselves and throw our future into the hands of the Gentiles who can and will do nothing for us. If it is true that we are like all nations and that only through leaning upon man, compromising, retreating, and betraying, will we survive, then know that *we will not survive.* If there is no Divine guarantee and if we must depend upon allies and the goodwill or change of heart of our enemies, then *there is no hope.*

For the enemies of Israel will never make peace; they will never seek less than the total elimination of the Jewish State. They do not want compromise because they look upon us as robbers and bandits. They speak not of a return to a particular year but of a return to a time when there will be no Israel at all. They are nationalists who will not compromise what they believe to be a sacred struggle for their own home; there is no hope at all that we will ever be able to live in peace with them. It is not a delusion of peace but a reality of existence that should concern us now: our enemies will have the world as their allies and we will have nothing. These are the facts, this is the reality for those who seek only "logic" and "rationality." If that is all there is, then flee to Canada or prepare to die bravely for the Land, bravely but hopelessly. If that is all there is, then there can be a Third Destruction and all the frantic programs and efforts and nonsense will avail us nothing.

But if that is *not* all there is; if the Jewish people did not survive impossible centuries of agony through natural means and did not outlive empires through ordinary, rational reasons; if the Jewish people is a Divine, Chosen People that *cannot* be destroyed, and this State that arose from the ashes is G-d's beginning of the Redemption and cannot ever be eliminated because it is part of the immutable and unstoppable Jewish Destiny—then the *only* hope for the survival of millions of Jews in the Exile and hundreds of thousands in the Land, and the only hope of a swift Redemption without agony, is to put our trust in G-d. To believe in the allies, the broken reeds that are men, is to believe in impossible miracles. To believe in G-d is to follow the natural, proven precedent that has served and saved the Jew throughout history.

Let us not be afraid. Let us, at long last, cease to repeat the errors of our forefathers. The Prophet Isaiah, 2,500 years ago, looked at the assimilators of his time and declared (Isaiah 31):

> Woe to them that go down to Egypt for help, And stay on horses, And trust in chariots, because they are many, And in horsemen, because they are exceedingly mighty; But they look not unto the Holy One of Israel, Neither seek the L-rd!"

And when King Asa of Judah turned to the King of Syria for aid, Hanani the Seer said (II Chronicles 16):

> Because thou hast relied on the King of Aram [Syria] and hast not relied on the L-rd thy G-d, therefore is the host of the King of Aram escaped out of thy hand. Were not the Ethiopians and the Lubim [Libyans] a huge host, with chariots and horsemen exceeding many? yet, because thou didst rely on the L-rd, He delivered them into thy hand. For the eyes of the L-rd run to and fro throughout the whole earth, to show Himself strong in the behalf of them whose heart is whole toward Him.

Today we tremble before mere men and place our trust in men. We tremble before our ally and prostrate ourselves and sell brethren even as we throw to the enemy parts of the Land of Israel. We lift our eyes unto Washington and from there expect our salvation. We place our hopes in political swindlers and diplomatic liars and snarling politicians. Foolish Jews, frightened Jews, Jews of little faith!

Do we believe that our ally that places its own interests above all else, is the worthy repository of our fate and trust? It will turn on us the moment it is convinced that its own self-interest demands it. We once trusted in France and it betrayed us, and we trust today in Washington and it will betray us because of self-interest. We, the people who survived a hellish Exile of two millennia *only* because of our deep and unshaken faith in G-d, suddenly forget Him, ignore Him, term Him irrelevant. One listens to the foolish speeches of the frightened Jewish leaders in Exile and in Israel and strains his ears hoping to hear a mention of G-d. There is none. Joy in the compliment of an obscure African leader; happiness in the support of bedraggled intellectuals; dancing for joy at the crumbs of politicians —but G-d is nowhere to be found. Foolish leaders who will bring destruction down upon those whom they lead . . .

The salvation of the Jew lies not in the foolish programs and realpolitik with which Jewish leaders in the Land and the Exile play. "These come from chariots and these with horses but we will remember the name of the L-rd our G-d." Are there really those among us who are so blind as to fail to see the mighty hand of G-d in the creation and sustenance of the State? Did we defeat armies and nations in a matter of days with the loss of a relative handful of men and then turn back awesome armies with a few tanks and weapons when the land stood open before them, because of our allies and our realpolitik or even *because of our strength alone?*

How ironic it is! After the Six Day War, Jews smugly proclaimed the invincibility of the Israel Defense Forces and there happily sprang up the myth of the Israeli superman. There was nothing the Israeli army could *not* do. After the Yom Kippur War, Jews brokenly spoke of the "blunders" of the same Israel Defense Forces and there was suddenly nothing the Israeli army *could* do! Strange and blind people. Those who understand, believe in the Israel Defense Forces today *exactly* as they believed last year and 10 years ago and 20 years ago. The Israeli army can do and cannot do *exactly* what the Almighty decrees for it; the miracles of 1948, 1956, and 1967 are only accentuated by the losses of 1973—which in the end proved to be the greatest victory and miracle of all.

The Jew never did understand the passage in Deuteronomy 8: "And thy say in thy heart: 'My power and the might of my hand hath gotten me this wealth.' But thou shalt remember the L-rd thy G-d, for it is He that giveth thee power to get wealth." It is He that implants terror in the hearts of Arabs in 1948 so that they flee in irrational panic and He that does not do the same in 1967, so that in the one case we are blessed with their absence and in the other G-d turns His face from us and curses us with their presence. It is He who allows us to defeat impossible numbers but then refuses to give us total victory, because we believe that it is only our right hand and power that gets us wealth. It is He who sees to it that terrorist effort after terrorist effort is foiled "miraculously," then turns His presence away when we refuse to believe. It requires a Six Day War to understand a Yom Kippur War and vice versa . . .

Let us remember the words of King Hezekiah, who faced the terrifying armies of the mightiest empire in the world, the Assyrians of Sennacherib. They stood surrounding the city of Jerusalem, armies that demanded Jewish surrender or they would slaughter without mercy. And Hezekiah told his people (II Chronicles 32):

> "Be strong and of good courage, be not afraid nor dismayed for the King of Assyria, nor for all the multitude that is with him; for there is a Greater with us than with him: with him is an arm of flesh; but with us is the L-rd our G-d to help us, and to fight our battles."

And the Jews believed and did not surrender and the hand of G-d smote the enemy and Judea did not fall.

We are not like other people, Bernie (did you know that your Hebrew name, Baruch, means "Blessed"?), and the norms and realities of the world are not for us. We are the Chosen People of G-d, the indestructible People of G-d, the people of G-d whose destiny is to see His kingdom on earth, and we live in the Era of the Redemption. Let us never forget that. Let us know it and believe it!

From that awesome moment when the mountains at Sinai burned and smoked and the lightning cracked and the terrible thunder boomed its fear into the hearts of the entire people that heard the voice of the Almighty Himself, the Jew believed. And believes.

Mornings he prays to the G-d "who chooses His people Israel with love," and Sabbaths he takes his cup and sings, "He who divides the holy from the profane, between Israel and the nations." On holidays he cries out, "Thou hast chosen us from all the nations," and when called to the Torah he pronounces, "Who hast chosen us from all the peoples."

For two millennia of an Exile that saw pogroms and Inquisitions,

Crusades and Auschwitzes, the Jew believed and proclaimed this uniqueness. It was only *this belief, this certainty* that allowed him to survive, that gave him the will to stand irrationally and illogically against impossible odds and against a whole world and shout: I am right and you are wrong; I will emerge victorious and you will be defeated; I will return home and there is nothing you can do to prevent it.

There is a guarantee, a solemn oath, a divine bond that the Jewish people cannot ever be destroyed but, rather, that they and their G-d will emerge triumphant in days to come. Zion will and must emerge as the mount to which all people will turn and L-rd will be the One before whom all knees will bend. Jerusalem *must* be rebuilt as the throne of the world and the Exile must end with the Jews returning to an eventual glory and majesty, to their Land and to an eternal peace based upon the acceptance of the dominion of the L-rd.

That final day will come and the beginning of the final era is upon us, and debate borders on the absurd. The one who doubts is not even a scoffer, he is merely pitifully blind. The rise of the Jewish State from the dungheap of history; the Return of the people ground into dust and scattered to the winds; the miraculous victories over overwhelming enemies thirsting for bloody destruction and Holocaust; the fulfillment *before our own eyes* of the promise in Leviticus 26; that "a hundred of you shall chase ten thousand"; the coming to life of the visions of the prophets—these are the first and irresistible steps into the final chapter of Jewish triumph and heavenly kingdom. This is the State of Israel.

This State of Israel *cannot* be destroyed because its creation and existence are the decree of G-d who prepares to bring the final Redemption. "After two days will He revive us, On the third day He will raise us up, that we may live in His presence," says Hosea. And the commentators state: "He has sent us a revival from the two periods of exile that afflicted us, the Exile in Egypt and the Exile in Babylonia. In this third Exile, in the future, He will raise us up and we will never again go into Exile."

The Prophets, each and every one of them, speak of the great Return from the Exile, the return home and the Redemption. They do not once speak of another destruction and Exile. We have seen the fulfillment of the prophecies of final Redemption begin. We have seen, with our own eyes, the words of the Bible come into being. This era, this return, this state is what the Prophets spoke of. To claim that G-d has ended 2,000 years of Exile, created a state, wrought miracles that saw the Jews return to the lands of Judea, Samaria, the inheritance of their fathers, with smashing victory over hordes of enemies, and to fear that this will be a temporary phase of 30 years, is to be of little faith with a vengeance.

The State of Israel is the beginning of the final Redemption and neither Gentile nor Jew can stop that prophecy from being fulfilled. If we only wish it and believe in it, then each war that the enemy begins must end in his defeat and in ever greater majesty for the Jewish people, and must return more of historic and promised Eretz Yisrael to Jewish sovereignty. For each defeat for the enemies of the Jews is part of the awesome sanctification of G-d's name on His march to the final day when the world will acknowledge Him. The State of Israel is testimony to the invincibility of the Jew and his Destiny.

But all this will come in its swift and glorious way only if we merit it through our unshakable faith and trust in Him and our willingness to stand firm against betrayal of Land, people, and destiny. All this will come only if we stop placing our faith and lives in the hands of the Gentiles and their Gentilized lackeys. It will come when those who cry "Give peace a chance," and then risk their future on retreat, concessions, and trust in Arab intentions are prepared to risk their future by doing far less dangerous things such as putting on *tefillin* and observing the Sabbath.

Faith in the Almighty! Faith in Him who spoke and the world was! Faith in our Maker before whom foreign ministers and great missiles are but as the withered grass, the cloud that disappears. Faith in the Jewish G-d so that we cease sighing and asking fearfully, "What will happen?" Faith in the Jewish G-d so that the answer will be shouted forth: The Messiah will come and bring Redemption!" Faith and knowledge that *how* that Redemption comes and *when* it comes depend completely upon us, on whether through our pure and total trust in Him, it comes gloriously and "hurriedly," or with needless suffering and delay, with terrible tragedies and losses, because we did not merit it.

What will happen is that we will behold all the pent-up hatred for the Jew *as a Jew* burst its bounds and civilization will collapse as the eager nations and religions band together to attack the Jewish State. It will be religious war in its fullest and most emotional sense—a raging, irrational, hate-filled assault on the Jew and Judaism and the Jewish State. Muslim and Christian and atheist communist, European, Asian, African, and American will join in a furious crusade against Jerusalem and the State of Israel.

How unnecessary and foolish, as I hope you can see by now. For it is in our hands to prevent it through our faith in the L-rd of Hosts. Given this trust in G-d, the very dangers that rationally seem insurmountable become impotent. If we trust in G-d and at the same time use natural efforts to achieve victory, the impossible becomes possible. The Jewish way of struggle is always to combine trust in G-d, standing firm and commiting oneself to dangerous risks rather than desecrate the Torah, with all natural means of struggle. This joining together of faith and natural action removes us from the realm of the injunction against relying on miracles. That adage does *not* mean that if one sees a terrible danger that apparently can be overcome only by sacrificing principle and Judaism, that one must do so. It does mean that if one sees a terrible danger from which natural means afford no salvation, one should not simply look for a miracle but should rather look to Heaven, refuse to compromise on principle, and *then* go out and struggle. That struggle, which without faith in G-d would have been doomed, will now be crowned with success. This if the meaning of G-d's call to Moses as the Jews stood at the Red Sea with the Egyptian army upon them: "Wherefore criest thou unto me? speak unto the children of Israel, that they go forward." To pray and cry to G-d and depend on His miracles alone is not enough: let them go forward. But how does one go forward into a sea? How does G-d expect us to plunge into an impossible situation? He does. Trust in Him, look to him, and plunge into an *obligation*. The combination of faith and action will work. We do not rely on miracles, we trust in them *and aid them*.

If we truly believe, instead of prostrating ourselves and collapsing in political fright, instead of sitting dumb with lack of initiative and imagination, always waiting for the enemy to demand and then defensively refusing and being dragged into compromise and concession, we will turn to the world—and our ally—with a bold and confident foreign policy, and say: "Do not delude yourselves and do not delude us. Do not attempt to impose a Munich on us, for we know the reality of the Arabs. No amount of compromise will bring us peace with them. The Arabs did not want peace when we were flexible in 1947; when we gave back the Sinai in 1956; when they had all the "occupied territories" in 1967; when there was *no state* and they rioted and murdered Jews in 1920, 1921, 1929, and 1936. The "Hebronism" of 1929, the slaughtering of Jews, is what we can expect from them and the only difference between Arab "Moderates" and the "Extremists" is one of strategy. They do not mean a Jewish State in the boundaries of 1967, 1957, or 1947. They

seek *no* Jewish State, they seek to eliminate the smallest and least
significant of Jewish States.

"The problem is that too many people do not have the least
understanding or respect for the Arab nationalist, thinking that
there can be "compromise" with him so that he will give us parts
of what he considers his birthright.

"The Arab is also a "Zionist"; he considers all of "Palestine" to be
his and is prepared to wait and fight a thousand years if necessary.
Who thinks that we can offer him Hebron and not Jaffa; Shchem
and not the wealthy villas of Savyon? If he has a right to Shchem
wherein lived our fathers Abraham, Isaac, and Jacob, then certainly
he has a right to Jaffa where 100,000 Arabs lived in 1947. If he has
a right to Hebron where our patriarchs lived and died, then how
much more so to Savyon where they did not build villas. If the
Arab declares that there is no difference between these places, that
the land is one and that not one inch must be given up, he is
correct. There is only one Land, *the Land of Israel*, and not one inch
is not ours and not one inch dare be given us. Tragic as it may seem,
there is no hope for peace with the Arabs as long as one inch of a
State of Israel exists and the Arab national pride sees both Jews
and Jewish State as robbers.

"To return anything to them is to have them see in this modera-
tion not good faith but *weakness*, and for the Arab the slightest sign
of weakness means a tremendous increase in his own confidence and
a whetting of his appetite for aggression. Our weakness is a
guarantee of war. Our return of land is a strengthening of the Arab
hand with no price paid by him; a loss of strategic, military, or
psychological value to us and a corresponding gain to the enemy,
with nothing assured except that the next time the Arab will
demand more.

"It is madness to return anything to an enemy who is sworn to
destroy us and will do so if we allow him the slightest opportunity.
It is insanity not to punish the enemy for aggression by making him
realize that his crime means loss of territory. It is beyond compre-
hension that we return the enemy's losses and give him no reason
not to attempt aggression again. It is beyond belief that our soldiers
regularly fall for the same land that the politicians have returned.
International law clearly recognizes that the aggressor pays for his
crimes by loss of territory; who swiftly seizes more enemy territory
than the Soviet Union?

"No amount of land can compensate for the blood of our soldiers
who fell in wars of aggression started by the enemy. But at the very

least, let the state that was attacked and whose soldiers fell be compensated to some extent, and not only by retention of those lands that are clearly part of the historic Land of Israel, but of any other parts that are strategically or economically vital, because of their natural deposits, particularly the important oil resources that are so essential for growth and industrial existence. The proposition that every enemy adventure is doomed to meet with tough and uncompromising resistance as well as the loss of more and more territory and resources—this is the only normal and logical reply to the butchers and rapists of Hebronism."

And the Jew who has faith and trust in G-d will continue: "We are not fools and we do not collapse before foolish arguments; we know that in the end the argument that we must submit to pressure because "there is no choice" is absurd. If this is really so, how can we ever say no when we reach the point where pressure is placed upon us to give up that which even the most "flexible" among us agrees cannot be surrendered? Every demand for concessions today is only the prelude to another demand tomorrow, only the first taste of the bitter hemlock cup that will soon be filled to overflowing. We refuse to be in the position of the foolish servant who was sent by the king to purchase a fish and who returned with one that stank. In anger the king offered him three choices: eat the fish, be whipped for it, or pay for it. Refusing to pay, the servant attempted to eat it but after several mouthfuls could not continue. He then chose to be whipped but after several lashes could not continue. In the end he paid—a fool *who ate the fish, was whipped for it, and ultimately had to pay anyhow!* We will not be the fools who eat the stinking fish of pressure, get whipped for it, and in the end have to say no anyway and fight inevitably, but from positions and lines infinitely weaker and more dangerous than those we hold today.

"Each retreat will leave behind it a depressing knowledge of impending disaster, a feeling of defeat and coming tragedy. The rush to leave Israel and to find a safer country will grow and Aliyah, emigration from both the West and the Soviet Union, will dry up, along with investment and capital. How bitter the hemlock will be when we lose confidence in ourselves and aid the slide down the road of retreat and defeat. Sanity requires us to cease the small retreats that make up disaster. It tells us to say *no* now, not later when we look about us and see that our backs have been pushed to the sea. It demands that we say *no* now because every *yes* today insures a further demand tomorrow, and an inevitable day when *no!* will be shouted by every one of us—and it will be late.

"We are not fools. If we cannot say no because of our need for allies, weapons, and aid, because allies will stop helping us, we will not be able to say no when they demand a return to the 1967 borders—as they surely will—or when they demand a change in the status of Jerusalem—as they surely will also. Then, according to the forecast of the timid ones, they will stop their aid, weapons, and support—and what will we do? If our yes today is only to gain time, then know that time is running out and the day of reckoning will come. For those who say that we cannot say no, the choice is clear: Leave for Canada today or join the demand to become the 51st American state. There is no other way."

But there *is* another way—the way of no to concessions now, and if stated with faith in G-d, this no will certainly not lead to disaster.

With deep and unshakable faith and trust in G-d, one becomes dynamic and imaginative. One speaks to an ally as an ally, not as a supplicant, as a giant to a giant, not as a grasshopper. One reminds the ally that all nations are moved by self-interest and that its self-interest, not its goodness, moves it to aid the Jewish State. One makes it clear that we are not naive, that we know how the supposed self-interest of the "champion of the free world" led it to enforce a "peace" in Southeast Asia that sold the interests, lives, and freedom of people; and that this is the kind of a "peace" Israel will get should the United States think that this is in its interest.

One tells our ally: "We know that the State Department and the Pentagon and the banks and the business interests consider U.S. interests to be oil (and we do not have oil); the opportunity to get billions of dollars worth of contracts in developing Arab states; the desire to keep the Soviets out of the Arab world by giving the Arabs what they could not get from the Soviets—Israeli concessions. If this is what America considers to be its interests, it will betray Israel with elegance and with ever-lessening qualms. And knowing this, we do not rely upon you and we do not trust you. Most important, we do not *ask* you for help, for it is not Israel that needs the United States but the American people and the American nation that will survive or fall depending upon their attitude toward the Jewish State."

And here, Baruch, is the major point. Here is the major message that the Jew, *who knows the L-rd*, will deliver to the Christian American.

Above all, one turns to the Christian American and stops speaking in terms of foolish realpolitik and nonsensical diplomacy. One points out the *real* interest that every believer in the Bible has in supporting the Jewish people and state. One says to the Christian: "Let the others speak to you of oil and ports and trade and "interests." They come with a sword and a spear and a shield but we, the Jewish people, come in the name of the L-rd of Hosts, the G-d of the armies of Israel. If you, the Christian, really believe in the Bible, in the prophecies that are written therein, that speak of the return of the Jewish people to Zion before the final Redemption, of the creation of a Jewish home before the coming of the Messiah, if you really believe this and you know that G-d is the only ultimate interest that you and your country have, then you will stand by the side of Israel and demand that your government and nation do the same, lest, on the Day of Judgment, when G-d counts those who believed and stood by His people's side and His prophecies, you will be found wanting.

"The final Era is at hand; it is the beginning of the final Redemption. We have seen the incredible events of our times: The terrible Holocaust that ripped through the Jewish people, tragically mirroring the words of the Prophet: "And I will bring you out from the peoples, and will gather you out of the countries wherein ye are scattered, with a mighty hand, and with an outstretched arm, and with fury poured out" (Ezekiel 20). The incredible blooming of the desolation of the Holy Land, envisioned in the words,

> But ye, O mountains of Israel, ye shall shoot forth your branches, and yield your fruit to My people Israel; for they are at hand to come. For, behold, I am for you . . . and the cities shall be inhabited, and the waste places shall be builded (Ezekiel 36).

The unprecedented return of a people, exiled for 20 centuries, to their ancient homeland, a return from a hundred lands and more as the prophecy of the Bible unfolds before our eyes (Jeremiah 31):

> A voice is heard in Ramah, Lamentation, and bitter weeping, Rachel weeping for her children. . . . Thus saith the L-rd: Refrain thy voice from weeping, And thine eyes from tears; For thy work shall be rewarded, saith the L-rd; And they shall come back from the land of the enemy.
>
> Behold, I will bring them back from the north country, And gather them from the uttermost parts of the earth. . . . He that scattered Israel doth gather him, and keep him, as a shepherd doth his flock (Jeremiah 31).

The resurrection of the destroyed and fallen Jewish State as decreed by G-d:

> Thus saith the L-rd of hosts: I am jealous for Zion with great jealousy, and I am jealous for her with great fury.
>
> Thus saith the L-rd: I return unto Zion, and will dwell in the midst of Jerusalem. . . . There shall yet old men and old women sit in the broad places of Jerusalem. . . . And the broad places of the city shall be full of boys and girls playing. . . . Behold, I will save My people from the east country, and from the west country; and I will bring them, and they shall dwell in the midst of Jerusalem; and they shall be My people, and I will be their G-d, in truth and in righteousness (Zechariah 8).

The exclusive right of the Jewish people to the Holy Land and the indivisibility of the Land of Israel, as solemnly pledged by G-d:

> And I will give unto thee, and to thy seed after thee, the land of thy sojournings, all the land of Canaan, for an ever-lasting possession. . . . Sarah thy wife shall bear thee a son; and thou shalt call his name Isaac; and I will establish My covenant with him for an everlasting covenant. . . . And as for Ishmael . . . twelve princes shall he beget, and I will make him a great nation. But My covenant will I establish with Isaac" (Genesis 17).
>
> Unto thy seed have I given this land, from the river of Egypt unto the great river, the river Euphrates (Genesis 15).

"And the Gentiles? What of them? There will be those who understand the decree of G-d, and who will remember the eternal promise of Heaven: "Blessed be every one that blesseth thee, And cursed be every one that curseth thee" (Numbers 24); "And in thy seed shall all the nations of the earth be blessed (Genesis 22).

"And remembering this, they will be part of the righteous who leap to do G-d's bidding (Zechariah 8):

> In those days it shall come to pass, that ten men shall take hold, out of all the languages of the nations, shall even take hold of the skirt of him that is a Jew, saying: We will go with you, for we have heard that G-d is with you.

And happy will those Gentiles be as they are blessed by sharing in the Kingdom of Heaven (Isaiah 2):

And many people shall go and say: "Come ye, and let us go up to the mountain of the L-rd, To the house of the G-d of Jacob; And He will teach us His ways, And we will walk in His paths." For out of Zion shall go forth the law, And the word of the L-rd from Jerusalem.

"Blessed and fortunate will be those that understand and leap to aid the redemption of the Jewish people, to hurry the final Redemption of mankind. And how cursed and destroyed will be those individuals and nations who do not understand, who defy the Divine decree, who refuse to stand totally at the side of the Jewish people, who attempt to thwart the return of the Jewish Nation to its Land and to diminish the sovereignty and territory of the Land of Israel as the exclusive Holy Land of the Chosen People.

"Upon them will the awful and terrible curse be realized (Obadiah 1):

But thou shouldest not have gazed on the day of thy brother In the day of his disaster, Neither shouldest thou have rejoiced over the children of Judah In the day of their destruction. . . . Yea, thou shouldest not have gazed on their affliction In the day of their calamity. . . . Neither shouldest thou have stood in the crossway, To cut off those of his that escape; Neither shouldest thou have delivered up those of his That did remain in the day of distress.

For the day of the L-rd is near upon all the nations; As thou hast done, it shall be done unto thee; Thy dealing shall return upon thine own head.

"Woe unto the nations that join together, actively or indirectly, to hurt Israel and to thwart G-d's will:

For thus saith the L-rd of hosts who sent me after glory unto the nations which spoiled you: "Surely, he that toucheth you toucheth the apple of his eye" (Zechariah 2). Behold, at that time I will deal with all them that afflict thee (Zephania 3).

"There it is, Baruch, the certainty and the immutable historic destiny of the world; nothing else is of any relevance. And what is at stake for the United States and for each and every citizen within it is nothing less than a choice of survival or destruction, life or death. The awesome question is: Will this country choose life and greatness or will it follow the historical examples of empires that preceded it and die a fearful death, consigned to the graveyard of historical rubbish?"

This is how a people with confident faith speaks to a world. This is a Jewish foreign policy that is imaginative, bold, dynamic, and based on belief in the Jewish G-d of History. This is a natural policy that will succeed because its faith in G-d will make Him turn it into success.

Then one presents the *Jewish* program for survival in the Chosen Land, as follows: The home of the Jewish people is Eretz Yisrael, the Land of Israel. It is the Chosen Land, chosen by G-d above all others, hallowed and given by Him to Abraham, Isaac, Jacob, and their seed, the Chosen People, after them. *This* is our claim to Israel. The first commentary by Rashi Genesis 1:1, says:

> Rabbi Isaac said: The Torah should have opened with the first law that the Jews were commanded; why then did it begin with the story of Creation? Because of the verse (Psalms 111): "He hath declared to His people the power of His works, in giving them the heritage of the nations." Meaning—if the nations of the world say to the Jews: "You are thieves for having conquered the land of the seven Canaanite nations," the Jews reply: "All the land belongs to the Holy One, blessed be He. He created it and gave to those whom He chose to give. He desired to give them the land and He desired to take it from them and give it to us."

This is our claim to the Land of Israel. Not a nationalist one, not simply because we *once* lived there, not because of a Balfour or a League of Nations or a United Nations or an America or a Russia. Ours is not a request for the Land of Israel, but a claim based on the Divine grant to us.

The Land of Israel is the home of the Jewish People and of no one else; there has never been a "Palestinian" people and never will be; the non-Jew is welcome to live in the Jewish State as an individual, but not as a sovereign people. The boundaries of Israel are those that are indicated in the Bible and Eretz Yisrael cannot be redivided.

The return to the Land and the miraculous victories that saw us liberate Jerusalem, Judea, Samaria, Gaza, and the Golan—all the Jewish lands within historic Eretz Yisrael—are decreed by G-d and part of the final Redemption.

The murderers of Jews do not want peace. Yet not "peace" but *existence* must be our immediate goal, and we must do several things in order to affirm, proudly, our legitimate claim to the entire Land. We must declare immediate Jewish sovereignty over all the territories liberated since 1967 (and what a magnificent opportunity we threw away then!); unrestricted Jewish settlement in every part —city and countryside—of the liberated areas under a planned, enthusiastically supported government program; a challenge to the youth of the Exile to come home, strengthen the Jewish fighting forces, and settle in the liberated areas; a mass campaign for more Jewish births and one for birth control among Arab women; and a plan for Arab emigration to Western countries while there is still time and the older Arab is not as nationalist as the younger one.

The Jew realizes that it is foolish to trust in the ally who today gives weapons and tomorrow withholds them, demanding a political price. Israel must not depend upon the ally, or upon miracles in general, and must begin an immediate development of mass weapons of mass deterrence, including nuclear, chemical, and biological ones. Surely the Arabs are not waiting for Israel to begin. Let us not be the immoral moralists we too often are.

Does the enemy have demands? We will boldly and confidently present demands of our own. Demands for the return of all the lands that are part of historic Eretz Yisrael: the major part of "Jordan," Lebanon, a large part of Syria, as far as the Tigris and Euphrates in Iraq. There must be Jewish determination never to forget or concede the lost territories. Two can—and must—speak of "lost territories."

There should be other demands: for the repatriation of Jews in Arab lands; for compensation of all Jewish refugees who fled from Arab terror; that the Arabs clearly state that the Jewish State is the beginning of the Jewish Redemption, the start of the fulfillment of the Divine return of the Jews to their Land as the first stage to His Kingdom of heaven on earth.

For the Jew in the Exile as in Israel, the choice is inescapable: refusal to merit Redemption, and thus Holocaust outside the Land and agonizing suffering within; or meriting it, and a swift, majestic end to suffering and tragedy. The way of merit is clear: *tshuva*, the return to G-d, tradition, and the commandments of the Torah. And the most vital element of that return is faith—belief and trust in G-d manifested by clear commitment and action. In the Exile, commitment means the admission that every day we sit in the Galut we violate a cardinal commandment and desecrate the Name of G-d; the decision to leave the comforts and the illusion of safety and come home to live in the Land of the Jews. In Israel, commitment means ceasing to fear some men and trusting others; standing fast in the face of pressure, threats, enemies, and allies; refusing to profane the Land of Israel by returning any part of it; refusing to limit or narrow the victory and miracle of G-d; refusing to desecrate His Name that was so sanctified by the rise of the State and the miraculous triumphs of the wars. In both Israel and the Exile, commitment means a refusal to betray or abandon Jews despite the risks that our aid to them may entail. In short, the Jew merits Redemption—immediate and glorious—by turning from man, in whom there is no salvation, and returning to the Jewish Destiny and the Omnipotent Jewish G-d. "If they merit it—I will hurry it; if they do not merit it—it will come in its time."

When a Jew dies and stands before the Heavenly court, he is asked: "Did you look forward to salvation?" The wise among us, those who understood the Chosenness and uniqueness of the Jewish people, those who *truly* believed, who scorned leaning upon the broken reed of Gentiles and Gentilized Jews, will say yes. Of them it will be said: "Surely this great nation is a wise and understanding people."

The others, the nonobservant and observant disbelievers, those who bowed and scraped before "allies" and who betrayed people, land, and destiny in the process, will be punished by having branded on their souls the words: "For they are a nation void of counsel, neither is there any understanding in them."

We watch as we become increasingly isolated, our enemies growing and our "friends" deserting us. We stand alone and we are terrified and thrown into panic. The children of that Abraham who stood isolated and alone, apart from the *entire world*, are thrown into despair because they stand alone against the Gentile, of whom cleverer Jews once warned: "It is a law, it is known that Esau hates Jacob."

Foolish frightened Jew! For the Jew to stand alone is a *blessing*, not a curse. Had the Gentile not forced us to be separate from him, we would not have survived the Exile as we did, but would have rushed to intermarry, assimilate, and disappear. To stand alone against all our enemies is to have the Jewish G-d of History, the angry G-d of vengeance, fulfill His pledge of final redemption (Ezekiel 38):

And it shall come to pass in that day, when Gog shall come against the land of Israel, saith the L-rd G-d, that My fury shall arise up in My nostrils. . . . And I will plead against him with pestilence and with blood; and I will cause to rain upon him, and upon his bands, and upon the many peoples that are with him, an overflowing shower and great hailstones, fire, and brimstone. Thus will I magnify Myself, and sanctify Myself, and I will make Myself known in the eyes of many nations; and they shall know that I am the L-rd.

The greater the isolation of the Jew, the greater the awe of G-d's ultimate victory. The more we stand alone and the less who stand with us, the more astonishing is G-d's majesty. And when the day comes that there are no allies for us to lean on, even though we desire it, then we shall see the Sanctification of G-d's name and the establishment of His kindgom on earth. Then will come the final Redemption.

Balak, the King of Moab, once sent Balaam to curse the Jews and Balaam desired to deliver himself of the most powerful and devastating of curses. But G-d forced him to bless the Jews instead, and he uttered the most powerful and devastating of *blessings*: "Lo, it is a people that shall dwell alone, And shall not be reckoned among the nations" (Numbers 23).

It was the greatest of all Jewish blessings. To be alone is not a curse; precisely the opposite. To be alone is the salvation of the Jew and the sanctification of G-d's name. "Asshur [Assyria] will not save us," cried Hosea. Only faith, belief and trust in the King of Kings, the Holy One, blessed be He, and a willingness to go out and act on this faith and trust.

If we understand this, we ourselves will bring about the Redemption, and in our time. If we understand this, we understand everything. But if we do not understand, we will bring disaster upon ourselves and our children as we dabble in foolish irrelevancies and ignore the truth. If we do not understand this, we understand aboslutely nothing. "Who is wise and will understand these things? . . ."

One final word, Baruch:
The very different and special laws that define the conduct of the Jew as an individual and as a nation, we call the Torah. It is this Torah that the Jew carried with him into Exile and into suffering, into pogrom and Crusade and Inquisition, and, not least, into Auschwitz. It is the Torah that he studied on bitter-cold wintry nights in Russia and on stifling summer days in Yemen. It is

this Torah that turned his poverty-stricken hovel into a palace every Friday night, when the Sabbath meant more than an occasion to exhibit an obscene $10,000 ritual of bankruptcy called a Bar Mitzvah. It is this Torah that made the Jewish family a warm and close unit where respect and love dwelt in necessary harmony. It was this Torah that turned out youngsters whose passion in life was not drugs and kicks and violent sadism, but the famous *kometz, aleph-aw*. And it was from the little Torah *cheder* that scholarly giants of the earth came forth to teach sweet morality and true goodness.

If you want an answer, do not seek an easy one. If you want to be a Jew—be the one that always existed. Seize the mainstream of Judaism, no matter how difficult it may be. Let me suggest to you a few points of departure:

1. That life is short and meaningless if its purpose becomes the mere pursuit of pleasure. That unless we are to go mad, there must be something more to this brief candle.

2. The knowledge that the Jew is different and exclusive; that he has a role to play which will determine his and the world's destiny; that the Torah turns him, his people, and in the end all humanity into a holy and meaningful entity.

3. That Torah cannot endure with simple practice, but is based upon deep and never-ending study, and that without scholarship, Judaism degenerates into the joke of the Long Island temple.

4. That only if we believe that the Torah is Divine will we submit to its will, for it is just a product of "clever" rabbis, and surely you will be convinced that you are as clever as they.

5. That the Jewish people is bound together by common destiny, and that this imposes upon each one an obligation to love and rush to the aid of each and every other Jew; that the Jew has no permanent allies except his own people; that for the Jew, Jewish problems come first; that we measure our responses by the yardstick; Is it good and right for the Jew?

These are the principles; now go and study them. Study; learn. Learn Torah, for only Torah and Torah knowledge can make you the kind of Jew that you must be. "The ignorant Jew cannot be pious"—this is the deepest of all truths. So find yourself a rabbi, a teacher. But make sure that he believes in what he is teaching. Make sure he is an honest man who does what he preaches and who can give you the truth that he has in his heart. Torah: go drink deeply from its waters.

You are young and you have the choice that the Almighty gives to all, young and old: life or death, good or evil, truth or illusion. If you choose the transitory pleasures of your present chapter of life, you will awaken some day with the taste of ashes in your mouth. If you really believe that the things for which our people struggled and fought and died and then continued to live for so long, are so cheap that they can be thrown away for a job or a girl—surely you will awaken one day with a broken heart and a broken soul. And you will follow the path of all the foolish and disillusioned Jews who saw in Emanicipation and Enlightenment an opportunity for "freedom" and "growth." Their paths led to the dead ends of Auschwitz or the bankruptcy of lives that give neither satisfaction nor permanence.

Consider what you had and threw away! You were part of a people that was trampled upon, spat upon, burned and drowned, hanged and shot, gassed and buried alive. And they existed in spite of all these. You were part of a people that did not fall prey to the moral disasters of crime, immorality, and cultural anarchy, but created geniuses and men of morality and ethics. While others beat their wives, Jews respected them. While others rolled in the gutter drunk with whiskey, the Jew raised his Kiddush cup to G-d. While others dabbled at Inquisitions and conquests, the Jew bent over his Tadmud and created warmth, kindness, and scholarship. While others worshiped idols, the Jew embraced the One G-d.

In a sense, you have no *right* to run because you owe an obligation to the unborn child who will someday come from you, to remain with his people—the people of his grandgarents and great-grandparents and ancestors from Poland and Russia and Yemen and France and Spain and Babylonia.

We lose so many of our best sons and daughters. Some die as those in Munich, in a blare of publicity, but many more are buried quietly and we never even know they are gone until we suddenly find them missing. These are the ones who fall before the enemy called Assimilation. These are the ones who never knew or, worse, forgot that Jewish is, oh, so beautiful. The ones who sell their precious birthright for a few cheap coins and pleasures. They think they are finding freedom and happiness; only later, too late, do they realize that they died in the bloom of youth.

Young Jew, Baruch, whom I have never met, come home. Return to your people and their destiny. It is beautiful. You are young and for you, Return is simple. And know that your life can only be lived in one place. Home. The Land of Israel. It is a large land. Extending from the Mediterannean to the Jordan, from Hermon through Sinai to Sharm-al-Sheaykh. It stands, capable of absorbing millions, many millions of its sons and daughters who have not yet come. It is the land where one cannot move without colliding with the Jewish past. This is the land where Abraham walked and Isaac and Jacob traveled; where David and Saul fought the enemy and Deborah and Samson smote the foe; where the Prophets raised their eyes unto the heavens and spoke to the people; where the Maccabees preserved Judaism with the sword and where the Sanhedrin and Ben Zakkai continued it with the book; where Bar Kochba died and where his children will return. Here is Eretz Yisrael; here is your home.

What a glorious challenge you have been given! The gauntlet has been thrown down before you, and you must climb the heights of greatness! Aliyah, going up to the land, this is the task at hand. Leave behind the dust of Exile, the terrible fate that awaits us, our enemies of the Diaspora who thirst for our blood and plan yet another Auschwitz. Make your plans to leave the graveyards of Galut and live in our own land—free, a majority, alive. Guarantee the preservation of your children and children's children. Watch them grow tall and tanned, strong and proud, secure and sovereign.

You need this land and it needs you, many of you. Millions of new Jews pouring into Israel will fill up its empty spaces, guarantee the retention of all the liberated lands of Judea, Samaria, Golan, Gaza, and Sinai; assure a vast Jewish majority despite the addition of a million new non-Jews; add Western democratic and technical skills to the land. Eretz Yisrael will never again be lost to us.

Above all, Aliyah will assure that the liquidation of the Exile—*which is underway regardless of our wishes*—will be completed with joy rather than with tragedy, with return rather than with disappearance. What a moment in history! How wonderful it would be if we were to understand it, clutch at it, become part of it.

Jewish happiness is looking at the teeming streets of Zion and remembering the Talmudic Aggada:

> Rabban Gamliel, Rabbi Elazar Ben Azarya, Rabbi Yehoshua, and Rabbi Akiva went up to Jerusalem [after the destruction of the Temple]. When they reached Mount Scopus they rent their garments [since they saw the Temple despoiled]. When they reached the area of the Temple Mount they saw a jackal run out of the site where once the Holy of Holies had been. They began to weep, except for Rabbi Akiva who laughed. They asked him why he laughed and he asked them why they

wept. They said to him: "This is the place concerning which the Torah says "and the stranger who enters it shall die" and now a jackal runs through it—shall we not weep?" And he replied: "This is exactly why I laugh. For it says (Isaiah 8): "And I will take unto Me faithful witnesses to record, Uriah the priest, and Zechariah the son of Jeberechiah." What connection is there between these two—did not Uriah live during the days of the First Temple and Zechariah during the Second Temple? But the answer is that the prophecy of Uriah was tied to that of Zechariah. Uriah said: "Therefore, because of you Zion shall be ploughed over as a field." And Zechariah said: "There shall yet old men and old women sit in the broad places of Jerusalem . . . And the broad places of the city shall be full of boys and girls playing." Until I saw that the prophecy of Uriah was unfulfiilled, I feared that that of Zechariah would not be, either. Now that I have seen the fulfillment of the words of Uriah I know for certain that the prophecy of Zechariah will come true." And hearing this, in this language did the rabbis respond: "Akiva, you have comforted us."

Jewish happiness is standing on Independence Day in the streets of Jerusalem and being comforted . . .

Baruch! Jewish—*real* Jewish—is beautiful.

Index

Jaffa, 228
"J" document, 37, 38
Jeberechiah, 241
Jenkintown Methodist Church, 128
Jephthah, 212, 213
Jeremiah, 192, 231
Jerusalem, 107, 117, 205, 213, 225-26, 232-34, 240-41
Jesus, 19, 29, 30, 31, 33, 94, 125-26
Jewish Affairs, 26
Jewish birth rate, 12
Jewish Board of Guardians, Court Clinical and Court Liaison and Referral Services, 157
Jewish Center (Manhattan upper west side), 46
Jewish Center of Long Island, 61
Jewish Community Center of West Hempstead, 79
Jewish Community Centers, 13
Jewish Community in America, The, 85
Jewish Community Relations Advisory Council (Pennsylvania), 144
Jewish Congress, World (See World Jewish Congress)
Jewish destiny, 177, 198, 199, 203, 206, 207-08, 212, 216, 220
Jewish Education Alliance, 157
Jewish Forum, 148
Jewish Herald Voice (Houston), 53, 64
Jewish Intermarriage in the United States, studies of (See Studies of Jewish Intermarriage in the United States)
Jewish Journal, The (Brooklyn), 111
Jewish nationalism, 28
Jewish Population Regeneration Union (PRU), 12
Jewish Post and Opinion, 7-8, 44, 55, 60, 62, 82, 84, 109, 134
Jewish Press, 148, 158
Jewish Reconstructionist Foundations, 144
Jewish Socialist Bund, 3
Jewish Teachers Association, 132
Jewish Telegraphic Agency (JTA), 93, 131
Jewish Theological Seminary, 62
Jewish Times, 39
Jewish war veterans, 144, 158
Jewish Week, 47, 112, 154
Jews for Jesus, 13, 29
Jews, self hating, 27
Joffe, A.B., 156
Johnson, President Lyndon B., 21, 115
Jonah, 191
Jordan, 116, 212, 235, 239
Journal of Jewish Marriage and the Family, 10
Judaism, 90, 114, 149, 158

Judea, 193, 234, 240
Judges, 11, 212
Junior High School 271 (Brooklyn, 24

Kaddish, 3, 43, 88
Kagyu, 34
Kaplan, Mordecai, 46, 47, 51, 61, 65
Kashrut (See Kosher)
Kastner, 220
Katz, Shlomo, 164
Kedusha (See Holiness)
Kellman, Rabbi Wolfe, 109
Ketubot, 204
Kiddush, 88, 239
Kiddush hashem, 196
Kissinger, 114
Klein, Siggy, 22
Kneset, 215
Kohanim (Priests), 66
Kohler, Kaufmann, 106
Kollin, Rabbi Gilbert, 13, 14
Kol Nidre, 56
Koran, 38
Kosher, 29, 39, 45, 54-56, 64-65, 75, 81, 85, 89-90, 103-04, 118, 130, 140, 156, 187, 198, 204, 209
 Non, 54, 118, 142
Koufax, Sandy, 89
Krishna consciousness, 33
Ku Klux Klan (KKK), 87

Lamm, Bob, 21
Landis, Dr. Joseph, 165
Landsteiner, Dr. Karl, 26
Law Committee (Conservative), 62
Law of Return, 215
League of Nations, 234
Lebanon, 191, 235
Le Burkien, Rabbi Michael P., 52
Lehrer, Tom, 21
Lelyveld, Arthur, 57, 59
Lenn Report, 40, 52
Lenn, Theodore I., 40
Lerner, Rabbi Stephen, 63
Lettuce boycott, 57
Leviticus, 125, 191, 216
Levy (See Caplovitz and Levy)
Lewin, Kurt, 26
Lichtenstein, Seymour, 91
Liebman, Charles, 103, 114
Lilienthal, Rabbi Max, 120
Lipshutz, Robert, 123-24
Lisberger, Carolyn, 103
Loeb, Seymour, 121
Look, 12
Long Island Jewish Hospital, 156

About the Author

Rabbi Meir Kahane (1932-1990) - As founder of the JDL, he coined the slogan "Never Again!" (referring to Jewish passivity during the Holocaust). He dedicated his life to the Jewish People; his emphasis on Jewish pride restored dignity, identity, and self-respect to an entire generation of Jews in the Diaspora, and his unprecedented efforts on behalf of Soviet Jewry infused millions of Jews behind the iron Curtain with hope and courage.
He made aliya in 1971, and was elected to the Knesset in 1984 as head of the Kach party, which called for an unabashedly Jewish state, expulsion of the Arabs, and annexation of all parts of Eretz Yisrael under Jewish control. He was murdered by an Arab terrorist in Kiddush Hashem.

Rabbi Meir Kahane: His Life and Thought
volume one, 1932-1975
by Libby Kahane

Hardcover, 761 pages (includes index)
ISBN 978-965-524-008-5
Distributor: Urim Publications www.urimpublications.com

Praise for Rabbi Meir Kahane: His Life and Thought (Volume One: 1932-1975):

"This is an extraordinary tale of a man with a vision and a mission, whose life's journey was passionately directed to promoting Torah, Jewish pride and power, and the Zionist dream. Rabbi Meir Kahane, teacher, writer, and activist, is portrayed in exceptional detail and vividness, a kind of day-to-day serial drama. His boundless dedication to the Jewish people, skillfully animated and painstakingly documented in this comprehensive biography, can serve as an inspiration for Jewish youth today, as he did in his lifetime. A major figure in modern Jewish history, Meir Kahane can now be judiciously assessed and appreciated through this new and gripping volume."
– Dr. Mordechai Nisan, author of Toward a New Israel: The Jewish State and the Arab Question

"The combination of memoir and biography works well, and the narrative is struc- tured around a combination of interviews and careful archival research... A work of scholarship that attempts to contextualize his actions both personally and historically, and let readers draw their own conclusion.... It will be a major addition to our knowledge of a very turbulent period in Jewish history."
– Dr. Peter Eisenstadt, editor in chief, Encyclopedia of New York State

About the Author:

Libby Kahane was married to Rabbi Meir Kahane from 1956 until his untimely death in 1990. Together with their four children, they moved to Israel in 1971, where Libby was employed as a reference librarian at the National Library in Jerusalem for twenty-seven years. Her research experience combines with her first-hand knowledge of events to present a comprehensive survey of Rabbi Kahane's ideology and political strategy, beginning with the childhood experiences that shaped him.

Books in English
by Rabbi Meir Kahane

Forty Years. Miami Beach: Institute of the Jewish Idea, 1983. 82 pp.
2nd edition: Jerusalem and New York: Institute of the Jewish Idea,
[1989], c1983. 112 pp.
Israel: Referendum or Revolution. Secaucus, N.J.: Barricade Books,
1990. 185 pp.

The Jewish Idea (Translation of Or Haraayon). Jerusalem: Institute
for Publication of the Writings of Rabbi Meir Kahane, 1996-1998.*
2 vols.

The Jewish Stake in Vietnam, by Meir Kahane, Joseph Churba and
Michael King. New York: Crossroads Pub. Co., 1967. 224 pp.

Listen Vanessa, I am a Zionist. Tucson, Ariz.: The Desert Ulpan for
the Institute of the Jewish Idea, 1978. 163 pp.

Listen World, Listen Jew. Jerusalem: Institute of the Jewish Idea,
1983, c1978. xiv, 145 pp.

Corrected edition. Jerusalem: Institute for Publication of the
Writings of Rabbi Meir Kahane, 1995.* 236 pp.

Never Again: A Program for Survival. Los Angeles: Nash
Publishing, 1971. 287 pp.
Softcover edition. New York: Pyramid Books, 1972 c1971. 256 pp.

On Jews and Judaism: Selected Articles, 1961-1990. Jerusalem:
Institute for Publication of the Writings of Rabbi Meir Kahane,
1993.* 168 pp.

Our Challenge: the Chosen Land. Radnor, Penna.: Chilton Book Co.,
1974. 181 pp.

The Story of the Jewish Defense League. Radnor, Pa.: Chilton Book Co.,1975. 338 pp.

Enhanced edition. Jerusalem: Institute for Publication of the Writings of Rabbi Meir Kahane, 2000.* 344 pp. www.bnpublishing.net 2008,

They Must Go. New York: Grosset & Dunlap, 1981. 282 pp.
Softcover edition. Jerusalem and New York: The Jewish Idea, 1985. 282 pp. Reprinted: 1987.

Time to Go Home. Los Angeles: Nash Publishing, 1972. 287 pp.

Uncomfortable Questions for Comfortable Jews. Secaucus, N.J.: Lyle Stuart, 1987.
324 pp.

Why Be Jewish? Intermarriage, Assimilation, and Alienation. New York: Stein and Day, 1977. 251 pp.
www.bnpublishing.net 2009.

Writings (5731): Selected Writings by Meir Kahane from the Year 5731 (1971-72). Jerusalem: Jewish Identity Center, 1973. 126 pp.

Writings (5732-33): Selected Writings by Meir Kahane from the Year 5732-33 (1971-73). Jerusalem: Jewish Identity Center, 1973. 264 pp.

Writings (5734-5-6): Selected Writings by Meir Kahane from the Year 5734-5-6

(1974-6). New York: Jewish Identity Center, 1977. 379 pp.

• Posthumous publications by the Institute for Publication of the Writings of Rabbi Meir Kahane, P.O.B. 39020, Jerusalem, Israel. The Institute is a non-profit foundation; Israel registration no. 58-120-521-9.

Breinigsville, PA USA
01 December 2010
250434BV00002B/418/P